the
beauty
of what
remains

Also by Susan Johnson Hadler

Lost in the Victory:
Reflections of American War Orphans of WWII
with co-author Ann Bennett Mix

the
beauty
of what
remains

Family Lost, Family Found

Michelle,
Enjoy your
new found
family!
Susan

Susan Johnson Hadler

SHE WRITES PRESS

Published 2015
Printed in the United States of America
ISBN: 978-1-63152-007-5
Library of Congress Control Number: 2015935222

For information, address:
She Writes Press
1563 Solano Ave #546
Berkeley, CA 94707

She Writes Press is a division of SparkPoint Studio, LLC.

Names and identifying characteristics have been changed to protect
the privacy of certain individuals.

To Sandra, who never lost hope.

Hold on to what is good
even if it is
a handful of earth.
Hold on to what you believe
even if it is
a tree which stands by itself.
Hold on to what you must do
even if it is
a long way from here.
Hold on to life even when
it is easier letting go.
Hold on to my hand even when
I have gone away from you.

PUEBLO BLESSING

Contents

Prologue

There was no before. Everyone in my family, which consisted of my mother, my older brother David, and my father's parents, was transfigured by grief by the time I was three months old, when my father died "somewhere in Germany" near the end of World War II. Yet the past was well hidden even before the war took my father's life. Family feuds and the shame of mental illness guaranteed that I would never see my mother's two sisters.

When I was three years old, Mother remarried and I was given an instant family. Dick, whom I learned to call Dad, was the youngest of five siblings. Their families became our family and our lives were punctuated with festive gatherings several times a year. Except for my father's parents, my stepfather's family was the only family I knew. My father had been an only child and Mother had almost no contact with her family. Nothing was said about the missing people, and I learned from the beginning not to ask.

Both Mother and Dad had lost a parent during childhood and were devoted to producing a large, loving family and to giving each of their seven offspring a happy childhood. It *was* a happy childhood, filled with music, theater, and picnics, and every two or three years Mother held a new baby for us to see, cooing and smiling. She laughed when he or she bounced up and down on pudgy baby legs and twirled and said funny baby things.

Years went by with birthday parties, Halloween costumes made of cast-offs, and sugar cookies decorated with sprinkles at Christmas. Then came piano lessons, ballet lessons, and guitar lessons. Mother loved to make things, and she taught us how to knit and sew. She read us stories and tucked us in with prayers.

Wherever we lived Mother made friends, good friends for life. I found them in our kitchen when I was a teenager and rose late. Mary perched on the redwood picnic table, the one table big enough to hold all nine of us. I slipped in beside her and made piece after piece of raisin toast while Mother stood at the sink washing the breakfast dishes, turning her head to laugh and talk.

The theater, Dad's passion, formed the backdrop of our family life. I sat in the grass and fed him lines for the part he was memorizing while he stood on a ladder in his T-shirt and rolled-up khakis, painting the garage. Green paint dripped on his khakis; he was focused on repeating the lines and never noticed. Mother and Dad were partners; he acted or directed and she helped with costumes and props. We kids found ourselves in the play, backstage, or in the audience. The family often gathered around the piano: Amy played while we sang show tunes. Dan accompanied on guitar and John on drums while Ellen's sweet soprano floated up to heaven and Clare danced. David, our older brother, raced. He raced through the house, he raced his home-made soapbox cars around the neighborhood, and he raced his motorcycle.

It was a happy time—so why did tears fill my eyes every time they played "Taps" to signal the end of the day at scout camp? Why did I lie down on the ice skating rink in winter and look up at the stars night after night? Why did I wonder about not looking like anyone in my family, and long for cousins whom I resembled when we got together with Dad's nieces and nephews? Why did I feel like an outsider in the family and everywhere else?

I preserved my longing to know the lost members of my family for nearly fifty years. It was as if I had a special womb in which I nurtured small seeds of possibility when all around me there was little hope of finding out anything about my father and my two aunts. The seeds grew from drops of Mother's hidden love for my father and her sisters and with my belief that these missing people were family with whom I belonged. My desire to find out who they were was stronger than their absence.

I lived my early years in a kind of pentimento. On the surface was the portrait of the family that existed after Mother married my stepfather, while underneath was another, older painting where traces of my father and Mother's sisters were still slightly visible. Eventually I spent hours, days, and years uncovering the original, following faint lines and pale colors until the older figures emerged one by one.

This is a story of developing connections with those not physically present and finding out that nothing is irrevocably lost. It's the story of a trek into the unknown, a search that reunited a family broken for four generations.

1

Questions

My father was neither alive nor dead in my mind, but existed some-where between a ghost and a god—ever present, never visible. Until I began my search I knew only three things about him: his name, David Selby Johnson, Jr.; that he was an only child; and that he was killed by a mine on April 12, 1945, somewhere in Germany.

I had only a few details and many questions. Was he serious or funny? What had he done before the war? What did he want to do after the war? I began my quest for information about my father as my fiftieth birthday and the fiftieth anniversary of his death drew near. Since then, the explosion that had blown him to bits had been happening in reverse for me. Bits of information about him had begun to fall into my hands, my mind, my heart. I'd gathered fragments from his life, dug up records, studied photographs and letters, tracked down people he may have known, pursued clues, memories, and emotions. The pieces arrived with burned and jagged edges, missing chapters, pictures that clarified, horrified, and confused. Each was a part of my father.

There were several photographs in a white cardboard box on the bottom shelf beside the fireplace. I loved looking at the one of my father smiling at my mother, who was facing him. He had pushed his soldier's cap to the back of his head; his hand was in the pocket of his trousers. Mother looked young and thin. She was wearing a dark skirt and jacket, a light shirt. Her hair was

longer than I'd ever seen it. She tilted her head and there was a hint of a smile. Only their eyes were touching. Once upon a time he was alive, and he and my mother were in love. They were married and they had a child, my brother David. Three years later, when Mother was eight months pregnant with me, my father left for the war. I was born in January of 1945. The next month he wrote me a letter of welcome. The V-Mail letter was taped into my baby book.

> *Dear Susan,*
>
> *Since I can't be there in person, this is a sort of "welcome" letter. Yours is a pretty good family as families run. Your dad is a bit on the off side, but your mother and brother and now, you, more than make up for that.*
>
> *Your brother is quite a guy. Of course, he's quite handsome and smart—will he get around—but I know he'll always be ready to guide you and protect you in every way.*

Your mother is the most wonderful person I've ever known. I've always marveled at my great good fortune to have loved her and been loved by her. If you will follow her dictates and examples, you may expect to meet life in the best possible way and your path will always be the right one.

Your family believes in living life to its fullest. We enjoy all good things and live well—in that you're fortunate.

For me, adhere to a belief in tolerance, a genuine liking for others, and always give to life to the fullest.

Your father, Dave

Black on white paper, the words were my father. They were his voice and his fatherly guidance. They proved that I had a father and that he knew I was born. From his words I forged a loyalty and a love and silently protected his place in my unearthly family.

I longed for stories that would bring him to life, but knew only one. It was a story that summoned his absence and a silence as cold and deep as the night sky in winter. When I was a six-year-old with freshly cut bangs, Mother put David and me on the train in Oshkosh, Wisconsin, where we lived, with a shoebox lunch of fried chicken. She tipped the conductor to watch out for us until we reached Chicago, where Granny, my father's mother, lived. My tall, white-haired grandmother met us at the station and drove us across town to her apartment in Evanston. She treated us like grown-ups, serving dinner on trays in the living room. The china was thin, bordered with a delicate purple and gold pattern—the silver, heavy.

After dinner David ran outside to play and I pulled up the stool with a needlepoint cover and sat in front of Granny. She was talking about "Daddy David," her name for my father.

"Daddy David and his two friends were out in the fields, making sure the way was safe for the others to follow. The area had been cleared, but your father and the other two men wanted to go first, just to make sure. All of a sudden there was an explosion. All three of them were killed." Granny looked down, stroking one thin hand with the other. I longed to put my head in her lap. There were no words, only silence.

I didn't know what to call my father. Granny told me to call him "Daddy David," which was awkward. David was my brother's name and a daddy was someone you knew who was endearing and familiar. I didn't know the man in the picture. I didn't know how old he was when he died, or where he died or was buried. I didn't know his birthday or even that I could know these things.

My father was killed less than one month before V-E Day, the end of the war in Europe. The family learned of his death as people were celebrating victory, dancing in the streets, wild with relief and hope. Sons and husbands were coming home. Ours was a reserved midwestern family for which politeness and concern for others took precedence over our own emotions. Expressions of grief in the midst of joy weren't possible. On Memorial Day, my grandfather reached into the back of his closet for the army jacket he'd worn in World War I, buttoned it up, and marched in the parade, his face wet with tears he couldn't hold back.

My father's parents didn't know what had happened to their only child. They were told he was killed in action in a town near the western border of Germany. Hovering over an atlas on the kitchen table, they searched for the place their son died. In January 1946, my grandmother wrote to the Office of Graves Registration: "Will you kindly give me any information you may have concerning my son, Lt. David S. Johnson, Jr.? I am anxious to know where he is buried."

The government replied: "It is with deep regret that you are advised that, up to the present time, information pertaining to the burial of the remains of your son has not been received in this office."

On Valentine's Day of 1948, Mother remarried. My stepfather had grown up in Oshkosh and returned from the war in the Philippines. David, my six-year-old brother, and I watched our new dad, the tall man with dark hair and glasses, open a can of paint, dip his brush in, and draw a gigantic red heart on the dining room wall of our apartment.

Eventually there were nine of us—three sisters and two more brothers. Life continued in the new family with almost no trace of my father, except inside of me. It was understood that my mother needed to live without being reminded of a time that had wounded her almost beyond repair. As soon as I could talk I knew that mention of his name upset her, and I didn't want her to be sad. I needed her too much. I imagined that my father was the love of her life and that she loved him still, an unspoken secret she and I shared.

Although he was rarely mentioned, sometimes the world offered a hint of his invisible presence. When I sat beside Mother in church and listened to her soft alto voice as she sang the familiar hymns, I knew she was singing to my father. I too sang with silent devotion: "This is my father's world . . ." and "Land where our fathers died . . ." I prayed fervently to "Our father who art in heaven." At those holy moments the dead and the living converged.

During our weekly spelling test, when my third grade teacher called out the word "mine," I froze and then wrote the word in tiny letters. It was a word that spelled death.

November 11—Veterans Day. Every year I stood with my class for two minutes of silence. One annual moment when soldiers like my father were remembered by everyone. I knew the silence meant death—soldiers, men being shot and blown up, their lives over as quickly as the two minutes elapsed. We went on living, but the soldiers and my father never did. I wanted the silence to last for a long time, and then I wanted to tell my friends and my teachers about my father. I wanted people to know that he was one of the soldiers we were remembering. I wanted someone to touch me on the shoulder and say, "I'm sorry your father was killed." Then I could say, "Oh it's all right, but thanks." I kept my secret safe for fear people would have nothing to say and I'd want to disappear, lost beyond hope that he could ever be mentioned in this world again.

The Fourth of July began in the garage. All of the siblings who were old enough to walk met there after breakfast to help Dad carry the ladder around to the front yard and lean it against the tallest tree. David was a Boy Scout and knew how to tie knots, so he took one end of the giant flag that Mother held, pulled a rope through the metal circle in the top corner, and tied it with a square knot. Dad climbed the ladder that towered above our heads and threw the rope over a sturdy branch. When he was on the ground again six or seven pairs of legs walked the ladder across the lawn to the other tree. David climbed the ladder and threw the rope over that branch.

All of us stood back and looked up at the flag flowing down between the two trees. It was almost as big as our house. Within a minute, the little kids dashed from one end of the yard to the other, running through the scratchy wool flag, making it ripple and wave. Soon, all the kids in the neighborhood were in our front yard running back and forth through the flag.

I was quiet standing there. I had seen the newsreels that appeared before the movies at the Saturday matinee, showing boxes, coffins covered with flags lying in rows, waiting to go into the ground during the Korean War. What about our father? Did he have a box? Did they wrap him in a flag?

Every year before the fireworks began after dark, we stood and placed our hands over our hearts and sang the national anthem. Listening to the words "*the bombs bursting in air gave proof through the night that our flag was still there*," I felt the thud of fireworks in my heart and thought of my father exploding to bits.

The flag and the war combined in the song with the coffins of the men who had died. I wanted to run joyfully through the flag like my brothers and sisters, but I knew too much about that flag. I looked over at Dad and David standing together beside the tree. They were proud of their work and they were proud of our flag hanging there boldly in the front yard.

David was happy to have a new dad. He earned his God and Country Boy Scout merit badge, and when he graduated from high school, he joined the Navy—his way of being close to our father.

Although David and I never talked about him, I thought about our father who never came home. Never came home. Why? Where was he? I knew he had been hit by a mine, but what if he'd been thrown off to the side? What if he had amnesia from the blast and was wandering the world, as lost as I was without him? We'd find each other. My father had decorated the pages of his books with little penciled sketches when he was a child. It was a clue that he loved books as much as I did. We'd meet in a bookstore in Paris, or maybe Buenos Aires, one evening at dusk. Glancing up from his book, he'd recognize me, see himself in my brown eyes, and know that I was his daughter.

———

Silence prevailed into my twenties. A vague feeling of living my mother's life haunted me when I became the mother of two small children and expected my husband, Jack, to disappear at any moment.

When my therapist asked about my father, I blithely answered, "Oh, he was killed in the war."

She pursued, her eyes full of concern. "How were you affected by his death?"

It was a question I'd never thought about. I told her about Mother, that she couldn't speak of him; her loss was too great.

"It's all right to be open," she said. "Look at the dogwood blossom. It's wide open to the wind and the rain and not even the fiercest storm can tear it from its branch."

In August my family—Mother and Dad, David, Amy, Dan, Ellen, Clare, and John—visited us at Jack's family's cottage, one big, open room with a fireplace, a row of bunk beds, and a screened-in porch facing the Chesapeake Bay. Everyone else was at the beach when I was working on a jigsaw puzzle and Mother came in and picked up a piece. It was a rare moment when the two of us were alone together.

"So, Mother, I'd really love to know about my father. What was he like?"

Mother looked at me, the warm atmosphere gone. "How can you ask me that, Susan? You know it's too painful for me to relive that time; you're smart and successful and have two beautiful children. You don't need to know that."

"But I *do* need to know. He was my father."

"Don't be foolish. You have everything you've ever needed. Why are you ruining this happy time together? Leave it alone."

———————

I kept my questions to myself for years after that. My father's parents had died, and my mother was the only one I knew who had the answers. When I was forty I invited her to spend the weekend with me in Pittsburgh, halfway between Indianapolis, where she lived, and Washington, DC, where I lived. We flew in from our separate lives, met at the airport, and stayed in a majestic old hotel. In between shopping and movies I asked about her life, hoping to learn little things about my father's. She told me about her childhood on the Ohio River, her mother's death when she was ten, and her older sister, who was a gifted pianist. "I left home," she told me, "when my stepmother burned my high school yearbook and all of my mementos."

I listened eagerly. We were getting close to the time she met my father. I wanted to break in and ask what she loved about him, what made him laugh, if I was anything like him. I held myself back, fearful of ruining the relaxed environment. She moved too slowly toward him. The stories were about her. She said nothing about my father.

Sitting across the table from me in the hotel dining room, Mother brushed the crumbs from her sweater and told me that she didn't remember my father very well. "I knew him for only five years. We were young and the war imposed on every aspect of our life together." She didn't remember the man who was like a god to me, a mysterious source of life whose presence I could sometimes sense, but whose actual life I couldn't fathom. She couldn't remember the things I needed to know to help me see my father as a human being who walked and ate and slept on this earth.

———————

Every Veterans Day, I thought of my father. I didn't know where he was buried, and I had no place to go to acknowledge his life or death. November 11, 1992, I decided to visit the Vietnam Veterans Memorial. Joining the slow line of silent people moving toward the Wall, I noticed men in old army jackets crying and hugging other men in uniform, people grieving openly. Names of the dead surrounded me—names engraved on the smooth, black, deepening wall, names read out loud, a never-ending litany of death mingling with thoughts of my father.

I knelt to read a poem. Red and white carnations rose out of a beer mug beside the piece of paper. The poem was written to a father who never came home. Pictures and medals were scattered below other names on the wall. Those expressions of sadness seemed like a bond, more like a caress than the isolating silence I'd come to know. Leaving that sacred wall, I vowed to begin to search for information about my father.

The next morning, I looked up a veterans' center in the phone book. I felt eager and pathetic—pathetic that I was nearly fifty years old and so unresolved and needy and alone as to look in a phone book for someone to talk to about an event that had happened half a century ago. I was afraid they'd tell me it was the wrong war or that I was too late.

A man with a voice like a cello answered the phone. I told him my father was killed in WWII, and I wanted to begin to know him.

"When it hits, it hits hard," he said. He referred me to Ann Mix, a woman in Washington State who had started a network for people whose fathers were killed in World War II.

I spoke with her that same day and told her the three things I knew about my father: his name, David Selby Johnson, Jr.; that he was an only child; and that he was killed by a mine in Germany.

"Do you know his serial number or his rank?"

"No, I don't."

"What battalion was he with?"

"I have no idea."

"Where did he fight?"

"It must have been somewhere in Germany, where he died."

"Do you know where he's buried?"

"No, I don't even know that."

She was asking for details I'd never thought about. Then she told me about her own father, who was killed on a mountaintop in Italy when she was four. She'd grown up with silence, as I had. She told me where to send for my father's military records, and gave me the phone number of organizations that listed reunions of military groups so I could contact men who might have known him.

2

Twenty Pairs of Socks

My father's military service records arrived on a wintry Friday in January. Sitting at the kitchen table in our Washington, DC apartment, I opened the large brown envelope. The first four pages were burned along one edge. His records had barely survived a fire in 1973 that consumed over three-quarters of the military records held at the National Personnel Records Center in St. Louis.

Within two minutes I knew more facts about him than I'd ever known. He was born on July 17, 1919. His birthday! That meant he was twenty-five years old when he died. He was five foot eleven and weighed 140 pounds when he entered the army in 1943 as a second lieutenant. He majored in history at Carlton College in Minnesota. Shaking my head in astonishment, I realized that I'd married a man whose height, weight, and college major were exactly the same as my father's.

Dates were missing where the fire had licked the page, but his handwriting revealed that he rode and trained horses. That made sense. His father, my Poppy, owned horses. He listed sailing and swimming as sports he was proficient in. That was another connection—we both grew up sailing on Lake Winnebago. Under "Main Civilian Occupation" he wrote: "Dairy manager. Worked in every capacity in milk plant: procuring, processing, sales, credit, firm policy, purchasing, advertising, and personnel, Guernsey Dairy Co., Oshkosh, Wis." I could now imagine my father as a boy working beside his father, who took pride in his son's eagerness to help. I'd never before thought of him as a child. He had no brothers or sisters to tell me stories. I knew no one who'd grown up with him, no one who could tell me about his childhood. A few simple words on a government form had given me enough to see him as a boy riding horses, sailing, and working with his father.

He joined the 782nd Tank Battalion on May 22, 1943, three months after it was formed at Camp Campbell, Kentucky. By Christmas 1944, they were in Camp Kilmer, New Jersey, preparing to go to Europe in the wake of the Battle of the Bulge. They sailed from New York Harbor on January 3, 1945 aboard the *USS Henry Gibbons*, and landed in Le Havre, France on January 16.

My hands grew cold as I read the entry for April 12, 1945. Under "Incidents. Messages. Orders," someone had written: "Place: Mechernich. Germany. Deceased: 2nd Lt. David Selby Johnson." There it was in black and white, irrefutable evidence of his death, the words recorded by someone who was there when the mine exploded.

I read on, "Men were searching for mines and tripped a release wire, igniting a German mine. [The wounded man] was sitting nearby in vehicle 1/4 ton). Non-battle casualties—all are eligible for Purple Heart Award (due to enemy action). Reports and action taken: Remains of deceased taken to cemetery at Ittenbach."

The major wrote to my mother thirteen days after my father's death:

Dear Mrs. Johnson,

I desire to convey my sincerest condolences at the death of your husband, Second Lieutenant David S. Johnson, Jr.

Your husband served honorably in this organization and passed away in the performance of duty.

Your husband was killed in action by an enemy mine explosion in Germany on April 12, 1945, while clearing an area. He was killed instantly.

The officers and enlisted men of this Organization were proud to have your husband serve with them and join me in expressing their sympathy in your bereavement.

If I can serve you in any way, please call upon me at any time.

Sincerely,
EDWARD INGLIS
Major, Infantry,
Commanding

I stopped reading and toyed with the saltshaker. The letter sounded flat and impersonal, as if my father had just drifted off ("passed away in the performance of duty"), but he was dead, exploded to bits, along with two other men. The major had been there—couldn't he have given my mother more information, told her something memorable about my father? Why were the men proud of him? Did they have a moment of silence, stand with their caps in their hands while "Taps" was played? Or were they in a dangerous situation with no chance to say or do anything more?

My thoughts switched to my mother and her story of how she found out he'd died: In the middle of the night on April 12, 1945, she woke with a start. She sat up in bed, knowing that her husband was dead. Over the next eleven days, she waited for the telegram. I can see her taking care of my brother and me—dressing us in the morning, looking out the window, watching, waiting for the doorbell to ring, hoping beyond hope it wasn't true, unable to tell anyone her fears.

Suddenly hungry, I reached for the refrigerator and noticed the photo of our daughter Sarah and her dad riding bikes. After downing a carton of yogurt I picked up the next set of papers. The documents sent by the Mortuary Affairs and Casualty Support Division of the Army were dated April 13, 1945, and they listed every item my father possessed at the time of his death. In addition to two uniforms, he'd had "two toilet kits, one pair of

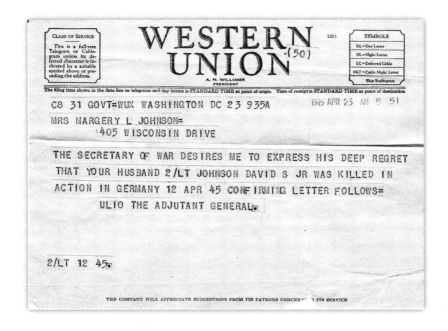

shoes, dress, with shoe trees, an electric razor, two wool scarves, two wool and three cotton undershirts, 20 pairs of socks, a pair of eyeglasses, a sewing kit, five snapshots, a picture portfolio with pictures, one photograph, a Bible, five neckties, a fountain pen, a wallet with cards and $38.67." The items were recorded, then packed and sent to my mother. Later his bedroll, which had been in the laundry at the time of his death, was shipped home.

"Twenty pairs of socks?" I asked out loud. Did Mother and Granny send him all those socks? I could almost hear my father laugh when another pair of socks arrived from home. The picture of him was shifting. He wasn't a god, just an unlucky guy with lots of socks and $38.67 when he died.

The next set of documents referred to an investigation into his death by the American Graves Registration Command. In April 1949, an inquiry was conducted in Mechernich, Germany, the town listed as the place he died. After detailing conflicting accounts of the incident, the investigator wrote, "Conclusions and Recommendations: That no useful information can be obtained from residents of Mechernich, and that further efforts at locating the remains of Johnson be made through the records of American burials and disinterments at the temporary cemetery established at Ittenbach, Germany.

"From the facts herein presented, it can only be concluded that 2nd Lt. David S. Johnson Jr. was killed in the action mentioned above and that his remains were completely disintegrated by the explosion of the mine, thus precluding recovery. This conclusion can be further substantiated by the fact that the remains of [the other man killed] were mutilated and the remains of [the other man killed] consisted of the left leg only, and after the incident no remains of Lt. Johnson could be found."

In January 1951 my mother received a letter from the office of the Quartermaster General of the Department of the Army:

Dear Mrs. Johnson:
 Several years have elapsed since the cessation of hostilities of World War II, which cost the life of your husband, the late Second Lieutenant David S. Johnson Jr.
 It is with deep regret that your Government finds it necessary to inform you that further search and investigation have failed to reveal the whereabouts of your husband's remains. Since all efforts to recover and/or identify his remains have failed, it has been necessary to declare that his remains are not recoverable.
 Realizing the extent of your great loss, it is with reluctance that you are sent the information that there is no grave at which to pay

*homage. May the knowledge of our husband's service to his country
be a source of sustaining comfort to you.*

Sincerely yours,
JAMES B. CLEARWATER
Colonel, QMC
Chief, Memorial Division

Putting down this last page of my father's records, I looked at the shelf above the table that held Granny's spoon collection. "No grave at which to pay homage." There was no place on earth that marked his life and death. No place to go to feel close to him. It seemed shameful that there was no grave, no final spot that belonged to my father, to his family.

Granny had shown me a picture of a white marble cross when I was a little girl. A friend of hers had been to Europe after the war, taken the picture, and sent it to her. She was planning to take me to the cemetery in Europe where she believed there was a cross with my father's name on it. We were going to take flowers, kneel on the earth, and say good-bye. Although the picture wasn't labeled, I'd always believed it showed my father's marker, the one solid thing left of him. After Granny died, I imagined my mother, my brother, and me standing by his marker, our heads bowed, the four of us together for the first and last time.

I'd been wanting to call a man named Frank, who was in my father's battalion, ever since the woman who kept track of battalions gave me his number, but I hadn't been able to gather the courage, afraid he wouldn't remember my father or wouldn't want to talk about him. I finally decided it was a risk worth taking and dialed. A woman with a Southern accent asked why I was calling. After I told her, she called her husband to the phone. I could barely breathe, waiting to speak to this man who served with my father.

"Yes, I knew your father. We were in the same Headquarters Company. He was in reconnaissance, fine gentleman, good officer. Not as mean as some. In our outfit only three of the officers were worth a damn, and your dad was one of them. And we were a tough bunch—wild, young. He was firm and we needed the discipline."

I gripped the phone and listened hard. "We lived for nearly three months at Camp Lucky Strike near St. Valery-en-Caux. We were refurbishing men and equipment after the train wreck. Can you wait a second?" Frank asked. "I want to get the troop history so I can tell you something you'll want to know."

When he returned he told me about a train wreck the morning after the battalion landed at Le Havre, France. "Midnight, 16 January 1945, we were loaded onto antiquated French boxcars. They were called 40-and-8s because they could haul forty men or eight horses. It was a short, frigid trip to St. Valery-en-Caux, our destination forty miles north of Le Havre. About 10 a.m. the next morning, the train finally pulled up the last hill before coming into the station at St. Valery, a dead end. The story goes that this was the first trip for the French engineer over this line. Either the brakes failed or the engineer applied the brakes too late. The train continued to gain speed downhill and crashed through the station. Two cars piled up on top of the station; several others jumped the tracks and turned over, crumpling like matchboxes.

"Lives were saved by the quick thinking and actions of men in the battalion who escaped from the wreckage uninjured. I was not injured and worked to take care of some who were. In all, three officers and fifty-one enlisted men were killed. It was a tragic blow to an outfit well trained and ready for combat. This wreck caused a long delay in our moving into Germany and taking our part in the war. I feel sure your father was in this wreck."

A fire engine blared in the street outside our apartment. He waited for the siren to fade and resumed, "Your father didn't go for long without a bath or a shave. He was so clean; he took baths in the freezing weather. Outside of his tent, clean clothes were always hanging out to dry."

Frank talked about my father as if he was alive, as if it had happened yesterday, as if I knew him too. "Me and another kid were out to steal soap one night," he continued. "We were going into the next town that wasn't yet liberated to find some women to wash our clothes or trade the soap for whiskey. Your dad caught us in the mess stealing the soap. He was on duty and could have turned us in, but all he said was, 'You have to be a little more careful. Anybody can see you coming in here. You could get caught.' He didn't make us put it back and we went on into town."

I told Jack and my children and my friends the soap story, and laughed about it over and over. It revealed more about my father than anything yet, and brought him a shade closer to life. He would have enjoyed my brother's mischievousness. He'd understood human foibles, and he'd been psychologically minded, too, like me.

Frank continued, "I remember the 'incident.' The Jeep driver was seriously wounded when the force of flying rocks hit him. He was sitting in the Jeep at the time of the explosion. Your father and two other men were searching for mines when one of them tripped a release, causing the mine to explode. They never knew what happened. It was an instant thing. Those German land mines were designed to put tanks out of action. That mine was apparently booby-trapped with a tripwire. Most mines were set off when a vehicle ran over them."

Frank told me that after my father was killed, the captain had them all trained to identify mines and bombs, "so it wouldn't happen again. Your dad did not die in vain. His death saved others' lives."

I looked out the window. So it wouldn't happen again? Did that mean it was a mistake, or an accident?

"There are a few other men I know who may be able to help you. I'll send along their names."

Jack walked into the room after Frank and I said good-bye. He crouched in front of me and put his hands on my knees. "How was the phone call?"

I told him everything Frank said, the phone still in my hand. I didn't want to put it down. Frank was a lifeline to my father.

Later that week I opened the letter from Frank with the names, addresses, and phone numbers of men he thought might have known my father.

◄ ►

I called the captain of Headquarters Company on a rainy Saturday afternoon.

"Sure, I knew Dave!" he answered. The way he said "Dave" sounded casual and immediate, as if Dave was right around the corner, a good friend he'd just left—as if Dave was someone I knew, too.

"In 1943, I took over the company. Dave's job was to train recruits, a difficult job. They were not the best-prepared men, and it was technical work. We had lots of training in radios, communication, encoding. Dave learned and then trained the others.

"We embarked from Fort Kilmer, New Jersey for England. The trip took ten days longer when we were blown off course three days out. Docked south of Hampton, England, we heard U-boats scuttling around all night. The next day we crossed the English Channel and disembarked at the port of Le Havre, France. That night during a blackout we boarded trains to St. Valery-en-Caux. Bridges were out and it took us all night to get there. After the train crashed into the depot it took a long time to retrain replacements for the men we'd lost. By early April we moved into Germany, up to Aachen, then fifteen miles south to Mechernich."

Thunder rumbled and rain splashed the window.

"Dave and I were two officers who had trained to locate, recognize, and disarm mines. The replacement officers were like college boys—no attitude of discipline or channels of command. That first morning in Mechernich they assigned Dave and three other men to go on a reconnaissance mission further into Germany. I was in headquarters talking when it felt like an 88-millimeter shell hit the building. It came from the direction we'd sent Dave in, so we ran over there. The Jeep driver was eight to ten yards behind the blasted area, between the Jeep and Dave, and two other noncoms. The driver told me, 'Johnson said, "I'm going to cut this wire. If it fizzes, duck."' Nothing was left of him. The driver had holes blown into him from the blast. The mine was a yard long, six inches wide, six inches deep, a high explosive. It would explode if you picked it up or cut it. He forgot that in the midst of things."

Shame and panic swept through me. He'd been trained; he should have remembered how the mines worked. How could he forget? It had cost him his life and two other men's lives. Was I picking up the captain's anger at my father's mistake, one that had made the captain look bad? Was the captain implying that the new officers were responsible for sending them out on an unnecessary mission? Was he shifting the blame to my father? What were they doing there? It was their first day in Germany—was my father so eager to play the hero?

The scenario flashed through my mind. After receiving orders to clear the area he rounded up the Jeep driver and two other men. They drove out of the camp and followed the road into the forest, where they parked. With a map in his hand he led the two men deeper into the woods while the driver lounged by the Jeep. Something ahead glittered in the morning sunshine. Kneeling to examine it, he brushed away leaves and studied the oblong metal bar with wires at each end, the two soldiers hunching over him, watching to see what he was going to do. He was twenty-five years old, in charge of even younger men, holding life and death in his hands for one small second, needing to know more than he knew despite all of his training. He felt light-headed, short of breath, and a little sweaty as he took the tools out of his pack and laid them on the ground. He tried to remember what he had learned about the wires, how they were connected to the explosives, so he'd know where to cut. He swiped his brow with the back of his hand and looked at his watch. 10:10. Thoughts cascaded: *Mail call. Maybe a letter.* He wiped his hand on his pants and picked up the wire cutters.

Didn't he know the power of the explosive? Why didn't he tell the others to move back? My father who was a god in my mind suddenly became an overeager, reckless kid who made a fatal mistake.

"I had given Dave $125 of the company's money," the captain continued, "to keep for transport. That was all gone. Not a shred left. I had a hard time explaining how it got lost!" He chuckled. "Dave was lighthearted, carefree. Nothing bothered him. He enjoyed everyone and everything. He joked and laughed. I judged he'd be a pretty good dad. Do you know what scrounge means? Your dad could scrounge. He persuaded the mess sergeants to give him bread and cheese. Then he made grilled-cheese sandwiches for everyone over the little flat-topped wood-burning stoves at Camp Lucky Strike."

He ended the conversation with, "I hope I gave you the information you wanted, with compassion."

The picture portfolio of the battalion, a souvenir from the 1988 reunion that Frank had promised to send, arrived. I opened the extra-long and wide booklet and examined pictures of tanks and soldiers standing in front of Jeeps. The baseball team looked like a bunch of happy, young guys ready to play ball. I skipped over the next page to inspect the official company photos, pictures of men who might have known my father. Long ago my grandmother had unrolled a wide photograph of his company and pointed him out. I'd never seen his face, and it looked like all the others. Granny, though, recognized him, tilted her head, and smiled tenderly. It almost seemed as if she were caressing him as her long, thin finger pointed him out. I nodded and pretended I knew him too.

In the reunion book there were snapshots of the train wreck that showed the engine bisecting the depot, the crush of wheels and wood, crumpled boxcars, and debris everywhere. Turning the page, my eyes focused on a large picture of my father squatting in front of a tent, a bandage on his right wrist, a cigarette in his left hand. Undershirts hung on ropes tied to the tent poles behind him. I studied my dad, his boyish smile, his eyes squinting into the sun. He was smiling right at me. They remembered him, even in 1988, so many years later. If he'd really been shameful they wouldn't have included a picture of him in the reunion book. Beneath that picture was another one of my father with two men, the three of them crouching shoulder to shoulder, tents and soldiers behind them.

The package contained a history of the battalion and a map of their

journey across France, through Belgium, and into Germany. Many of the pictures, including the ones of my father, were taken at Camp Lucky Strike, where the men waited for replacements after the train wreck. The history mentioned the "snow, mud, and cold tents of Camp Lucky Strike."

Camp Lucky Strike was where my father's last days were spent—grilling cheese sandwiches, throwing horseshoes, washing undershirts, receiving yet another package with another pair of socks. I wanted to stand where he stood, to see the views he saw in his last days on earth. I wanted to participate in his life the only way I could, by bringing myself into closer contact with what he'd seen and done. Jack and I decided to spend the month of July following the route of his battalion.

In preparation, I wrote a letter to the captain asking for the exact locations and he replied with detailed directions. On the side of the page, almost as an afterthought, he wrote, "Your dad was killed about four miles out of Mechernich, on the road to Eisenkirche."

3

Camp Lucky Strike

From the window of the airplane, the sea looked solid, like slate, its surface a gray, wrinkled pattern. Impenetrable. We were flying over the same Atlantic Ocean my father had crossed by ship nearly fifty years earlier on his way to war. He and his short life had always seemed impenetrable until recently. As we started descending, floating down toward the wind and waves, and the storms he knew, I wondered what lay ahead.

Our first day in Paris, Jack and I crossed the wide stone bridge over the Seine River and made our way to Notre Dame. Entering the cathedral, I became one more pilgrim as I began an odyssey born of loss and hope, a search for a lost part of myself. Notre Dame, Our Lady. The central sculpture at the right altar was a pietà. I noticed Mary first, the mother mourning her son whose head and shoulders rested in her lap. Her grief was immense and immortal. She had thrown back her head and opened her arms to grief, a grief that is the soul of Notre Dame. I stopped at a side altar and lit one candle for my father and one for the journey.

We rented a little red Peugeot. Jack slid the seat back as far as it would go, tucked his legs under the steering wheel, and checked the mileage. I folded myself into the front seat beside him and we set out for St. Valery-en-Caux, the seaside town on the north coast of France where my father lived for three months in the winter of 1945.

We had a hard time getting there. We lost our way. We fought. Like most couples, Jack and I are different and we are alike. Numbers and rules comfort him, while I live by words and intuition. He keeps notes and papers for years and I am quick to toss out yesterday's scribbles. You can tell which desk and bureau belong to him, which are mine. His are neat inside but every surface is piled high with trinkets and books and magazines and old newspapers and boxes of licorice. Mine are tidy on top and messy inside. These days, when I rummage through the jumble of forty-odd socks in my top drawer to find one matching pair, I think of my father and laugh.

I married a man confident in himself, a man who traded nuclear physics for history after spending his middle year of college teaching in East Africa, a man with a touch of the eccentric who wears vests, sweater vests, fleece vests, vests from Guatemala, Ireland, and India, and never a white shirt. I was first attracted to Jack's confidence and his willingness to be himself regardless of social pressure. Maybe because of my legacy of loss I was extra sensitive to the emotional environment and tried to intuit what was needed to keep everyone alive. Bursts of wanting to help overpowered my introversion and drew me into relationships when I yearned for a good book and free time. I could cope with anything when I had a book, one peopled with characters who didn't need my help, waiting for me. Now, finally, I was helping myself by doing what I always needed to do—search for the missing characters in my own family.

Jack and I both like to walk through cities and browse used bookstores. When we travel he reads history books and guidebooks, while I turn to novels and poems. Generally, during our twenty-seven-year marriage, I've been content to follow his well-researched plans for the places we visit, and I learn things. Often we go our separate ways for part of the day. He visits museums, stores facts, and takes notes while I wander, notice the ordinary and the odd, poke around markets and shops, and fill my bag with small treasures—turquoise earrings for a friend, a red scarf for myself, and always a new book. As different as we are, at the end of the day he listens, and he learns as much from me as I do from him.

I realized that this trip was different from all others when I got angry with Jack for questioning my decisions and blamed him for trying to take over. We stopped at Giverney to see Monet's home, Jack's idea. He read every inscription in every room and I was itching to be on the road to St. Valery. When we reached the parking lot I was angry. "This is my trip." My voice was loud. "I have a strong inner sense of where we're going. You can come along only if you can support me without trying to take charge. I know what I'm doing and if you can't follow you can leave now."

"I want this trip to go well," Jack said, "I'll be your right-hand guy and make sure we don't overlook anything. I want to help you find everything to do with your father that's still here."

I smiled, stuck my thumb in the air, took the keys, and we were on our way.

———

Late that morning we arrived in Le Havre, drove to the port, stumbled on a railroad yard, and found two vintage WWII boxcars made of wood with rounded tops. I realized they must be the 40-and-8s Frank described, boxcars that could hold forty men or eight horses. We were in my father's territory. Gray, choppy water splashed against iron embankments behind the railroad tracks. That cold January night after sixteen days at sea, all those seasick, travel-weary men stepped onto the earth right where we stood. They were rushed from ship to train, crammed into boxcars like these, and sent up the coast.

On the road again, we followed signs for the "Museum Ancien Le Havre" and stopped in front of a tall, ivy-covered building. After passing by endless exhibits of boats, I found the pictures I was looking for on the top floor. Photographs depicted the citizens of Le Havre building their city with care and pride. Architectural plans for the new library and the opera house were displayed beside photos of the completed buildings; people strolled through the shining, sculpted city and tidy parks. The last pictures showed the rubble after the Allied bombing. Heaps of bricks lay at the base of ruins; fragments of doorways, windows, and walls stood alone against the sky, the destruction of a city built brick by brick, lived in and loved. I mentally entered that time when no one was safe from horror and death and began to see through my father's eyes.

We left Le Havre and found our way to Goderville. A picture in the reunion booklet showed an American tank with a white star parked in downtown Goderville. We looked around for the place where the photo might have been taken and found the exact spot. Nothing had changed. Rooftops and the names of stores were identical to those in the photograph from 1945. Only the tank was missing. Bar des Halls, the same bar depicted in the photo, was still there, and we went inside.

The room was dark and empty except for the bartender and an old man sitting on a stool at the counter across from him. I showed the photograph to the bartender, who took it and handed it to the man who was shrunken and wrinkled with age. His gnarled hand reached for the picture, and the two spoke excitedly—too rapidly for me to understand every word, but I knew they were talking about the time American soldiers and tanks surged through their town.

We left Goderville and headed for the train station in St. Valery-en-Caux, hoping to find Camp Lucky Strike—where, according to the history of the battalion, the soldiers ended up after their first fateful night in France:

> *After the wreck the Battalion reassembled at Camp Lucky Strike, a veritable mud hole, 4 miles south of St. Valery. Most of our individual equipment had been lost in the wreck and a major job of reequip- ping lay ahead . . . Battalion Headquarters, and Service Companies remained at Lucky Strike. Lucky fellows!!*
>
> *As soon as all the companies became settled in their new quarters a vigorous training of all the reinforcements was started. The new men, being eager both to learn and to cooperate, soon were filling their jobs with great efficiency. The old spirit came back to the Battalion in full force. Training was carried on for two months while we waited in France for the call to the front.*

My father was stationed there when he learned of my birth and wrote me the letter of welcome. Camp Lucky Strike was the place that linked the two of us. If I could stand where he stood when he first knew of my existence, I would be able to mentally, spiritually, bring us together and complete the link in reverse. Never having had the chance to exist in the same place, I wanted to view the horizon he saw and visit the places he lived and worked and walked.

Jack and I found a room in a hotel across the street from the train station. After unpacking I took my photos of the train wreck downstairs to show the hotel manager, hoping he'd give me directions to Camp Lucky Strike. The manager, a burly man with a paunch, left his office when I knocked, then stopped in front of me to light a cigarette. After a few puffs, he reached for the pictures, took a quick look, scowled, and handed them back to me. Without a word, he walked away.

We were on our own with only two clues. The battalion's history reported that the camp was outside of St. Valery-en-Caux and that it was located on the site of what had been a German airfield. We followed railroad tracks out of town hoping to find something resembling it. After hours of looking at maps and driving along roads no bigger than paths, it was mid-afternoon and we were frustrated and discouraged. We decided to return to the hotel for a nap and head to Germany the next morning.

Refreshed from the much-needed rest, I roused Jack to go for a last walk around town. We climbed steep wooden steps that led to the top of chalk cliffs high above the sea and stopped to inspect a War Memorial. It was dedicated to the cavalry who died defending St. Valery when the Germans invaded in 1940. Following a narrow dirt path up beyond the memorial, we found tall, square concrete posts, shelters, and lookouts dug into the earth and covered with concrete, remains of the German army. Fifty years later, plants and vines grew wild on top of the dugouts, almost burying them from sight. It was easy to imagine D-Day and the fighting, soldiers scaling the cliffs to face German guns.

There the sky was a lighter shade of gray than the sea, which darkened into a melancholy blue-gray where sea and sky intersected. Sea gulls floated and dropped and swooped. I followed one as it flew over the concrete and sand harbor, all brown except for tiny red and yellow and blue and white square flags flapping in a row on thin white posts. The gull rose and cleared the rim of chalk cliffs, cliffs that curved around the edge of the sea and thinned like a line of soldiers marching into the horizon.

We descended the narrow stairs into town. Making a picnic of baguette, Camembert, and tomatoes, we perched on a park bench and found ourselves part of the local crowd cheering a bicycle race. I caught sight of a seventeenth-century, half-timbered house with wooden logs that formed diagonal stripes and diamond shapes in the white plaster. Intricately carved pillars and beams surrounded the doorway. A sign outside read "Bureau de Tourisme."

Lured by the enchanting building, we entered and greeted the frizzy-haired woman behind the information counter in English.

She peered over reading glasses tethered with a beaded chain as she handed me a map of the area. "I'm closing the building," she said, "at this very moment. And furthermore, speak French, s'il vous plaît."

Jack had his back to us as he studied a watercolor map of the area's chateaux on the wall opposite the counter. Excited and speechless, he tapped me on the shoulder and pointed to a picture of a tiny airplane on a runway labeled "aerodrome" just outside St. Valery. I strung together enough French words to ask the woman the name of the airfield.

She stood and stared over her glasses without replying.

Jack blurted out, "How old is the aerodrome?"

The woman replied, "1944. There was a camp there during the war."

I was breathless.

"American soldiers camped there," she continued. "Camp Lucky Strike."

I shook her hand and told her my story. The three of us, suddenly allies, leaned over the counter inspecting a small, detailed map of the local area on pink paper that showed us exactly where to find Camp Lucky Strike.

She invited us into the museum in the back of the building, to see an exhibit marking the fiftieth anniversary of Camp Lucky Strike. Stepping into the room, I found myself in the middle of the camp. Poster-sized pictures and text filled one entire wall. I read that Camp Lucky Strike was the largest of five "Cigarette Camps" built in France at the end of 1944 to deal with equipment and troops going to and returning from the war. The camp housed four hospitals, four theaters, a court, a post office, ball courts, bars, and stores where the men could buy "charms of the French capital: perfumes, handkerchiefs, lace, and jewelry."

I read on: 89,000 men stayed at the camp on their way home from the war and 3,000 German prisoners of war cooked, washed, and cleaned for the soldiers. Nurses and other women served hot coffee, cakes, and magazines in the Red Cross clubs. The exhibit described the traffic as being as "intense as the traffic of New York. Here one was more likely to encounter trucks, tanks, bulldozers, and Jeeps than Pontiacs or Cadillacs."

It was a city teeming with action and boredom and corruption, a place where people lived on the border of life and death and grabbed what they could to slow time down or speed it up, depending on whether they were coming or going. American and European cultures and languages mixed in the air, in the bars, in the shops. It was a place where soldiers, prisoners, women, and men were thrown together at the edge of war, a temporary place; buildings were temporary, relationships were temporary, lives were temporary.

The camp described in the exhibit was far different from anything I had imagined. As a child I had pictured my father in his tent, sitting on his khaki sleeping bag with the plaid flannel lining, cleaning his fingernails with a twig, dreaming of my mother, my brother, and me. I thought his camp was like the one I went to in the Smokey Mountains, where I sat on his khaki sleeping bag in the brown canvas tent with a tilting wooden floor and wrote letters to Granny.

Looking at the pictures of Camp Lucky Strike, I wondered if he thought he was going to die. He saw men die in the train wreck, he saw the wounded at Camp Lucky Strike, and he met men who had barely escaped death. He had plenty of time to see the effects of the war while he was there.

Beside the article about Camp Lucky Strike was a poster-sized photograph of the train wreck, the same picture that was in the reunion booklet, showing the engine protruding through the center of the station. Boxcars lay broken and scattered. Another poster-sized picture showed American soldiers lined up on the airfield wearing helmets and combat boots, hands

clasped behind backs. Four American flags waved over the rows of soldiers.
What I had learned never to speak of was public here, history for the world
to see.

The next morning I woke early and hurried to the hotel down the street for
thick, rich coffee. Soon after, we drove off in our red Peugeot and headed for
Camp Lucky Strike. The road passed through farmlands and crossed railroad tracks. This time, we saw the arrow-shaped sign pointing the way to
the aerodrome and stopped in front of a small airport and hangar. The old
airfield.

We parked and walked over to explore what remained of Camp Lucky
Strike. The ground was dry and cracked. Weeds had broken through slabs of
concrete; blood-red poppies sprouted through bits of rubble. I walked into
the fields where army tents once covered the ground. Prickly thistles rose in
clumps beside bunches of scraggly grass, the same scraggly grass that had
grown in front of my father's tent and was pictured in the reunion booklet.
Half-buried pottery shards and pieces of green and white glass lay scattered
about like raisins poking through the crust of a loaf of bread. Stooping to

touch the earth, I picked up a small piece of green glass worn smooth with age. Something to see and hold, a relic from the time my father lived and walked on this ground.

I visualized the place filled with tents and tanks and a thousand young men in uniform, restless to get into the war and yet scared to go, waiting for news from home, waiting for news from the front, waiting to know what would happen to them. My father was alive when he stood where I was standing. He saw the same villages and red-roofed farmhouses in the distance, the same clusters of trees and black spire against the same gray-blue sky. It was where he lived when he learned of my birth and wrote to me. Our bodies would never exist in the same place and time, but standing there on that bit of earth and slipping into the time he lived there, I could almost picture him looking out over the flat plain toward the spire, thinking of me as I was standing there thinking of him.

We decided to visit the aerodrome before leaving. Inside, we met Tomas, a dark-eyed young flyer in charge of the airport, and Philippe, lanky and grinning through black-framed glasses. Both were curious about us, so I showed them my photos of Camp Lucky Strike and told them my story. When I finished, Tomas pointed to the picture that still hung in its place on the wall behind the counter, an advertisement from the forties that showed Jean Harlow in a sultry pose, hand over heart, a pack of Lucky Strike cigarettes brushing against her bare shoulder.

Tomas told us there was someone who would like to meet us. "Madame Presidente, the president of this aerodrome, usually stops by the airport every day around this time. She's planning a formal ceremony later in the summer to mark the fiftieth anniversary of the camp. I'm sure she'll want to see your photos and hear your story. I hope you can wait for her. She'll be here any minute."

After waiting half an hour we were eager to be on our way and were in our car when we were called back. Madame Presidente's daughter had arrived instead of her mother. Philippe introduced us to Brigitte, a woman with a determined manner. Her blond ponytail bounced as she shook our hands. "My mother has a book about Camp Lucky Strike you'll want to see. We live nearby. She'll meet us there."

Following Brigitte and Philippe, our car meandered through the countryside on a road so tiny we could almost touch the low white farmhouses and billowing gardens along the way. Brigitte turned into a long, pebbled driveway lined with trees and stopped in front of a yellow stone chateau. She beckoned us into a lofty room with a slate floor and a stone fireplace. Small pots of wildflowers sat on the deep windowsills and brightened the room on that cloudy day.

Madame Presidente was not home, but Pierre, Brigitte's stocky eighty-four-year-old father, stomped in to greet us wearing green rubber hip boots and carrying a shotgun. With a look of disapproval, Brigitte signaled her father to put away his gun. Grinning, Pierre told us that he had been shooting moles in the front yard. We settled in to listen as he talked about his life during the war and Philippe translated:

"We were defending St. Valery from attack by the Germans in 1940 and the lot of us were taken prisoner. We spent the next five years in a German prisoner-of-war camp. When the camp was liberated in May 1945, thirty-four bicycles were unloaded in front of us. The Russians grabbed the bikes, but never having ridden in their pre-war days, they promptly fell off, to the amusement of us Frenchmen. We snatched up the bikes and rode off.

"I rushed back home to my family's farm only to be confronted by American soldiers commanding me to halt. The Germans had confiscated the farm when they seized St. Valery in 1940 and built an airfield on the land. After liberating that part of France in 1944, the Americans had built Camp Lucky Strike on the airfield. My father worked at the camp, on his own land. I began to work there too." Pierre walked over to his desk, took out a slip of paper, and showed us a faded green card, soft with use: his pass to enter and leave the camp. On the back an officer had written in script that was still legible, "This man lives on the post and should be permitted to leave and enter the post with his car."

Pierre invited us to sit down and have a drink as Brigitte handed us a large brown paperbound book about Camp Lucky Strike. The end papers displayed pictures of tree trunks carved, as high as a man can reach, with the names, dates, and home states of American soldiers—graffiti from the time old men like Pierre were as young as Tomas and Philippe.

It was almost noon and Madame Presidente still had not appeared. I relished the novelesque atmosphere of the chateau, Pierre's stories, and the book that connected me to this family and my father, but we were anxious to reach Germany before nightfall. As we turned to the door Madame President arrived, her golden hair upswept, her bearing dignified. She showed me a detailed 8 x 12 photograph of the train wreck and I showed her the pictures of my father.

She examined them. "Would you leave them with me so I can make copies?'

"Copies? Sure. You keep these. I have extras with me."

After exchanging photos of the camp, we followed her back to the aerodrome and climbed the stairs to the flight tower. She had something she was eager to show us. I watched her spread out the architectural plans of Camp Lucky Strike. Together we identified the various sections: the officers' section, the theaters, hospitals, and ball fields. Madame Presidente rolled up the plan and handed it to me. When we said good-bye, she grasped my shoulders firmly with both hands and spoke to me fervently in French about something I must know when I got to Germany. I was so overcome with emotion, I didn't understand, but I felt her words and her hands on my shoulders and her gift as deeply valued companionship. Meeting as strangers, leaving as friends, we were connected through our stories and the history of Pierre's family farm, a small plot of land where armies came and went—armies made of men like my father, men who ate and played ball and wrote letters home. I was lightheaded with joy, as it had been my lifelong wish to talk with people who were as interested in my father's story as I had always been.

4

Sorrow Flies Up to a Branch and Sings

Ⓦe left St. Valery from the airfield and drove through France, across Belgium, and into Germany, following the route my father's battalion recorded in their history:

> *At last the waiting and expectation ended. Before dawn on the 7th of April, we turned over the tank engines and assembled at Goderville for a long road march up to the Rhineland . . . We passed through Amiens and Cambrai in France. Cathedrals and cemeteries from the First World War blended into our impressions. In Belgium we followed the beautiful Meuse River Valley through Mons, Namur, and Liege. On the morning of the 11th of April we crossed the German border with all guns half-loaded and were soon in Aachen.*

From the car window I saw the same cemeteries from World War I that my father had seen—tidy, square patches of graves enclosed by iron fences resembling well-kept gardens bordering the road, gardens of the dead. I took a deep breath as I realized that each gravestone held years of suffering. I knew the endless sorrow of just one family where one young life was lost. Multiply that by the millions who died in wars in this century and the suffering was unfathomable.

After France we drove through Belgium and entered Germany before nightfall. Our destination was Aachen, or Aix-la-Chapelle, as it was called before it fell into German hands. The different names paralleled my sentiments. Aix-la-Chapelle evoked a painterly lightness that matched my feelings about France, where I had been met with graceful help and found the background for the stories I'd heard about my father. Aachen sounded hard and threatening, like metal. During an earlier trip, in the seventies, when I was reading the literature of the Holocaust, I left Germany soon after arriving, with the past horrors of the country haunting me. This time I would stay long enough to try to find where my father died or where any of his remains might lie so that I could pay him homage as close as I could get to the place of his last bodily existence.

Before leaving for Europe I had learned that Charlemagne made Aachen the center of the Holy Roman Empire and built the cathedral in which he was later entombed in 804 CE. Because of that, Hitler considered Aachen the First Reich and vowed to defend it at all cost, and the cost was exorbitant. When the fighting ended, 10,000 people had lost their lives and the city was in ruins, but the cathedral was still standing. Stocks of food were discovered and passed out to refugees, electricity and phone lines were restored, and Aachen became a center of rest for those, like my father, on the way to the front.

Jack and I settled into a hotel late in the afternoon and set out on foot to explore Aachen at sunset. As we walked and talked quietly about my father's last night on earth, spent right here, I reached for Jack's hand.

"He may have walked these streets. They're pretty now, with splashes of red geraniums under every window, but he must have seen nothing but wreckage. I read that some of the buildings were habitable and the men slept in beds for the first time since arriving in Europe."

Jack squeezed my hand. "Let's hope your dad had a good, warm night's sleep."

We sat at a table in the open square and ordered drinks.

"Your dad and his buddies may have sat here in this plaza in front of the cathedral, drinking beer and talking about life after the war. Maybe he showed them the most recent photo of his family—your mother, David, and little Susie."

"Look over there." I pointed to a group of young people dressed in black, playing music, dancing, laughing, and kissing on the wide stone steps. "They remind me of our two children." The sky had turned a golden pink and my thoughts returned to my father. "He was their age, twenty-five years old, when the world went crazy with killing and death. He had to use his exuberance for life to fight a war. And then the fighting stopped less than a month after he died. The war in Europe was over and he and so many others were left where they died."

The kids on the steps scattered in groups as darkness entered the plaza. Jack raised his glass. "To David, who sat here with his friends on his last night. We toast you with love and sadness."

I woke the next morning filled with dread. My father had awakened in Aachen and driven down to Mechernich, where he was killed later that day. After breakfast we walked over to visit the cathedral, which had been closed the night before. While we lingered in the nave, a service began in German. I sat quietly, thinking of Granny. I was doing what she'd wanted to do: find out what happened to her son. I prayed for courage to face what lay ahead.

There were three clues about the place where my father died. His military records stated, "Men were searching for mines and tripped a release wire, igniting a German mine. Remains of deceased taken to the cemetery at Ittenbach." The second piece of information came from the Graves Registration Command, which investigated his death four years later, in April 1949. Mechernich Police Sergeant Marko testified at the time that "the area in which the accident occurred was in a wooded section just outside of Mechernich." The report noted that the area had been used by the Germans to store ammunition. The third clue was from a letter the captain sent me, which said, "Your dad was killed about four miles out of Mechernich on the road to Euskirchen."

We left Aachen and arrived in Mechernich shortly after noon on a still, hot day. Behind the broad, flat main street, narrower roads wound up and down the hills. I walked up the steps to a small, tidy hotel and rang the bell. No one answered. Apprehensive, tired, and hot, we looked around for a place to sit with a cold drink. We found a grocery store, but it had nothing cold to drink. The town seemed immaculate, sterile, and shut down, eerily rejecting.

Finally we found a bar that was open. Since there were no other customers, we were alone with the bartender, a hefty man with blue eyes who greeted us in English.

Jack thumped his palms on the counter and leaned over. "Do you know where we can find a cemetery in Ittenbach? There were three American soldiers who were killed near Mechernich close to the end of the war. They were buried in Ittenbach and we want to find their graves."

I stood behind Jack, a sense of danger lingering for me in hearing him say those words out loud in this place.

The bartender tossed down the rag he'd used to mop up a spill on the counter. "I've never heard of Ittenbach, but you could visit the cemetery over the hill where German soldiers are buried. You can also try the tourist bureau. Take a right at the corner. It's in the next block on the left."

My fear was somewhat relieved with the friendly human contact. He hadn't tried to shoot us or threaten us. We were still alive. The war was over.

After speaking with several people at the tourist bureau, we were ushered into an office crowded with papers and books. A man with graying hair was hunched over his desk. He looked up when we entered, listened, frowned, pulled a map out of a drawer, and pointed to Ittenbach. "It's across the Rhine, about sixty miles to the east. The 'wooded section' is now an amusement park over near the grocery store."

I was skeptical about his idea of the wooded area, but he'd helped us as much as he could, so I thanked him and left. We were at a loss about where to get the information we needed and considered driving to Ittenbach. I turned to Jack. "It may be the closest we can get to my father's remains."

We were about to get in the car when Jack noticed a police station across the street from the parking lot. "Let's ask them to help us locate the old German ammunition dump."

My first reaction was horror. To walk into a German police station felt like walking into the jaws of the enemy, yet I knew that if we were going to find anything, we'd have to ask for help.

The first person we met was a short, round, bald-headed policeman. Jack spoke to him in rusty college German and I showed him my copy of the 1949 investigation report that contained the interview with Police Sergeant Marko from Mechernich. Bobbing up and down with excitement, the officer shouted, "I knew Sergeant Marko. Sergeant Marko worked here."

Our conversation attracted two other officers. One was a broad-shoul-dered younger man with rumpled black hair and a faint smile. In English, he invited us into his office, where I told him my story, including the three clues. When I finished he reached up to the wall behind his desk and pulled down a large map of a restricted area around Mechernich.

"The Belgians occupied Mechernich until 1992. Their headquarters were in a secluded area about four miles out of town on the road to Euskirchen. Before the Belgians, Americans occupied that spot, and before the Americans came, Germans built their headquarters on the site in the beginning of the war. An ammunition dump stood there." The man rolled up the map and handed it to me. Infused with anticipation and gratitude, I remembered the two words of German my stepfather taught me: *danke schoen.*

We returned to the hotel we had chosen and this time when I rang the bell, a smiling woman with an ample bosom answered and showed us a small room. We tossed our luggage onto the bed, clutched the map, and set off.

The road out of Mechernich reminded me of rural Wisconsin, where my father grew up, with gently rolling, greenish-gold cultivated fields on one side, rock formations spiraling up from the earth on the other. Tall, sparse pine trees grew between the brown-layered rocks. As in glacier-scarred Wisconsin, we could see both the gentle and the violent hands of nature. I was comforted thinking that my father's last journey might have seemed familiar to him.

I studied the map. The area we were searching was a wobbly circle of green with a cleared space in the middle. Several roads led into the center of the circle. I couldn't have found this place or even known its importance without the map. We drove around the entire circumference, about twenty miles. The roads leading in were small and crumbling from disuse. Signs warned that the area was closed to the public. I chose one of the roads, and we entered the prohibited area, driving over rough terrain and through forests. I was vitally alert, determined to catch any sign of a wooded section. We came to the clearing, a wide meadow with golden grass and flecks of bright yellow and white wildflowers. To the left was a small brick structure surrounded by a wire fence and street lamps. Beyond that, down the road and past the fence to the left of the building, stood a large clump of trees. I looked over at Jack. "That's it."

I was not yet ready to enter the little forest without considering the whole area. There were several smaller clusters of trees to the right of the building, and we explored those first. Bracken scratched my legs and I picked a few wildflowers to press between the pages of my journal, something to keep from the earth that held my father. Leaving that group of trees, we hiked to the crest of the hill and discovered a wooden lookout tower. From the top, I spotted several bunches of trees, standing as islands of green in the middle of the golden meadow. I focused on the forest I had first noticed and saw a dirt road cutting through the center of the grove.

We climbed down from the tower and headed for the grove. A sense of certainty filled me as I walked down the neglected road, which looked as if no vehicle had used it for fifty years. In the woods, it narrowed into two dirt ruts, with grass reclaiming parts of the old road. I felt outside of time as I looked for signs of the past.

Several yards in, I noticed two jagged concrete blocks lying together on the right side. "They could have been blown apart," I told Jack, "thrown there by an explosion." I turned off the road and walked up an incline, Jack behind me, and came to a place surrounded by barbed wire. Below me lay a crater where the earth had been carved out. The right edge of the crater was steep, and a bowl-shaped area had been formed in the center. The bottom of the crater was filled with ferns swaying gently in the afternoon breeze. Three trees in the center of the crater were smaller and younger than those on the outside.

Jack pointed out that the barbed wire encircling this spot ran right through the middle of the trees. "They've been growing around the wire for fifty years."Across the crater there was a concrete post much like the posts the Germans built on the cliff above St. Valery. I took a picture of the crater and tried to take another. I thought there were several pictures left on my roll of film, but the sound of rewinding was unmistakable.

I sat down cross-legged and looked into the crater, the spot where my father—who was half my age, but always my father—died. I read a poem and Jack said a prayer. I was six years old, and twenty-five, and fifty. I talked with my daddy for the first time in my life. I told him that I missed him and that I loved him. I told him about his grandchildren, in whom he would have delighted, and how they would have loved him as I loved his parents, Granny and Poppy. I told him about Jack, who would have felt accepted by him, as he would have seen Jack as his own son. I told him about all the people who helped me find him, and that I used my pain in my work as a therapist with people who needed to talk so they wouldn't feel utterly alone.

As I talked to my father, my eyes were drawn to a white birch tree on the far hill. It was radiant, with white-gold light shining from its center. Beneath the light, long, grassy weeds were becoming a mauve brightness. Beauty was in me and around me. Heaven had opened.

"He's all right. My father is all right." I didn't realize until then that I needed to know he was all right. It was more than a thought; the words came from somewhere inside.

I sat there for the rest of the day and watched the light dance with the trees until darkness began to enter the grove. Sorrow flew up to a branch and sang. That little spot in the woods was everything—all time, all life. He was gone and yet he was there. I couldn't bear to leave. I wanted to stay forever. I was whole there with my father. I poured water on the ground to bless it, Jack said a prayer, and we said good-bye. We walked down the road to the car, away from that spot of violence, beauty, and holy light.

5

Requiem

We left Mechernich the next day and drove the eighty miles to Luxembourg, where my father's name was on the Wall of Missing in the American Cemetery. After finding a room near the train station and dropping off our bags, we headed to the cemetery. It was dusk by the time we entered, and the cemetery was about to close. We rushed inside through the blue iron doors. After passing the visitors' center, I found myself in front of the chapel looking out over a valley of white markers—rows and rows of white markers, uniform, like the soldiers they once were. Hundreds and hundreds, thousands of white markers—crosses and Stars of David, each one representing someone who was once a son, a brother, a husband, a friend, a father. I walked among the rows reading their names, the states they came from, and the dates of their deaths. Almost every one had died near the end of the war, in '44 or '45, most of them in the Battle of the Bulge. Too sad to weep, I read on and on. One more from Michigan, another from New York, Nebraska, North Carolina, Ohio again—a story of death and sadness with each marker.

The last light of day whitened the wall where I found my father's name. JOHNSON DAVID S JR – 2 LT – 782 TANK BN – WISCONSIN. I touched the letters carved in the stone. Now I knew a little more about him than his name and the date he died. I had stories. I knew where he worked and where he went to school. I knew his birthday. I knew that he was all right.

After breakfast the next morning I wandered the streets near the hotel looking for flowers. I wanted to bring my father roses, red for his life and the

blood we shared. Mother liked daisies. I bought daisies for her. We arrived at the cemetery around ten on an overcast day. The brilliant greens and whites of the day before had turned to shades of gray. It began to rain.

I knew exactly where to find him, and I ran my fingertips over his name again. I belonged there in that place of loss and memory. The flowers brightened the stone beneath his name. When Jack took a picture of me standing beside my father's name I felt a little silly, but at the same time thought of all the family pictures that were never taken. As I walked away from the wall, I looked back and saw a group of people gathering where I'd left the flowers. A few would read his name.

We traveled back to France the next day feeling lighter, deeply contented, and tired. A few days in one place to rest and catch up with ourselves sounded heavenly. We headed for Rouen and discovered a city bursting with people from all over the world who had come to attend a music festival. There was no place to stay. Caen became our next destination. From there we could explore the Western Normandy coast. Colorful buntings welcomed Americans, Canadians, and British, those who had liberated France fifty years ago.

Every hotel was full.

Discouraged, we left Caen for Chartres. After nightfall, we spied the ubiquitous bed and breakfast sign hanging from the gate of a farmhouse and turned into the long gravel driveway. A cheery, plumpish woman met me at the door, wiping her hands on her apron. The one room left, up in the attic, belonged to her son the artiste who was away, sculpting in Paris.

"But," she cautioned, "the room is full of termites and they have begun to fly about."

I assured her that if there was a bed in the room, we could manage.

She led us single file up steep rickety stairs, charged into the room, and began spraying the windowsill.

After she left I studied the termites crawling around the sill and flying over the bed. Their wings were delicate slivers of silver that shone in the moonlight. They were almost too tiny for their heavier bodies, yet they rose up and flew away, if they could, after the deadly spray. I felt sad for the fallen termites and happy to watch the rest fly off. Turning from the window, I scanned the room. Indeed it was an artist's room—charming and romantic, filled with dusty pink sculptures of naked women. A tattered tweed coat hung on a wooden peg and worn leather boots huddled on the floor beneath the coat. Pen-and-ink drawings and clay pots lay scattered around the room. The bed was hard and sleep was good.

The next morning, after café au lait sipped from bowls in the garden, we left for Chartres. Soon I spied cathedral towers and spires rising in the distance. Chartres, the destination for pilgrims since the tenth century, was just ahead across the flat plain. Modern pilgrims, we approached the holy site by car.

Our first day in Chartres was Sunday, July 17th, my father's birthday. He would have been seventy-five years old. Jack and I set out to explore the cathedral and stopped before entering to read a poster taped to the iron gate. I could hardly believe what I read: "Dimanche 17 Juillet 1994 a h. 00, a 9 PM, CATHEDRALE DE CHARTRES, REQUIM: DURUFLE." Pictures of Churchill, Roosevelt, De Gaulle, and Eisenhower adorned the four corners of the poster.

We looked at each other in amazement and then Jack threw an arm around my shoulder. "A recognition of those who died in the struggle to liberate France fifty years ago and a requiem for your father on the night of his seventy-fifth birthday!"

We arrived at the cathedral gates well before nine o'clock. Jack waited until most of the people had entered the cathedral and then carefully peeled back the tape, rolled up the poster, and slipped it into his sack.

The cathedral at night appeared even more vast, ancient, and holy than during the day. The stained glass windows seemed etched in shades of blue and black. Carved figures cast and held deep shadows, and the stone walls had turned a soft gold where light touched them. Throughout the requiem I relived the drama of death, sadness, and peace. When it was finished I thanked the host, a gaunt man with dark hair and dark eyes. When I mentioned my father he took my hand firmly in both of his. He didn't speak, but in his eyes I saw my own sadness. I left the cathedral warmed by the music, the remembrance of those who died, and the sadness in the man's eyes.

6

Reunion of the 782nd

We all understand about relating with people we can see and hear, but the search for my father opened up a new way of relating to myself and to someone I'd never seen, heard, or touched. My earliest sense of him was a mixture of feelings that I inherited from my mother and grandparents—sadness, love, and loss. Then I found the letter he wrote to me. He knew my name. He wrote that we were a family—my mother, my brother, David, and me. Best of all, he signed the letter, *Your Father, Dave.* My father. I belonged to him and he was mine, a secret inner atmosphere of unknown wonder. I came from him and even though I didn't know him in the worldly sense, I knew he was part of me and I was part of him. He didn't exist and yet he didn't really not exist. His body was gone, yet I knew it wasn't over.

Searching for him meant that I lived with him in my mind day and night and related much of what I read and felt and thought and did to him. Vestiges of his life and death began to emerge. Looking back, it almost seemed as if the three of us—my father, Jack, and I—worked together to find Camp Lucky Strike and the grove of trees where he died. My father had become a true part of me and I had become a true part of him. The more I discovered about him, the happier I became and the more I wanted to know the men he'd lived with during the winter of 1945. After returning from Europe in the summer of 1994, Jack and I flew to Oklahoma City to attend a reunion of my father's tank battalion.

We arrived late and went straight to the room where the ceremonies were being held. I stopped outside the door, weak-kneed, and looked to Jack for courage. One kiss and we entered. The hotel conference room was large and dark. People were watching a video. Jack and I found chairs at the back and unloaded our packs. There I was, sitting among men my father knew, men who were with him during the last days of his life. Would they remember him? Would I be received as a stranger, unwanted, because his death caused too much guilt or grief?

A thin, gray-haired man in jeans and a white shirt leaned over and tapped me on the shoulder, "Are you David Johnson's daughter?" he whispered. I turned around and smiled, thrilled to be known as my father's daughter. The man showed me photographs of the train wreck and gave me the pictures to keep.

The video ended and the lights came on. Several men walked over to us and introduced themselves as having known my father. One of them was Frank, the first man I'd called who knew him. Frank had invited me to the reunion, and here he was in person, a big man in a plaid shirt, reaching for my hand with both of his, grinning widely. Other men joined us and we stood in a circle and talked about my father as if talking about him was natural, as if he were real.

"Dave was a quiet man. Kind. Respected."

"He was slender, sandy-haired, slouched a bit, smiled. There was no other like him."

"He was a prince. Johnson pitched in with work to be done. He didn't just give orders, he worked with us. We had laughs together. Others were jealous of him, the way he treated us. We were shocked by his death. We hated to lose him."

I looked around the circle. "I thought maybe he was full of youthful recklessness."

"No!" they insisted. "He was confident, one of the officers we liked best."

"Your dad," Frank smiled remembering, "came into our tents to talk. He'd sit down and put his glass of whiskey on the table. When he left, the glass half full of whiskey was still there for us to finish. It was a cold winter and that whiskey warmed us up."

A man wearing overalls ambled over to us. He was huge and he had no teeth. "You look like your father." He shook his head from side to side and tears rolled down his face. "The eyes," he said, "your eyes are like him."

That night I could barely sleep as I thought about spending the next day with these men who knew my father. Saturday morning, Larry, the master of ceremonies for the weekend, introduced me to the battalion. He told them how hard I'd worked to get information about my father, and he invited me to speak. Reserved by nature, I was eager to address this group of a hundred men, many of whom knew my father. Standing in front of them in my black suit, I felt as if I were my father. Maybe it's how they looked at me, with soft, open eyes—eyes that knew death. Or maybe it was their acceptance of me.

"Your stories are my stories," I told them. "I want to know as much as possible about those two years you lived and worked side by side."

After the meeting, Larry approached Jack and me. He shifted his weight from one foot to the other and looked at me with probing eyes. "Your father's death caused me lots of guilt." He took a long breath. "I shouldn't be here. I was supposed to drive him in my Jeep that morning. I missed roll call because I was shaving, so they sent someone else instead. After the explosion there was chaos, and before the remains were identified, my buddy ran into the room where I was lying on my bed and he was yelling that my Jeep was blown up and I was dead. I yelled, 'No! I'm here. I'm alive!' I don't know why it wasn't me. I've been troubled by this ever since, but I'm very thankful to have had my life with my wife and my children."

I looked down and then raised my eyes to meet his. "You've had a good life, Larry, and I've found my father. Now I'm here with you and the others who are helping me know him. Everything's all right."

Frank stepped in beside me and walked me over to a group of men sitting in a circle. One of them jumped up and brought two more chairs into the circle. Frank introduced me to the wiry, white-haired medic, Snow, who was there just after the explosion. "You can tell her all you know about her father's death."

I leaned forward and listened to Snow with my whole being.

"I have never spoken about this before," he said. "Please stop me, Susan, at any point if it gets too graphic."

"I assure you I will."

"I heard the explosion and rushed over. The few remains were scattered to the four winds. All that was left of him was a bit of spinal cartilage, some flesh, and entrails hanging from the trees."

The trees. I thought of the tree on the far side of the crater and the three younger ones inside.

"Do you want me to stop?"

"No. I want to hear all of it."

"The only thing left of one of the other men was a foot in a boot. The third man was dead."

Another medic joined us. He was tall, thin, and dark with angry, sad eyes. One of the men who died was his best friend. "I accompanied his body to the cemetery across the Rhine where we buried him. When the war was over I visited his family and told them about their son." He finished speaking and left. I watched him leave, my sweating hands clutching the chair. I knew the explosion wasn't my fault, but I felt responsible for the man's loss.

Snow talked about the assignment my father was given that morning. "Dave and two other men were sent to a German ammunition dump to find mines to use in teaching the men how to identify and detonate mines. They found the mines stacked on a shelf. Dave told the others they didn't have to help him take the mines off the shelf, but the other two wanted to help."

I thought to myself that maybe if he had been less chummy and more authoritative, they wouldn't have wanted to help him. Maybe they would have walked away from that stack of deadly mines and survived the blast. Maybe his midwestern friendliness was fatal in war. As a father, his kindness might have nurtured me; as a lieutenant it was, perhaps, deadly. The explosion was either my father's mistake, lack of knowledge, or German soldiers had booby-trapped the mines. The picture of the aftermath was graphic and it was real. Knowing what happened brought relief, and it also brought my father's death into the human realm, a combination of errors—the hubris of youth, and war. My mother and grandmother didn't know this part; they couldn't have helped me with this. This was silence opening up. His death could live in the world, where it belonged. I was so thankful to be there with those men who didn't hold back. We could talk about it as much as we needed to, until it faded like the last red streak of light fades from the evening sky so that night and rest and the next new day can follow.

———————

All day long men brought me gifts: the battalion pin, a baseball cap with the battalion's insignia, pictures, and a cookbook the women put together. They showed me their photo albums and scrapbooks of the war and they voted to pay for our room.

Saturday night, at the banquet, Jack and I sat at a table with Frank and his wife, Jeanine. She was concerned about me, worried that the men had told me too much. Most of the wives had heard nothing about the war until 1987, at the first reunion of the 782nd, when they overheard the men talking. We chatted about the war between bites of chicken and green beans and choco-late cake, and Frank told us about another dinner long ago and over there.

"I was invited to eat at the home of a French family. The daughter was a schoolteacher the same age I was then, eighteen years old. I stole food from the mess to take to that family who invited GIs to eat with them even though food was scarce."

Larry asked me to stand. After introducing me, he hesitated and stopped, having forgotten Jack's name.

Jack chuckled and leaned over to Jeanine, his blue eyes shining. "I feel like you, Jeanine, one of the wives who can listen and overhear, but it's Susan who's trusted with their stories. She's one of them."

7

Old Friends

A pale purple line divided the frozen lake from the winter sky. Geese whirred through the cold air in an almost perfect V of small black dots. Behind me stood the great stone hospital in Oshkosh, Wisconsin where I was born in the dead of winter while my family waited for the war to end and my father to come home. Victory came with spring and peace settled in over the summer. For us the effects of the war continued as, one by one, my father's family died, beginning with my father's death in April 1945. Returning to his home town, Oshkosh, more than fifty years after his death, I hoped to find out about his life before the war, unearth the silence, and gather the fragments that remained before they turned to dust.

Jack and I left the lake and set off to find a place to stay. Our choice was a hotel in the heart of town with Main Street two blocks away. We took a walk to see what was there and discovered practical things in old-fashioned red brick buildings on Main Street: paper and pens and shoes and aspirin and vacuum cleaners—nothing fancy. Windowless taverns popped up on street corners, and the library, courthouse, and town hall stood like prominent citizens with stately columns and matronly domes. Near the hotel we found the New Moon, a bakery-café with high ceilings and oak tables, and we went there often to strategize, reflect, drink tea, and watch people. I couldn't get enough of the round-sounding words of my mother tongue.

"There you go," the waitress sang as she set mugs of steaming chai on the table.

We began our search at the library. The research librarian escorted us to a series of old books, and I looked up my grandfather's name in the 1945 city directory. There he was in bold letters: "David S. Johnson, President, Guernsey Dairy Company." Checking back through older directories, I found that my father left Chicago, where he was born, and came to Oshkosh in 1927 with his parents and his mother's parents. All five of them lived together in a house on Jackson Street—the two-story, white-shingled house with a front porch and a birch tree in the yard that we'd driven by earlier.

Jack read newspapers on microfiche, and he found my great-grandfather's obituary, dated November 7, 1933. It stated that George L. Meyer, my grandmother's father, was born in Bavaria, Germany in 1865 and came to America when he was sixteen years old. Astonished, I realized that for the first fourteen years of his life, my father lived with his German grandfather. Then, when he was twenty-five, he left home to fight against and then die in the country where his grandfather was born and raised.

———————— ❦ ————————

Earlier, when I had written to Oshkosh High School requesting my father's records, I had received a copy of his enrollment card. In the lower right corner, my fifteen-year-old father looked out at me. At once I saw my own round face, full lips, and serious, dark eyes. I looked nothing like my blue-eyed mother, whose face is long and narrow. Placing a school photo of my fifteen-year-old self beside my father's picture, the resemblance was unmistakable.

At the public library I asked the librarian for Oshkosh High School yearbooks for the years 1934–1937 and followed her over to a locked case.

"The yearbooks from those years are scanty," she said. "They didn't publish any during the depression years. None from 1934, none from 1935 or 1936." She removed a pamphlet covered in green paper with the title "Index–937."

I peered over her shoulder as she opened the book, and carefully turned the pages to the section listing seniors and their activities.

"There he is." She thumbed the page. "David Johnson."

The top row of a group photo showed my father wearing a V-neck sweater and a plaid tie, and it revealed a new similarity: we were both on the high school yearbook staff. The next page, labeled "Homecoming of 1936," showed hundreds of kids outside the high school building. There he was again in the write-up beneath the photo, living his teenage life: "Goal posts were decorated by Dave Johnson and his committee."

Our next stop was the University of Wisconsin, Oshkosh, where I told my story to the woman behind the desk, noting that WWII was her grandparents' generation.

"I'll need a death certificate to release his college records," she said.

"There is no death certificate, but I can bring you his obituary."

Jack and I headed back to the library. The obituary wasn't hard to find; we knew the date, April 12, 1945. Jack read through the newspaper just after that time and called out to me, "I found the announcement of his death—Monday, April 23, 1945."

It was the same day my mother received the telegram.

DAVID JOHNSON
KILLED IN ACTION
WITH U.S. FORCES

To the honor roll of Oshkosh
heroes in World War II has been
added the name of Second Lt.
David S. Johnson, Jr., 25. Infor-
mation was received here today
from the war department that
Lieutenant Johnson was killed
April 12 somewhere in Germany.

Staring at the tall black headlines, the happy, easy life I began to imagine for my father disappeared. I pictured my mother and my grandparents hiding their sadness in dark coats and hats, their shoulders bent in grief, as they went about their day's work, trying to bear up, answering questions, listening to condolences, touching hands and nodding, comforting those who tried to comfort them, sick inside, knowing he wouldn't return, hoping against hope that the war department was mistaken, knowing it probably was not, their lives suddenly frozen.

After we exchanged the obituary for the transcript at the university, my father was alive again, a student at Carlton College in Minnesota, where he spent the 1937–1938 school year. He made his way from school to school to marriage, entering Oshkosh State in September 1939 and withdrawing in

May 1940 when he met my mother. He was twenty-one and she was twenty when his other grandfather, a Presbyterian minister, presided at their wedding. A picture shows them standing under an arbor, their private closeness visible in the way he leaned toward her, the way they held hands behind their backs.

Recently Mother answered some of my questions about their life together in a letter. "He was the first of his crowd to marry, so our apartment was a gathering place until one by one the boys went off to war. We really had little time together in a normal, everyday marriage and those times were hard for me with little money. Because he was somewhat spoiled and doted on as an only child and grandchild, our bank account was often overdrawn or he forgot to deposit money, so I had to depend on the Johnsons and my dad who were always very supportive. There was no grave; we had only a memorial service in Oshkosh. The next year or so is dim to me—the first year of your life. I was numb and depressed and paid neighborhood children to play with you." Toward the end of the letter she wrote: "Please don't ask me for too many details—it is too shattering to keep digging into the past, even though I want you to be at peace."

———————◆———————

Announcements of other deaths in my father's family appeared in the *Oshkosh Northwestern* soon after the obituary, and Jack, who had become an expert sleuth, found them. In November 1945, my father's grandfather, the one who married my parents, died in Chicago. In December 1946, Granny's mother lay in her hospital room listening to carolers singing outside her door. "Angels," she said with her last breath, "have come to take me home." In July 1948 my father's father was stricken with polio. "Dear Ones," my grandmother wrote to her brother-in-law's family, "Just a note to tell you Dave is seriously ill with polio. He is completely paralyzed from the waist down. It is an unusual case, not easily diagnosed. The doctors say that if he lives through the next three days he has a chance to live. Please, please pray for him and me. We need your prayers as we never have before." He was sick less than a week before he died. My grandfather was the one we relied on—father to my mother, my brother, and me. My grandmother moved to Chicago and married a childhood sweetheart in 1950. Three years later, he died of cancer and my grandmother was alone again. I spent vacations and summers with my grandmother until her losses and loneliness became too much to bear and she took her life the summer I was seventeen. The family withered like leaves in fall and one by one floated down to death. Only my mother sprouted with love again when she married my stepfather.

———

Before leaving for Oshkosh, I looked up the phone number for one of my father's childhood friends, Bob. Afraid of rejection, I almost didn't call, but Jack's support and my desire to know my father guided my hand and I dialed the number.

Bob seemed happy to talk about that time in my father's life. "I gave Dave a pretty good picture of Carlton. He entered as a freshman when I was a sophomore. We'd go out and have a beer and Limburger cheese-and-onion sandwiches. He worked on the college paper. He was a good student and could have been at the top, but we showed him there were other things besides books. Dave was a combination of all—shy, funny, serious, a bookish kid as a young teenager. His senior year in high school he got to know people, got mixed in, a balance between introverted and extroverted, fun to be with and liked by all.'"

Bob's description of my father closely described our son, Jacques, who is both introverted and extroverted and liked by everyone.

"Every Friday morning," Bob continued, "all of us, the old gang, meet at Hardees for coffee. We've been meeting ever since the end of the war. Your dad knew all these guys. We'd like to have you meet us there when you're in town." Before he hung up he gave me the telephone number of another friend.

The next day I called her and she dove right in. "When Pearl Harbor happened, I was at your mom and dad's apartment and all the guys said, 'Let's go to Officer Candidate School.' I said to my honey, who later became my husband, 'Oh honey, no! Second Lieutenants are cannon fodder. Just go in and get it over and come home.' Your dad and my honey went overseas in winter. It wasn't a good time to be on the ocean. The German U-boats were out to sink our convoys. For a long time we didn't know if and when and where they landed. And your mom was expecting. It's not like now, when they tell you everything. All she got back was your dad's watch."

———

Thursday Jack and I had a free day and decided to drive over to the Oshkosh Museum hoping to see an exhibit about local dairies. Algoma Boulevard wound past houses with porches and gables that were built in the early years of the twentieth century. The Oshkosh Museum was in one of the grand old houses. When the woman behind the counter in the gift shop, about my mother's age, asked why I was interested in dairies, I told her about my search.

"Well," she said, "my next door neighbor, Ellie Baynes, knows your family. She's mentioned your father." The woman gave me Ellie's number.

"I know that name," I told Jack. "It's a name I've heard since childhood. Mother saw her whenever she went to Oshkosh, and they spoke often." When we got back to our hotel, I left her a message. Jack and I walked over to the New Moon Café, where the late-afternoon sunlight fell on our table as we talked. Just being in Oshkosh, windows into my father's life were opening.

The phone was ringing when we entered our hotel room. It was Ellie. "I've known all your family—your grandparents, your dad, your mother, and your stepfather, Dick. I could enlighten you about your dad. Would you like to meet for dinner?"

"Of course."

Jack and I had planned to see *The Glass Menagerie* at the Grand Opera House after dinner, but thinking Ellie might talk more freely if it were just the two of us, I kissed Jack good-bye and agreed to meet him at the opera house for the show.

Ellie was waiting for me inside the spacious wood-paneled restaurant. She was pretty, with white curly hair and pink cheeks. We slid into a booth and ordered. Right away she said, "On his last night home, your father left Margery and went out with the guys. She was eight months pregnant. She never said anything, but all the girls thought it was bad. His last night home. He flunked out of school," she continued. "His parents were disgusted. He went from one thing to another."

I was surprisingly happy to hear her talk about my father, given the disparaging picture she painted. She knew him then and she was talking about him as he was when he was alive. I loved listening to her talk about his foibles.

"He was bookish, a scholar until he met us," she added. "We broke him in and he came out of his shell. Made him well-rounded."

Ellie forked a string bean and looked at me. "I knew you when your family lived in Oshkosh. You looked like him as a little girl. You have his eyes. You still have his eyes." She smiled. "He was a good dancer. He loved to dance. I liked to dance with him."

I heard the softness in her voice when she said that and I thought of our daughter, Sarah, who is a terrific dancer.

"Everyone was surprised when he brought Margery home. We liked her. Your grandparents loved her." Ellie wiped her mouth with her napkin. "All the guys were so excited to go to war. The women in Oshkosh, their wives and sisters and mothers, wondered why. Your dad didn't know what he was about and thought the Army would figure it out for him."

We were coming to the end of our meal and the end of our talk. Before saying good-bye we ordered one divine chocolate dessert and shared it— like Mother and Ellie would have, like two friends. Before parting, Ellie asked me if my children had my father's eyes. "Our son, Jacques, does," I told her. My father's eyes and his dancing feet are alive in our family, in this world.

I said good-bye to Ellie at her car and walked to the opera house to meet Jack. The Grand Opera House had maintained its late-nineteenth-century style, and *The Glass Menagerie* was still relevant—what to do with ourselves, mothers who wanted us to be the way they needed us to be, absent fathers, and troubled siblings.

Before meeting my father's friends at Hardees, I put on a rose-colored turtleneck sweater, gray flannel trousers, and my warm peacoat with the collar turned up against the cold. I threw a red scarf around my neck, and Jack and I made plans to meet later at the New Moon Café.

Bob was at the door of Hardees, waiting for me. His body was slight, his white hair sparse, and his whole face wrinkled and twinkled when he laughed. He walked me over to the table where twelve men were sitting. I shook hands all around and pulled up a chair.

The guys were funny; they teased each other. "We come here every week and we say the same things," they told me.

Two men entered and walked toward us. One, gruff looking, wore glasses, a red sweater, and dark slacks. Bob introduced him. "This is Henry, also known as Mr. Oshkosh. He knew your dad well."

The man standing behind Henry reached up and tucked in the label on Henry's sweater, announcing to the whole table, "Hey, you've got a woman's sweater on. Liz Claiborne is clothes for women."

Henry frowned. "When my wife died the kids came and sorted through her clothes. Went through mine, too. Threw away a lot of things, gave the rest to Goodwill. When they left, I went down there and bought back all my own clothes."

The men laughed and shook their heads. My father would have loved to be sitting there with his old friends.

The youngest of the bunch rose from the table, excused himself, and left for work. A man at the far end of the table asked me if I worked.

"I'm a psychologist by profession," I told him.

"She's got you figured out, " another said.

"Well, all I do is help them be like you guys, able to laugh and have a good time."

Bob was goaded into telling me about the times Al Capone, the Prohibition-era ganster, came to Oshkosh. He pronounced the name the way they said it there, "Caponie."

"Every spring Al Caponie and his gang stopped in Oshkosh on their way up to their hideout in the north woods. They stayed at the Athearn Hotel downtown, where an underground tunnel led to the opera house so they could escape if the feds showed up. Al Caponie always bought a brand new Cadillac from the Oshkosh Motor Company. He was good for business in Oshkosh."

When the men left I asked Henry to stay so I could show him the book of documents and photos I'd collected about my father.

"What was he like?" I asked.

"He was a kid like the rest of us. I went sailing with him. We raced our sailboats every weekend. Dave had his own boat and I had mine. Look here. There's a trophy named in honor of your dad, The Lt. David S. Johnson, Jr. Trophy."

Henry handed me the book, *A Century of Sail on Winnebago 1869–1969*, and I read that my father was the only member of the club to lose his life in World War II.

Henry warmed toward me in a fatherly way when he mentioned that he was in Aachen about the same time my father was there. His voice was soft and the words came slowly. "I know that area. Your dad may have been deactivating a mine or he may have tripped a wire. The whole area was mined all around the ammo dump." His hands trembled when he read the morning report of my father's death.

He took a yellowed clipping out of his scrapbook and handed it to me. It was a newspaper account of a sailboat race in the mid-1930s, when my father and Henry were about the age I was when I raced sailboats a little farther north on Lake Winnebago. I read that Henry won the race and my father came in last.

"You can keep it," he said.

I took the precious remnant and put it inside my book. Later, when I wanted to show it to Jack, it was missing.

———

That night I sat with a cup of tea in our room looking out over Oshkosh— at the dark river flowing as it always had, the lights beyond, and the wide purple sky. Steel halyards clanked against metal masts. My father's friends had given me a sense of him before grief darkened memory. They couldn't welcome him home, but they had welcomed me, and they were now my friends.

For so long tragedy was all I'd known of Oshkosh. Lost happiness. After sitting with my father's friends, listening to their stories, hearing them laugh and joke, I felt affection for them and I had a new understanding of that family, my family, when they were alive and a central part of life in Oshkosh, Wisconsin, before the war. My family was simply part of the flow of life that was sailing and dancing and having lunch with friends, as well as war and sickness and death.

My father's friends had let me know that he and I were quite a bit alike in looks, activities, and interests. The unknown is within. All along my father had been right there in my eyes and my hands, maybe even in the ways I thought and saw things. He was now more of a person to me, a guy with dark, serious eyes much like my own, an easygoing, forgetful sort of guy, maybe like his grandson. I think he would understand his grandson, who is both quiet and people-loving, who believes in living life to its fullest and enjoys all good things. Jacques' playfulness would have matched his own. And he was like Sarah, who carries a natural goodness and a belief in tolerance, and who gives to life to the fullest. Words were life giving for him as they are for her, and their words have given life to those who read what they've written. Sarah writes letters and poems and lets people know what they mean to her, like my father did. They would have enjoyed each other. I never knew the search would lead me to this, seeing my father in my children and in myself.

8

The Ninety-Day Wonders

I'd heard several different accounts of my father's death: He was on a mission to clear mines in the area so the tanks of the 782nd could safely follow. Arrogant young replacements with little training were eager to give orders that first morning in enemy territory and sent him out. He was commanded to find and disarm mines to use for teaching purposes, stumbled onto the ammunition dump, and tread on a booby-trapped step of a wooden structure that housed mines. He was reaching for a mine in the ammo dump to use for teaching purposes when it exploded. He cut the wrong wire of an allegedly booby-trapped mine, or maybe it wasn't booby-trapped.

If anyone knew and was willing to tell me what really happened that morning, it would be Mike Rowlands. Mike and my father had attended the same officer training school and they'd been in the same battalion. And by an uncanny coincidence, he'd married a woman, Sally, who had been my mother's camp counselor when Mother was a teenager back in Ohio.

Sally read a *Reader's Digest* article I'd written about my father and called. She told me the remarkable story of how, ten years after befriending Mother at camp, she had seen her again. "Mike was in Officer Training School, in Louisville, and we were at a restaurant when your parents danced by. I told Mike I knew that girl. He said I didn't know anyone in Louisville, but it turns out I did. Your father was in the program with Mike and we shared housing with your mother and father until the men were shipped to San Diego and then on to Europe in the wake of the Battle of the Bulge."

"Everyone loved Sally, with her dark hair and sparkly eyes," Mother remembered when I told her I'd talked with Sally.

After Sally died, Mike and I stayed in contact. He was ninety-one and nearly blind when I called to see if he was up for a visit.

He responded as if he were expecting me. "You might have some questions I could shed light on."

From the airplane window, the land looked much as it did when the first people lived there. There were no highways or buildings, just hills, valleys, mountains, and the rivers that wound across the land like ancient paths.

In Seattle I picked up a rental car and followed the MapQuest directions to a bed-and-breakfast directly across the street from Mike's condominium. When I called him, he invited me over.

As I stepped into the room Mike inspected me from the side, explaining that he had only a bit of peripheral vision. "You *do* look like your father. You have his brown eyes."

I breathed more slowly and knew this was the right place to be. Mike was tall and slender, and he carried himself with an air of dignity and confidence, like the officer he once was.

It was easy to talk with him about the war and the 782nd, something we both wanted to talk about. Soon into the conversation I mentioned the stories I'd heard about my father's death and Mike responded.

"I saw Dave the morning the battalion reached Mechernich, April 12. I asked him if I could borrow his sergeant to drive me into Germany. I took the sergeant and the Jeep and drove through German towns. White sheets were hanging out of windows everywhere, from houses, hospitals, and stores. The Germans had blown up bridges and we were hell-bent on getting back to camp. That day was the first and only time I saw General Ike Eisenhower, who was out in his Jeep inspecting the damage. I was shocked to hear the news about Dave when I got back. I never asked for particulars. All I know is that Dave was sent out to disarm mines so the tanks could move into Germany. That was the same day President Roosevelt died. The sergeant was very thankful I'd taken him with me. Your father was a great fellow, open, good conversations, loved family. He did his duty with dignity and enthusiasm. We enjoyed each other and our wives got on great. "

A woman who looked like Jackie Kennedy walked through the front door and Mike introduced Jeannie, his daughter. "Ours is a family that tells stories," she said. "We're noisy, gossipy, curious, and we talk."

I was enchanted by that statement and with the playful way she related with her father—not filled with caution and fear and longing as I'd been in my family, wanting to know and afraid to ask.

"I'm the rebellious one," she went on. "My father was so powerful and controlling that I stayed away from the family for two years."

Is Mike the kind of man my father might have become? I wondered. *Successful? Confident? A bit reserved, but responsive, and maybe also domineering? Who knows?*

Mike was eager to show me his officer's uniforms, the same ones that my father would have worn, the kind that were shipped home in my father's footlocker. "We had to buy our own uniforms, unlike the enlisted men. They gave us money for them, $200 or $250, and Dave and I went together to buy ours. The training at the officers' school was intense and your father was intelligent. They called us 'The Ninety-Day Wonders.' We had to march around the parade grounds and be commanding. We had all kinds of tests and many of the men, maybe 20% or so flunked out, but your father and I made it. He expressed himself well. One small thing I remember is that he liked dinner rolls with plenty of butter."

Mike and Jeannie and I went into the bedroom where Mike's uniforms lay on the bed, cleaned and pressed. He showed me his "pinks," the light beige woolen trousers with a hint of pink, the dress shirts, and ties. I tried on the Eisenhower jacket and Mike adjusted his soldier's cap. "Your father always wore his hat cocked at a jaunty angle."

Jeannie picked up the dark green trench coat and slipped it on. "My brother would have loved to have had this coat, but Dad kept it just the way it was when the war was over. He put all of his uniforms away and only recently sent them to the cleaners."

"After Susan's visit I'm going to send my uniform to my grandson." Mike reached into the small wooden box where he kept his medals and gave me the 782nd patch, a triangle of gold, red, and blue with the picture of a tank and a streak of lightning.

The next morning the two of us sat in his living room overlooking Puget Sound.

"Sally loved this view," he told me. "She had the electric burners removed from the stove when I was beginning to lose my sight; she was afraid I'd burn this place down. I found out it would cost a fortune to get them put back in." Mike filled two mugs with water, added Postum, and put the mugs in the microwave. Sally had covered each button with Velcro so he could feel which one to push.

We took our mugs back into the living room and he began to talk about the war. "We left New York harbor in a fifty-ship convoy, sad to leave, but we felt pride when we passed the Statue of Liberty." As Mike spoke, a mixture of wonder and fear showed in his face. "The waves were ten feet high. I was so sick. We all were. I'm sure your dad was sick, too. We went as slow as the slowest ship in the convoy and it took a long time. We were in danger of being attacked and it was cold. We landed in Le Havre at eleven at night and boarded the train."

Mike described the train wreck. "We came back the next day and saw the unbelievable wreckage. If we hadn't gotten up to look out when the train gained speed, we would have been killed. Your dad was in the same car, the officers' car.

"Camp Lucky Strike was cold, twenty below. We slept in our clothes with our boots on. The Red Cross sent heavy gloves and the balaclavas we wore to cover our faces. We left Camp Lucky Strike around the beginning of April 1945. In Charles Le Roi we had ice cream with crystals of ice! We loved it! We'd had lots of ice cream at camp in Kentucky."

I laughed knowing that my dad, the dairyman's son, would have loved the ice cream, maybe as much as I did. When I mentioned Aachen, a look of horror passed across Mike's face.

"Death! Aachen smelled like death. Death in the rubble."

As we sipped our Postum, I thought of my father's last night on earth with the smell of death all around. I wanted to reach out and bring him home before it was too late. Call off the war. Come home. Stop! Don't go in there. We need you more than they do. My father was a speck in the war machine and yet he was a person, and that's where the collective and the personal overlap. I'd never know if some fatal thought entered him and took over when he was surrounded by death. First the wreck, then the rubble, and then death. My father failed to survive the war. As a child I felt a sense of shame that I could never quite name. It had to do with silence. No one helped us and no one helped me, not a teacher or a minister or a friend. No one talked about "it"—the war, my father, or his death. No one told us what happened, and that meant it was too shameful to talk about. It couldn't have been the war or the army because other men survived. My father was the only one I knew who didn't survive.

Aachen smelled like death. I knew from 9/11 a little bit of how death creeps into the mind and body. My father had a job to do that morning and his mind and his heart were permeated with death. I could only imagine what joy the new life, my birth, gave him in the midst of that cold winter, life and death so close.

———————

Mike and I helped each other lighten the darkness when we talked about a time both of us needed to talk about. I would never know the answers to some of my questions—the elusive nature of my father's death remained— but this newfound relationship brought me into the heart of the man who fathered me and into the heart of one who knew him. When I left, Mike told me that I was like one of his children.

9

Arlington

I always pictured Mother, David, and me putting flowers on my father's grave, the three of us standing together, heads bowed to the earth where he lay, a playful breeze ruffling our hair. Afterward, we'd go to a nice restaurant and Mother would tell us about our father, her first love. That small comfort ended when I learned there was no body and therefore, no grave. I called the Battle Monuments Commission for confirmation that there was no grave, and they explained that the government would provide a marker for anyone lost at sea, missing, or whose remains were unrecovered.

Right before Thanksgiving in 1996, I received a special entry permit and a location map from Arlington National Cemetery. The memorial marker I had requested had been installed. My first thought was that it was only a marker, not a grave. It took several weeks to gather my courage to go and see it.

Jack and I headed for Arlington on a rainy Saturday in early December. When I showed the guard the entry permit, he waved us through. We wound around Eisenhower Drive, where the road rises and falls over gentle hills, found section C, parked at the bottom of a hill filled with rows of identical white markers, and wandered up the hill reading names and dates of men who died so young. Then I saw it:

IN MEMORY OF
DAVID SELBY JOHNSON, JR.
JULY 17, 1919–APRIL 12, 1945

I touched the smooth, cold marble and traced the letters of his name. Stones of old soldiers and young ones dotted the hills and valleys all around. I belonged here with my father. In an odd way, he had come home. He was no longer lost "somewhere in Germany." I'd helped him home—not guiding him by the elbow, as I would have wished, but by marking his existence with this stone. He lived, this stone said, and then he died. His grandchildren could know he lived.

We planned to have his funeral in July. David and his wife would be in the area and would attend the service. Mother wrote to say she and my step-father would be there too.

———◀ ▶———

The night before the ceremony, six of us were seated around our dining room table: Mother and Dad, Jack, our daughter Sarah, and my friend Nick. His father was shot by a sniper in the courtyard of a village in Luxembourg and was buried in the American Cemetery where my father's name was on the Wall of Missing.

Seated at the head of the table, I glanced up at the wooden shelf on the wall to my left and noticed Granny's teacups. She was here, too in the dining room where the table was set with her china and silver. My father would have recognized the gold-rimmed plates and the silverware engraved with the initial "J."

Nick cleared his throat and began the dinner conversation. "There are many of us war orphans who know so little about our fathers."

Mother set her glass on the table and all eyes turned to her. "I hate that term. I've told Susan. I'm the one who suffered, not Susan. I had it rough, a widow with two kids, young and confused in a chaotic world. Susan was always well cared for. She was not a ragged, starving child."

Nick turned his dark eyes to me and then faced Mother. His usually mel-lifluous voice was tight with effort to explain. "My world was shattered. I was five years old and trying to be the man of the house, figure everything out."

Mother's fork hit the plate. "Susie always had enough to eat and nice clothes to wear and plenty of love."

I looked across the table at my stepfather, who was quietly spooning rice from his dish, and then glanced at Jack, who was sitting beside me. His nor-mally rosy complexion was pale.

She continued, "I never told her about him because I did not want her to know him. He was mine and I needed him for myself, so I would always have him with me. Now he is not mine anymore. Susan ruined my memories with her search."

Sarah, sitting across the table from her grandmother, was the same age now that Mother was when her husband died. Tears filled her eyes and spilled onto her cheeks.

Lying in bed that night, I fidgeted with thoughts of having been silenced yet again and tried to hold on to my wish to understand Mother. My father appeared in my mind with his wide, boyish grin. The thought came to me that he would have loved both of us. My parents were just beginning their life together. Mother wanted to keep him as he was during the short time they were together, when he was hers. She needed to keep the sense of her young self when she loved and was loved, before death took everything. I wasn't part of that early love, but a reminder of his death and her grief. Sharing him with me opened her to darker memories. Sarah understood Mother's fear of losing him. Without him, she had nothing. How could she go on if she gave in to grief? No wonder Mother fought my intrusions and protected her memories at all costs. I threatened her peace of mind with my relentless pursuit of him. She'd given me everything I needed to grow into a decent person, so why would I try to take that from her?

Turning my pillow over to find a cooler place for my head, I tried to hold my feelings of guilt in check, not wanting to lose myself to that demon. Mother's way and my way, though seemingly opposed, were part of the natural dance of life and death, one that took generations to complete. We both loved him in our different ways: Mother preserved him in her private memories, while I tried to find him by seeking out the people and places he knew. Understanding some of what it had cost her, I was grateful that Mother had come for the ceremony. The next day we'd meet David and his wife, Gloria, and gather at Arlington. Sleep came slowly.

In the morning I picked up flowers to carry for the family to place at my father's stone. As we pulled into the parking lot, Jack asked if I'd brought the flag. I'd forgotten the flag! We raced back over Memorial Bridge and up Rock Creek Parkway and then back to Arlington with the flag.

The reception house was filled with family and friends who had encouraged me and listened to my stories, and war orphans from all over who knew the same loss. We followed the chaplain to the road, where the procession began, and watched him place the flag inside a flag-draped caisson. Three soldiers on horseback led three riderless horses for the three men killed in that explosion fifty-two years ago. My father loved horses. Smiling, I imagined that he would have liked this day—the horses, soldiers, family, and friends gathered to honor him in that quiet place with tall trees. The band played "Amazing Grace" as we lined up behind the caisson. *I once was lost but now I'm found.*

I thought I should feel sad, but I felt triumphant walking down the road behind the soldiers and the caisson, Jack and our children, Jacques and Sarah, beside me, our family and friends nearby. Sarah carried the basket of flowers, and I carried the red roses I'd also bought. The procession wound through the cemetery and stopped beneath the hill where my father's stone stood. We were ushered to chairs set up on the lawn as the band played the familiar hymn, *Faith of our fathers living still in spite of dungeon fire and sword* . . . Mother loved this hymn, and I saw her trying not to cry.

In silence, the soldiers unfolded the flag and held it over the ground as Jack, an Episcopal priest, stood in front of us and began the service. "Blessed are you who mourn, for you shall be comforted." He told what we knew about my father's life. Several of the young soldiers smiled as Jack recounted how, in the winter of '45, my father left his glass of whiskey for his men. I reached for David's hand and we were two kids listening to stories about our father.

After the dedication of the stone, seven soldiers on the hill fired three rounds of shots. As silence returned, the slow notes of "Taps" drifted up from the bottom of the hill. While the band played "America the Beautiful," the soldiers folded the flag, each one touching it softly with white gloves. One of the soldiers held it to his heart before passing it to the chaplain, who presented the flag to us.

Mother, David, and I climbed the hill to lay our flowers at the marker that bore my father's name and the dates of his short life. Walking down the hill, Mother took my hand. "Thank you, Susan. I could never have done this."

The journey to find my father ended there in Arlington National Cemetery, where we were together for the first time remembering the eager young soldier who was my father.

Mother was going to our apartment the morning after the memorial service to look at the records, documents, and pictures I'd collected. As I leafed
through the book I'd put together, I tried to see it through her eyes. Many
of the pages held terrible reminders of his death. She would see the letter
that brought the news of his death and the letter six years later that told her
there were no remains to bury and no grave. There were pages with lists of
his belongings the Army sent home the summer after his death. She would
remember opening the packages, finding his shaving gear and his shirts, the
last things he touched. Would this book ease her grief or open wounds and
plunge her into darkness? Or would we be able to sit together and talk as two
grown women sharing stories about the life and death of someone we both
loved?

We sat at the table in the living room beside windows that looked down
on the busy street, drinking coffee and talking, until Mother asked to see
the book. I took the thick blue album down from its place on the bookshelf
beside the fireplace and set it on the table in front of her.

She opened it and turned the pages. "I love that picture of the two of us.

It was his first leave." Mother sounded teary and tender. "One night while we were at a camp in Kentucky or Tennessee I had a nightmare that something happened to Dave and he didn't survive the war. I told him. He wanted me to have more family, so we decided to have you. He wanted me to have another child."

I heard love in her story and in the tone of her voice. I was part of that love as I listened to her. We could never be a living family, but I was part of them at that moment.

"Dave had a sense of humor. And he liked guns. When he was in high school he shot off a gun in his bedroom. He showed me the bullet holes in the woodwork where the bullet ricocheted around his room. I left Davey, who was just a few months old, with Dave's parents when I went to visit him in camp. They couldn't wait to get their hands on the baby. When I came home Davey didn't recognize me."

My young mother faced loss wherever she turned. How divided my parents must have felt; there was no time for them to be together as a family. I could only imagine the dread that ran through their lives as the war intensified.

Mother took a sip of coffee and held the mug in her hands. "We were the first of Dave's crowd to get married. Our home was the place where everyone gathered before going off to the war. I was so angry when he died. I was angry that *he* was the one who died. He was mine and I needed him. If the war hadn't come we wouldn't have done everything so fast. But everything was speeded up."

Tears gathered in her eyes as she read the letter he wrote to welcome me.

> *Your mother is the most wonderful person I've ever known. I've always marveled at my great good fortune to have loved her and been loved by her.*

"His handwriting is so familiar and sad. He was a good letter writer. That's where you get it from." She looked up at me, then examined the picture of my father squatting in front of his tent at Camp Lucky Strike, cigarette in his hand, an open smile. "I like that picture of Dave. He'll always be twenty-five to me."

10

The War is Over

A little over a year later, the *Washingtonian Magazine* published an article I wrote entitled "Finding My Father." I sent Mother a copy, hoping it would help her understand why I'd wanted to begin the search and what I'd found. I was naïve, to say the least. The peace we'd found after the memorial service exploded. Mother was livid. She called me at work, shouting, "You have invaded my privacy. You had no right to publish those pictures of Dave and me."

The trouble between us escalated when *Reader's Digest* wanted to excerpt the article from the *Washingtonian* and called Mother to verify the story. She was furious, and my brother David threatened to sue. Mother and I stopped communicating when our talks ended in conflict. Once again the family circled its wagons around her and I was outside that circle. I was upset that no one understood what I was trying to do, only that I was hurting Mother. I felt mistreated, condemned, and rejected. I'm sure Mother felt persecuted, betrayed, and rejected.

During this time I relied on Jack and on meditation. Jack understood my search and my wretchedness. He was steady in his support and his love for me, never pushing me one way or another. When I needed to cut back on work, we changed our lifestyle to accommodate our changed financial situation. He accepted and supported my exploration of Buddhism and my practice of meditation.

In 1995, I had traveled to Ladakh in Northern India with a friend to join a trekking and meditation camp. Meditating in the thin Himalayan air with monks and lamas and eating and walking in silence day after day slowed me down and I entered a place of timeless peace. When I returned home I continued to mediate and I learned the ancient Buddhist practice of Tonglen, a way to touch suffering and transform it into something light and clear. I practiced Tonglen daily to keep my heart open to my family and myself during the almost four years we had little contact. First I breathed in Mother's suffering, recognizing the pain of being young and alone with two children, or the distress of having a daughter who hounded her when all she wanted was to preserve her memories in peace. Breathing out, I'd mentally send her a cup of coffee and wish her some peaceful moments to sit down and enjoy it, or I'd send her comfort and ease. I then did Tonglen for my stepfather and my siblings, one by one, and for myself.

Several years after the blow-up about the publications, I was sitting on my meditation cushion when a memory surfaced of sitting quietly beside Mother in church. I wrote her a note:

Dear Mother,

I know that I've hurt you deeply. We've both hurt each other. I miss the way you put your arms on my shoulders and look me squarely in the eyes. We'll always share the bond of our love for the old hymns.

You are still my mother and I am still your daughter and I love you.

All my love,
Susan

A few days later I opened a card from her:

Dear Susan,

Thank you for your beautiful note. I feel mended! We seem to always think of each other at the same times and that is a strong bond. I am still your mother and I have always loved you and I always will. Mother.

I wrote to my stepfather, who had tried to love the lost and silently rebellious child I was.

Dear Dad,

I have just seen a documentary about Jewish children who were sent out of Germany by their parents during WWII and taken into homes in England. I identified with a woman in the film who said that she had been difficult to live with. She said she was like a wounded bird. When you first pick up the bird you think it should rest quietly and thankfully in your safe, loving hands, but it struggles and wants to get free and is hard to hold, even though it needs to be taken care of. I have been like that wounded bird in your hands.

With love,
Susan

A little while later, I sent Mother a note and enclosed a picture of myself grinning like a five-year-old. I mentioned that we were planning to visit college friends in Wisconsin, people whose parents had known my parents. Several days later I was surprised to hear Mother's voice on our answering machine. I picked up the phone and heard her ask us to stop in Indianapolis on our way to or from Wisconsin. "It's time," she said.

Jack and I arranged the trip for the end of March.

I labored over what to wear, the place my anxiety showed up, and decided on a navy wool turtleneck sweater, short skirt, and gray tights. I bought Italian loafers and felt like a college kid going home on semester break. Saturday morning I woke up with energy, ready to go, feeling curious but cautious.

The flight was quick. We rented a car and followed their directions to their new home.

They were walking out the front door when we arrived. They'd aged since the memorial service, almost four years before. They looked frail. They shuffled. Dad planted one of his memorable wet kisses on my cheek. I turned to Mother and saw a bright eagerness in her eyes. She hugged me to her with the hunger of loss and return. When we separated I told her I liked her hair, which was pure white and softly curled under, different from her curly perms of the past.

She stepped back and stared at mine, which was rapidly turning gray. "I like your hair. Granny had white hair when she was young." We'd broken apart and mended and there we were talking about our hair. "Look," Mother pointed to her new Italian loafers. "We have the same shoes."

Mother and Dad led us inside and showed us their new home. It suited them perfectly. The rooms were spacious and bright and all on one floor. The living room opened to a patio, which the former owner had decorated with a weeping cherry tree and a winding brick wall. A little statue of a buddha sat in the garden.

My brother Dan, his wife, and their children were coming for dinner. I kept my guard up with Dan but melted when I saw their three children, whom I hadn't seen in four years. The oldest sat with us and talked about visiting colleges. "Carlton is a possibility," Dan piped up. "Where your father went to school."

Smiling, I noted that the silence had been broken in this poor war-torn family.

Sunday morning, Jack and I picked Mother and Dad up for church. Mother and I sat side by side in the pew. Her hymnal fell open to "Faith of Our Fathers," a hymn from our past, and she nudged me playfully. Sitting beside Mother in church was so familiar, like sitting beside her when I was a girl. Dad and my younger siblings attended the Catholic Church, so it was just David, Mother, and I sitting in the church of our ancestors.

The next morning, Jack and I arrived for brunch before leaving for the airport. Jack was talking with Dad in the living room when Mother came out of her bedroom with several framed portraits in her hands. We stood in the hallway and she showed them to me one by one. "This is Poppy, your father's father, and this is your great-grandmother. These are for you. And here is Sarah Ellen Sinclair, my father's mother. I'm keeping this for one of the other children, as she's their great-grandmother too." Her voice softened. "I found this one of Dave. It's my favorite. I want you to have it."

I took the portrait in my hands and looked at my father's warm, dark eyes. He was looking right at me, as he had looked at Mother all those years. My beautiful young father, so much pain in the wake of his death. Now it was over. The war was over in this family. Like the light in Mechernich, I didn't know I'd needed this. This gift was a sign of her love for both of us, a sign wrested from the despair and ruin of war, a sign that I was my father's daughter and that we were family. I was part of my mother and my father.

With the pictures in my bag, I walked into the living room to look at the albums from Mother and Dad's fiftieth wedding anniversary, which I hadn't attended. Underneath the two anniversary albums was another, older album. I opened the brown leather cover and looked down at the page of black-and-white photos. Mother pointed to a photograph from long ago. "That's me as a baby with my mother."

Her mother's head bent lovingly over the baby she held in her arms. Beside that was a picture of Mother when she was about four years old, sitting on the front steps with her father, Grandpa Ben. The next page was filled with pictures of Mother and her brother and two sisters. "That's Elinor." Mother pointed to a young girl with a feather in her hat. I recognized Mother in the next picture. She was tall and her face had narrowed. She was standing beside her little sister, Dorothy, and they were dressed up. "That picture was taken just after my mother died. I was ten."

I remembered that picture and the next one, the one of Mother and Dorothy behind the hollyhocks. The girls had almost disappeared behind the flowers, like Mother's sisters had disappeared. "Where are they now?" I asked.

"Elinor's probably dead and Dorothy's somewhere on the East Coast."

Other mysteries from the ashes of death, I thought to myself. "It's possible to make good copies of old photos these days," I ventured.

"Take the pictures you want," Dad said, "and have them copied."

"It might be safer to take them in the album."

"Sure. Take the album."

I couldn't believe my good fortune. Jack and I got our coats and I picked up my bag with the portraits and the album. I'd arrived at their home with painful memories of past battles, fear, and scant hope. I left with a heart full of gratitude. Mother had been generous and forgiving. She'd given us the ending to our fifty-six-yearlong war story, and it was one that I could never have imagined. Fragments of that young family had survived like fragments from an ancient text. As we walked toward the car, I looked back and saw a sparkle in Mother's eyes.

11

Plum Village

The *Reader's Digest* article not only unleashed Mother's fury, it also opened a crack in the wall of silence for many others whose fathers died in WWII. For over a month I received hundreds of e-mails a day from people who didn't know where their fathers were buried or much at all about them. The messages were heartbreaking. I let them know where to send for their fathers' records and directed them to the American Battle Monuments Commission, who told them instantly where their fathers were buried. That was good, but I felt as if I carried thousands of wounded, forgotten people with every step I took.

I began to search for something that could lighten my load, but after reading books and thinking about things, my exhaustion continued to deepen. I knew psychology inside and out but needed help of a different kind. I meditated in my room and that gave me some stability, but the pain was too great for me to carry alone. I looked for a spiritual community, but none of them resonated with my needs.

One fall day in 2000, a friend took me to a day of mindfulness where I met a young woman who told me about her stay in Plum Village, a Buddhist community in southwest France founded by the Zen peace monk Thich Nhat Hanh. The nuns had saved her life and given her a new way of seeing herself and the world.

That's it, I thought. *A new way to see myself and the world is exactly what I need.*

I'd heard about Thich Nhat Hanh and his work for peace during the war in Vietnam years earlier, when I was in college. Soon after the day of mind-fulness, while browsing at a bookstore in DC, I was drawn to a book with a cover showing Thich Nhat Hanh in a brown wool watch cap touching the names of the dead at the Vietnam Veteran's Wall. I picked it up and read:

> *We who have experienced war directly have a responsibility to share our insight and experience concerning the truth of war. We are the light at the tip of the candle. It is very hot, but it has the power of shining and illuminating . . . Practicing mindfulness we will know how to look deeply into the nature of the war and, with our insight, awaken our own people. We know what war is. We also know that the war is not only in us; it is in everyone—veterans and non-veterans. We must share our insight, not out of anger, but out of love.*

I bought the book and the next day wrote to Plum Village asking to stay for a month.

The train stopped at a small village about an hour east of Bordeaux. I stepped down and waited. A woman in a long brown dress walked towards me, her shaved head shining in the noonday sun. As I was about to extend my hand, she brought both of hers together in front of her chest and bowed. Smiling, I brought my hands together and bowed. It was spring 2001, shortly after the reconciliation with my mother and my family. We left the station in the sister's blue Citroën and set off for Lower Hamlet, the area of Plum Village where the nuns lived.

Trees planted in neat rows, vineyards, farmhouses, and villages whizzed by. The nun was from the States and today was her birthday. "My continu-ation day," she said. "It means we simply continue to manifest in one form or another and right now I'm happy to be alive sitting in this car with you driving to Lower Hamlet."

"Well, then, happy continuation day."

We turned into a long gravel driveway and stopped in front of a row of ancient stone buildings. A weathered wooden door leaned open on one; bushes grew beside an arched doorway on another. Small stones and white and yellow flowers bordered the paths leading from one structure to the next.

The sister disappeared into a low building with a sloping, red-tiled roof, and I followed until we came to a square room with plenty of space for the six beds. A window at the far end of the room opened onto a forest. I plopped my gear on the bed nearest the door, the only one left, and began to settle in.

———— ▶——

The first two days, a cold rain muddied the dirt paths and chilled every room in the monastery. I wondered if I would last. Then, sunshine and warmth. We were to walk to Upper Hamlet, where the monks and laymen lived, and listen to Thich Nhat Hanh give a talk. I followed brown-robed sisters and a few lay friends out the gate, down the road, up a hill, and into the stone meditation hall. When my eyes adjusted to the darkness, I found a cushion, sat cross-legged, and studied the ink painting over the altar. It was huge, delicate, and strong, simple and carefree, almost like a child's drawing; a bending branch circled the inside edge of the paper and two hastily rendered oak leaves met near the center. Beneath the calligraphy, a small buddha sat on the low altar table, a branch of bright yellow forsythia on one side, a bouquet of wildflowers on the other.

Thich Nhat Hanh slipped into the silent room and we stood and bowed. Monks and nuns gathered in front of the altar and began to chant, accompanied by guitars, drums, and bells. The soft, rhythmic melody pulled me into a peaceful place and I began to relax.

After three sounds of a big bell, Thich Nhat Hanh, or Thay, as he is called, spoke. "We're sitting for fun. Sitting is being here for yourself, your body, and your feelings, to nourish the pleasant ones and embrace and transform the painful ones." He seemed to live into every word, raising his eyebrows and widening his round dark eyes when he pronounced the word "transform." I trusted this monk from Vietnam who had experienced the sorrows of war and sat with an aura of deep calm.

After the talk, we gathered in a circle beside a gigantic linden tree and sang softly:

> *Breathing in, breathing out.*
> *I am blooming as a flower. I am fresh as the dew.*
> *I am solid as a mountain. I am firm as the earth.*
> *I am free.*
>
> *Breathing in, breathing out.*
> *I am water reflecting what is real, what is true.*
> *And I feel there is space deep inside of me.*
> *I am free. I am free. I am free.*

Tears swelled as we sang. Inner space was what I needed.

Thay began to walk slowly, and we followed in single file or two by two down a tree-lined path, about fifty men and women, over half wearing brown monastic robes. We stepped over roots, walked through mud puddles, dodged branches, and came to a meadow. After Thay sat down in the sun-warmed grass, the rest of us did, too. Sounds of zipping, swooshing, and crinkling gave way to chirps and twitters. Ping! The little bell signaled the end of our meditation and we were on our feet again, following Thay across the meadow, past the lotus pond, and back to the linden tree. Thay bowed, we bowed, and he floated away.

That afternoon I joined a discussion group. Sitting in a circle, we shared our experiences one by one. Roger, a man with a weathered face and gravelly voice, told us he spent five years in prison. Roger was changed, "got up different" is the way he put it, after being in a meditation group. He had tears in his eyes when he said that, and tears surfaced in my eyes, too, as I remembered getting up different after sitting with my father in Mechernich. My protective shell was beginning to dissolve, the armor that came from frustrations and hurt. Nobody spoke for a few minutes, so there was time to be with myself again after listening. Another person told of the joy she felt walking down the path hand in hand with a friend. This was a place where I could say what was true even when I was happy and another person was sad or upset. There was space to listen to what was inside. Space to be with myself.

We lived outside much of the day, eating under trees or in the open-sided pavilion when it wasn't raining and even when it was. I began to notice things like the changing light as spring deepened into summer, and the tiny round plums just beginning to form on branches in the orchard behind my room.

The next day's talk was in our hamlet. Something Thay said reminded me of my family and the ones who were missing. "To be present means to know that parents and ancestors are in every cell of our body and that maybe they've been waiting for us to be present. They hurried and never had time to stop. They were waiting for the moment to feel free from worry, projects, sorrow, and regret. It's wonderful to allow them that moment. It's an act of love to allow the ancestors in you to stop. When we walk mindfully, freedom is what we get—not political freedom, but freedom from worries. We know how to stop and be fully present. Because they are in us, we can do that for our ancestors when we do it for ourselves."

I thought of how my father and mother hurried into marriage and parenthood, how the war pulled them out of their youth and pushed them into fear, into ideas about sacrifice and patriotism that led them into deeper fear and death. I thought of my grandparents, whose later life was filled with anguish. They ended their lives in intense suffering, without the chance to enjoy old age and grandchildren, to slow down and enjoy the fruits of all they had worked to build. I would walk slowly and peacefully for them and show them the beauty of all I saw. This new way of slowing down was like having a roadmap for finding my way back to myself, a way to feel at home wherever I was.

That afternoon, the kitchen nun asked two of us to wash a basket of apples. Mia, my young, red-haired, freckle-faced roommate from Holland, and I sat on a step behind the barn with the basket, a bucket of water, and an empty box. She sang a song about a little boat on the choppy sea while I dove into the basket, pulled out an apple, dunked it in the water, and tossed it into the box.

"Whoa." Mia stopped singing. "You know what, why don't we hug these sweet apples and then lay them gently in the box one by one. We don't have to hurry. We have all afternoon, and it's so pleasant sitting here with you and the apples from the orchard." She picked up an apple, lowered it into the water, held it in her hands, and examined it all over before setting it down in the box. We took our time, and I felt happy sitting in the sunshine with Mia and the apples.

One morning I woke at five and started out in a soft, slow rain for the special ceremony beginning at six. I attuned my steps and breath and walked slowly to the meditation hall. Mist floated low in the trees. I slipped out of my clogs, entered the hall, and sat in the outside row close to the front. Suddenly I remembered the announcement from last night. Monastics were supposed to sit in the front rows, behind them lay people who had been ordained into the Order of Interbeing, then those who had made a public commitment to follow the Five Mindfulness Trainings, and the rest last. I was among the last, so I moved back toward the door. Monastics and lay people entered, robed, and figured out where to sit. Thoughts and feelings popped up one after the other: *I hate this. It's a hierarchy. Some are more special than others. I don't belong here.* I gave my chanting book to the woman in front of me and didn't join in with the singing, feeling more and more lonely and left out.

At the end of the ceremony Thay told us to walk mindfully from the hall. Slowly, I felt more peaceful and remembered that being present was all that counted. Then I saw the tricks my mind devised as a war orphan, the painful feelings I'd lived with as a stepchild and a half sister, unsure about where or to whom I belonged. Shadows. They were only shadows. The monastics and lay people were seated according to their level of commitment to practicing mindfulness. That's all. My emotions and judgments blocked the truth of the moment like tall buildings on a city street block the sun. I laughed. I knew well how to water the seeds of being an outsider, of not belonging. I could keep that going all by myself. I knew Thay wanted all of us to live happy, peaceful lives. It was up to us, up to me, to water seeds of happiness and peace instead of continuing to reinforce old habits of feeling left out and hurt.

We woke to pouring rain and wind trumpeting through trees. I took off my shoes outside the meditation hall. My socks were wet. Inside I found an empty cushion and sat down. Thay sat in front of us on a raised platform, erect and silent, a lit candle on his left, a tall, swooping branch of purple-and-white orchids on his right, and the big bell in front of him.

After three sounds of the bell and a few minutes of silence, Thay began to talk. "Father, Mother, your people, the world. They did not know how to transform their suffering and transmitted it to us and we did not know why we suffered like that. We can listen to our suffering and understanding is born in us and heals us and the world. You need compassion to heal.

"When we don't understand each other," he continued, "that means there are wrong perceptions. It's up to us to release our wrong perceptions; give up thinking the other is this or is not that. We may have inherited wrong perceptions from our ancestors who didn't know how to transform their perceptions into understanding. When the mind is free of wrong perceptions and habit energies it is new and fresh. We don't have to throw anything away. We can transform what we have. One way to do that and begin anew is to write a love letter."

Thay encouraged us to write a letter of reconciliation to someone who had made us suffer. "Even if your mother has already passed away, reconciliation is still possible. If we look deeply, we will see that she is still alive in us. We can't *be* without our mother. She is us and we are her. We are the continuation of our mother, our father. Reconciliation is made within oneself. To reconcile with our mother or father means reconciling with our self."

Surprisingly, as Thay talked, it was my father who came to mind. Maybe there was something more with him. I'd never thought of writing him a letter but the idea intrigued me. It seemed like a way of continuing my relationship with him. With raindrops splattering the window, I sat on my bed facing my father's picture and began to write.

Dear Dad,

I love calling you Dad. It's so easy now like we belong to each other. I'm looking at your picture, the one Mother loved best, and you're looking right at me. I can see your seriousness, so like my own. I see kindness in your warm dark eyes.

What a simple family we were with our small-town lives and friends and jokes and fears and dreams. And what a short time you had to live your life, to grow into yourself. We humans ripen slowly and you had so little time to ripen. And yet there was a hint of your full ripening in your letter to me when you wrote, "for me, adhere to a belief in tolerance, a genuine liking for others and always give to life to the fullest." I mourn the loss of your full ripening, for you and for all of us.

Finally, I am able to feel that I am your continuation. I feel your energy and your love, your being, in me. And what would you tell me about life and love and war?

First you would say that you love me . . .

Dear Susan,

Although I've never seen you, I've loved you ever since I knew you were on the way. When you were born I was one happy dad. I yearned for my family and my just-beginning life. I wanted to take your mother dancing, to teach you and your brother to ride horses, to read you bedtime stories and tuck you in with a kiss. I wanted to finish college and find work I liked and support my family in grand style.

All the young men in Oshkosh were eager to go to war. We believed the world and the country needed us and I was swept along. We got into something over there that just took over. There was so much death, it frightened me and sickened me and I couldn't leave. The men, Frank, Larry, and all the rest were swell, but I didn't want to die and I didn't want to be around death. Death was everywhere. I could just barely catch a glimpse of life—the church steeple across the field—and then it was gone and I was back with the wounded and news of the dead.

I wanted to help and do my part, but given a choice, I would use my youth, my energy, to support and enjoy life. That's what I meant when I wrote to you, Give to LIFE to the fullest. I never wanted to leave so much pain, grief, and sorrow.

You're all grown up without me. I love that you remember me and all of us who never made it home. Love is stronger than death.

And so, dear Susan, live fully and enjoy being alive. Enjoy the eagles and the birch trees. Keep a lump of sugar in your pocket for the horses. Walk slowly so you can hear the birds, and enjoy the blue sky at noon and the red sky at dusk. You can find me there and everywhere your heart is open.

Your mother needs your love. Reach out to your brother, and enjoy my grandchildren double for me.

Your father,
Dave

I tucked the letter away and went for a walk. The rain had stopped and the sun was out. Stepping around puddles, I found a large, flat rock and perched there, listening to the trickling creek. I never saw, or heard, or touched my father, but I knew him by giving him space to exist inside of me. Standing where he stood and being with people who knew him made him real for me, and that was enough.

There was a special program that night for those who wanted to make a commitment to follow the path of mindful living by taking the Five Mindfulness Trainings as a guide. After supper, I set out for the meditation hall. The moon was round and full, rising through the trees. Stopping to watch, I needed new words. It felt like love, but it came from taking the time to connect deeply with the moon, the trees, the night sky, and myself all as one. Maybe this was wholeness. In Plum Village I was not an orphan. I was full like the moon, the same moon my father had seen.

I found an empty cushion beside Mia and settled in for the talk. Thay told us that the practice was to arrive home in each moment, to touch the peace and joy that were within us, and to open our eyes to the wonders around us. When we did this, he said, we experienced real happiness. "Home is in the present moment, the only moment we can touch life. If you love someone, the greatest gift you can give is your presence."

He described a practice they'd use the next day in the ceremony called Touching the Earth. It was what the Buddha did to confirm his enlightenment when the great tempter, Mara, tried to pull him away. "The practice," he told us, "is to bow down and touch the earth and empty ourselves of any resentments, judgments, and discrimination we feel toward anyone. To do this is the best way to get replenished. If you do not exhale and empty your lungs, how can fresh air come in?"

I decided to take the trainings and rose early to walk slowly and mindfully to the meditation hall. The air was cool and fresh. Little purple flowers spotted the ground. When a flowering bush seemed to reach out, I touched it. The touching came from a deeper place than the feel of the leaves and flowers on my skin. It felt like we were sisters, part of the same whole.

This time I was invited to sit in the middle of the meditation hall, along with about fifty others. When we were given time to meditate, I thought of how enslaved I'd felt to others' emotional needs, fearing that if I didn't help them, they would die—another false perception I could try to let go of.

After the bell signaled the end of meditation, Thay invited us to bow and touch the earth four times in gratitude to our parents, who had brought us into life, to teachers who had shown us how to understand and love, to friends who guided and supported us, and to all beings in the animal, plant, and mineral world.

Just before touching the earth I thought, *I'm giving up my freedom to do as I please, to go around without awareness. From now on I'll have to be aware of everything. Maybe I shouldn't be doing this.* Then I remembered that living without awareness, I missed the deeper connections and wonder that came from paying attention to what was here.

When I touched the earth I thought of my father, who was always with me. I thought of my friends and of Mother and Granny and Jack, especially Jack, who supported me and loved me just as I was.

After the ceremony we were each given a name that reflected our main aspiration for the practice. Mia found me in the crowd and gave me a hug. "What's your new name?" she asked.

I chuckled. "Transformational Light of the Heart. At first I didn't like it. I thought it was about me transforming everything, but I think it means that the light of the heart, or compassion, is what transforms suffering. What's your true name?"

"You can call me Ha, short for Hugging Apple." We left the hall linking arms and laughing.

The next day I rose before the gong and came upon a nun standing in front of a tree where a large brass bell was suspended by a rope. Slowly and prayerfully she raised the stick. *Bong. Bong. Bong.* The clear sound flew out over the hamlet. A few minutes later I followed the brown-robed sisters into the stone meditation hall, where we sat in tranquil silence.

During his talk, Thay reminded us that we were not just our physical bodies. We were love, and we were light. He told us about a Vietnamese poet who wrote about love. I tried to capture his words in my notebook as he quoted the poet: "If there is a connection between humans, we can live, we can survive. The value of laughter and enjoyment surpasses all the gold and silver of the world. You see, human love is so beautiful and has the capacity to heal. Who can extinguish the fire of survival if the heart is still full of love?"

I thought about the invisible connections with my father and Mother's two sisters. It was odd; I had learned to relate to absence, the absence of my father and mother's two sisters, and now I was learning presence, the life-giving vitality of being present to what was within and around me, whether or not it was physically visible.

12

Love is Stronger Than Death

Home was the apartment on a busy street in Washington, DC where fire trucks blared and car radios blasted rap at the stoplight outside our third-floor window. Afternoon light poured into the living room. Everything it touched glowed—the wooden floors, books on the bookshelves, plants, my father's picture, the yellow teapot on the table by the window, and our two mugs, filled with homemade chai. I leaned over my cup and inhaled the aroma of cinnamon and cloves. Jack was eager to hear about Plum Village and I was eager to tell him.

"It changed the way I see things and the way I think about things. Perceptions. It's all about perceptions." Drinking chai with Jack, I put into words many of the perceptions I'd carried like stones on my back and blinders on my eyes. We talked about those and the new ways I now had of seeing my father in light of the search and what I'd learned at Plum Village.

Over the next few weeks we continued the conversation, discussing the debilitating ideas about life and death I'd inherited. Many of the ideas that were supposed to protect me actually caused me to suffer. What I'd thought was true and lasting I now saw as changeable notions that reflected society's ways of coping with traumas and tragedies. Jack and I talked about the fresh, new ways I was beginning to understand my relationship with my father and the impact of his death.

You can never overcome the pain; it will destroy you if you touch it was the first idea I found to be false. In the beginning of my search, heading into the unknown and frightening territory of trying to find out what happened to my father, I faced my family's grief, the suffering of war, and the sorrow inside myself and found that rather than destroying me, it made me less anxious. Those emotions connected me with my heart, and my love for my father was set free. Even when I was enveloped with sadness for all who'd suffered and died during the war, I was in touch with a truth I needed to feel and not push away. Suffering lay in the belief that I shouldn't think about him, whereas facing the reality of his death, I could finally let go of the dread and my connection with him began to grow.

You have no reason to suffer. As long as I believed that being loved and cared for prevented me from having emotional pain, I was cut off from myself, because I was alone with my sadness and didn't understand why I often felt lost. When I accepted that both the pain of losing my father as well as the joy of being loved and cared for were real, I was able to begin my search. I had found the way into my own life.

Avoid pain, be happy, and don't upset anyone. That was a warning from Mother and from society that had led to alienation from myself and inner isolation from my family. In a family that loved musicals and happy endings, I was drawn to tragedy. It was good to live in a loving family, but I had experienced unspoken undercurrents of unresolved grief. Dwelling on death was cast as something only morose people would do and I didn't want to be one of those people, so I kept my desire to know my father to myself. When I became an adult I discovered that exploring problems could relieve them, that emotional upsets were temporary and often necessary to break through to fresher ways of being. That opened the way to my search, but took me into conflict with my family, who forbade the revival of painful memories and left me outside the family circle. A combination of meditation, notes, and gifts kept the relationships alive, but I was devastated by the separation. In the end I was accepted back into the family and learned that we could all survive the tumult of digging up the buried past. We were closer because we were no longer silenced by the fear of buried emotions.

Questions stir up trouble and cause pain. I learned early that it was upsetting to ask questions about my father. For many years I asked no questions and nothing changed. When I found people who welcomed my questions, it was as if the wind had finally filled my sails, and I began to move. There was plenty of help out there, and when the answers to my questions about my father began to fall into my hands, I found each one to be a sparkling gem.

It's shameful to air your private sorrows in public; people will pity you. You should never speak of your father's death. This was an unspoken rule I'd inherited from my mother, who lived through the exceedingly difficult time when other soldiers stepped out of trains, home from the war, and she was alone with loss and grief. It was a rule that may have protected her and one that was supposed to protect me, but times changed and the rule never did. Having seldom talked about my father's life or his death, I held him inside of me as inexpressible sorrow. I didn't know how to talk about him or how to think about him. How could I remember him when I had never known him? I didn't know where or how he fit into my life.

The prohibition lasted until I saw veterans weeping and hugging each other during the tenth anniversary of the Vietnam Veterans Memorial Wall in 1992. I soon found others whose fathers had died in WWII, and we began to talk about our fathers and our lives without them. As we shared our stories I was amazed to discover how much pain I had. Sometimes it was sharp and raw like an open wound, sometimes soft like a long sickness. Experiencing that long-neglected pain was healing, somewhat like a bone that aches as it mends. I learned how to talk about my father and how to think about him and about my experience as a war orphan. I read the poetry and stories of others who had similar experiences of grief in war, and went to public ceremonies that acknowledged the deaths of soldiers. Slowly, what was once hidden and unspeakable became full of life and meaning and connection.

The dead are gone. It's the living that matter now. This idea confused me. I loved my family and I loved my father. He was dead but he was not gone. Slowly, as he became known and accepted by the family, I became less hidden, less divided, more alive, and more a part of family life.

Don't dwell on what can't be changed. Before searching for my father, I didn't realize that even though his body was gone, the meaning of his death could change and my relationship with him could grow. Learning more about him strengthened me. I became less fearful and more confident. My relationship with Jack changed into a partnership. I was no longer a girl looking for a father. I knew where I came from and who I was.

The past is over and done with is another false idea. My father still existed in the people who knew him and in the words he wrote to me. The past was alive in the present. I was probably quite a bit like him, and knowing something about him, I could see him in his grandchildren.

The past affected my relationship with my mother. If I had obeyed her wish never to speak of my father, our relationship would have stagnated. She couldn't open the door to her grief by herself, and although I was unskillful at times, we found our way through our differences to a deeper understanding and shared love.

You never knew him and you never can is an idea that filled me with sorrow.

I discovered that my father was more than his body and I could know him in ways other than through his physical presence. Reading his records, walking the ground where Camp Lucky Strike once stood, sitting on the edge of the crater, and talking with people he knew allowed me to know dimensions of him I might never have known even if I had known him in person.

—————◆▶—————

I will never see my father walk, or hear him speak, or take his hand—he will always remain unknown in many ways. I now value that as part of our uncommon relationship. The saying that "love is stronger than death" simply means being open to love and receiving it as it flows through us and changes us with every encounter, even death and beyond. My search for my father showed me that the ineffable is also real.

13

The Obituary

Tragedy can wither and scatter a family like dry leaves. Even so, seeds of love can survive in the warm earth of the heart. That was my hope when I listened to Thay tell us that we are the continuation of our ancestors—that they live in every cell of our body—and thought about Mother's sisters.

There were no letters or Christmas cards from them, they never set foot in our home, and we never visited or saw either of them. Elinor and Dorothy were names without bodily substance, like my father. Still, they were family, and I wanted to know them, to see if they looked or acted or sounded like Mother, to see her talking and laughing with them. Most of all, I wanted to be part of an ordinary family.

Browsing through the box of family photographs, I had often seen a picture of Mother and Dorothy as children. The two sisters stood side by side. They were dressed up but they were not smiling. My mother, Margery, a head taller than Dorothy, wore a print dress and a cardigan with a collar typical of the 1930s. Her arms hung at her sides as she squinted dubiously at the camera. Dorothy, in a polka-dotted dress and coat with matching floppy hat tied under her chin, stood like a soldier ready to march off. I studied the photograph, searching for clues about Mother's childhood. Where was Dorothy and why hadn't I met her? Why did the sisters look so solemn, and where was Elinor? There were no pictures of Elinor in Mother's album.

Once, when I was young, I asked Mother about Dorothy.

"Oh, Dorothy married a Brooklyn cop," she told me with a flick of her wrist and a tone that meant, "She's gone. Forget about it."

A few years later we were in the playroom, a room with long windows and shelves that held our toys, puzzles, games, and books. I was standing perfectly still while Mother sat on the floor pinning up the hem of my new blue dress. "Elinor, my older sister, played the piano. You have her hands, Susie."

"Where is she now?"

"She was sent to the hospital with schizophrenia," Mother told me quietly, almost as if she didn't want to speak the words out loud.

The tone of her voice let me know that she didn't want to say anything more about Elinor, and I didn't ask. It's only now that I understand the silence that surrounded my three missing family members and kept me in touch with the unknown, which is where they existed. It was a place that required no words and no earthly presence. Having loved my unseen father since birth, it was natural for me to think about Elinor and Dorothy, especially when they were evoked through experiences that related to what little I knew about their lives.

Books taught me about people and the world. My favorite class was library, when we picked our own books, sat on small chairs, and read in the middle of the school day. That joy ended when my third-grade teacher, a woman whose smile showed her teeth but never reached her eyes, appointed me class librarian. My job was to shelve books. I hated it. It was boring. One afternoon I stayed after school. Shy as I was, I stood by her desk and waited for her to look up. Twisting my fingers, I stared at the purple mimeographed pages she'd been marking and told her that I didn't want to be the class librarian. I just wanted to read.

Soon after that I read the story of a girl who grew up in Brooklyn, and thought about my Aunt Dorothy. Brooklyn was romantic for a kid from Oshkosh, Wisconsin. It was tall, skinny houses linked together with five steps down to the street and wrought iron railings. Brooklyn was downtown in the next block, riding the subway to New York City, where you could walk on crowded streets and not know anyone and no one would care how you looked. Brooklyn was full of immigrants, people I'd read about and wanted to know, people who had families scattered everywhere but who stood up for each other because they'd been through wars and troubles, people who spoke tough but you could see they were soft, people with accents.

In the Midwest, grown-ups didn't tell children anything about the world because they didn't want them to get in trouble. They wanted their children to be happy and play quietly so they could wash and cook and work in peace. In Brooklyn, adults had experience and helped children grow up knowing about the world. They didn't want children to get in trouble either, so they talked about life and answered questions. Brooklyn was the place I wanted to have grown up. Mother's sister, Dorothy, lived in Brooklyn, but I didn't know how to reach her.

Elinor was on my mind when the youth group I belonged to during high school was invited to a Christmas party at the county mental hospital outside of town. Driving down the tree-lined avenue, we approached the red brick building as the winter sky faded into darkness. We parked and walked toward the forbidding structure, snow crunching and squeaking under our boots. Inside, I tried to imagine living in a grim place like this, one with bare walls and fluorescent lights. Men and women in baggy clothes stood against the far wall and watched us watching them. I waited with my friends, anxious to see what would happen.

One of the nurses put a record on the record player and Frankie Avalon's voice rolled out of the loudspeaker. She told us to pick a dance partner, and within seconds, a short man with fuzzy hair shuffled over and held out his hand. I reluctantly took it and we rocked back and forth with the music. When the song ended, he smiled, and I noticed that several of his teeth were missing. I walked back to my friends, relieved that the visit was almost over.

New questions bubbled up on the drive home. What made people mentally ill? Why did they have to live in a place that looked like a prison? Did Elinor live in a place like that? What did she look like? Did mental illness last forever?

———◄ ►———

Elinor and Dorothy were Mother's sisters, and they belonged together the way David and I belonged together. I speculated that their absence from our lives must have something to do with their mother, who died of strep throat in 1930, when Mother was ten. Maybe that was when the sisters lost each other. Stories of death, grief, and madness invented themselves in my young mind. From an early age I could tell that Mother did not want to answer my questions, and I surely did not want to upset her by asking. All I could do was remember their names and wonder about them. They were family. I needed them, and maybe they needed us.

———◄ ►———

Sitting at the kitchen table, I opened the manila envelope from David and pulled out some family documents. Fishing through the pile, I picked up Grandpa's obituary. The paper was yellowed and brittle, thirty-one years old. Holding it carefully, I began to read the names of Grandpa's survivors. There was Mother's name, and Uncle Bill's, who was the only one of her three siblings I'd met. But wait! Here were the married names of Mother's sisters: Mrs. George Sasko of Brooklyn and Mrs. Floyd Del Vecchio of Stark County. That was news. My heart raced and I dropped the paper on the table. I didn't know that Elinor had married. Yet there was proof: she was Mrs. Floyd Del Vecchio of Stark County. If she left the hospital and married, why hadn't we ever seen her? It was probably too late to find Elinor alive, but maybe I could locate her grave, just as I found my father's name on the Wall of Missing. And Mother's younger sister, Dorothy, might still be alive. *There can't be many Saskos in Brooklyn, if she's still there*, I thought.

Picking up the obituary I continued to read, astonished to learn that Grandpa had fifteen grandchildren. There were seven of us, and Uncle Bill had two children. They'd visited when I was about eleven. Billy and David, who were the same age, raced motorcycles up and down the street. Those two cousins were not a mystery, but that only made nine. Who were the other six? Where were they?

Two aunts and six more cousins. *What happened to you, Mother? What went so wrong that we never saw your sisters? And why do I feel such longing to know these strangers?*

My father was an only child, so there were no cousins on his side. We didn't see much of his family after he was killed, only his mother, my beloved Granny. There were lots of cousins on Dad's side—girls my age who lived close by when I was growing up. They resembled my five younger brothers and sisters, and I longed for cousins of my own whom I resembled. But the only possibility was Mother's sisters, and she had no contact with them.

The year I read Grandpa's obituary, 1993, was the year I began my search for my father. I filed away the obituary, but kept Dorothy and Elinor's married names in mind and resolved to find them.

———— ▪ ▬————

The winter before I left for Plum Village I gave a professional genealogist friend the names of Mother's married sisters and asked her to help me find them. The next day I opened an e-mail message from her. "Elinor has probably died, but here is Dorothy's address. Her phone number is unpublished." On February 28, 2001 I wrote a letter to Aunt Dorothy:

> *Dear Dorothy Sasko,*
>
> *I'm the daughter of Margery Laughlin Johnson Henkel, whom I believe is your older sister. Among our family photographs is a picture of you as an adorable young girl. I found your married name in Grandpa's obituary and your date of birth in a Bible Mother gave me last year that belonged to Great Grandmother Sarah Ellen and to Grandpa.*
>
> *You may know that my father, David Johnson, was killed in WWII. Having known almost nothing about my father, I began to search for information about him several years ago. Thankfully, I was able to gain a picture of him, which gave me a deeper sense of wholeness.*
>
> *He didn't have any siblings and his parents have passed away, so*

the only relatives I have are my mother's family. You can get in touch with me by phone or mail. I am really hoping you will respond.

I had an emotional connection with Dorothy, born of wondering about her through the years. Knowing she was alive and I could write to her, affection for my almost reachable aunt spread through me. Picking up a note card, I wrote her a more personal message, thinking that this might be my only chance to tell her of my love for her.

———

The day after Dorothy received the letter, the phone rang and I answered.

"It's your Aunt Dorothy! I got your letter yesterday. I lost track of your mother. Is she"—hesitating—"still . . . ?"

"Yes. She's still alive."

"Tell her I love her dearly—always have. Sorry we haven't kept in touch. We drifted away like the kids."

Dorothy went on. She talked about her dad: "Grandpa Ben worked in the pottery—Homer Laughlin is the family pottery. We'd tease our father we never had one good set of dishes. Grandpa played the banjo, guitar, and mandolin. He wore a straw hat and bow tie and matching handkerchief."

I loved listening to Dorothy; she sounded a little like Mother, but more talkative and with a bit of Brooklyn in her speech. And she was funny. She told me stories about the day she and a friend joined the Marines and she left East Liverpool forever. "From the time I left for the Marine Corps I never went back home. I was based in New York and ran out of money, got a job, and a friend asked me to live with her in Brooklyn. My friend wanted me to meet her brother and I married him. George was a New York City cop. First a bus driver, then a cop, mostly in a radio car. I told him I didn't want to know what he was doing unless it was a good story. It's not my cup of tea."

"We raised our kids in the projects, in Brooklyn, in Canarsie. Our friends were all sorts, Jewish, Hispanic, Italian, Irish." She told me about her four children. "Mickey's the one who lives nearby. He's got a ponytail and personality. He has the Laughlin chin and the Laughlin ear for music. He plays guitar in a band and lives with his wife Dona in Long Beach."

What an adventure, growing up in the projects in Brooklyn by the sea with all kinds of people—so different from my small-town midwestern upbringing. "Darn!" I told Dorothy. "Think of all those years we lost being family together and the fun we could have had."

I asked her about Elinor.

"She married an Italian, Floyd Del Vecchio, greenskeeper of the country club. He had a heart attack on the green. Elinor had two children and managed the country club. She was in charge and it was too much work. After Floyd died she went into a sanatorium. I went with my father to see her and she didn't recognize me. She called Grandpa "Mr. Laughlin." We sent her clothes and she never wore them. Floyd's family adopted the two children. Elinor played the piano, classical music. She played on KDA radio in Pittsburgh."

Elinor had children! More cousins! I never imagined that Elinor had children. Where were they now? This was more than I'd ever known about Elinor. I'd always thought it was her mother's death that had left her crazy with grief, but it was the death of her husband.

Soon after finding Dorothy, I called my sister, Ellen. I was excited. Dorothy was a relative that we shared. Dad's large, loving extended family wasn't ours in the same way Aunt Dorothy and her family was.

"Ellen, I've found Aunt Dorothy."

"Who's Aunt Dorothy?"

"Mother's younger sister. She has four children, our cousins, and one of them, Michael, is your age. She calls him Mickey. He's musical like you and plays in a band."

"Don't tell Mother. Mother and Dad are pretty frail. He's almost blind and she worries. Don't tell her. It would upset her. I would never have thought to look for Aunt Dorothy."

I put on my coat and went for a walk to think about how to tell Mother when the time was right. When I was a child and asked about Dorothy, she dismissed the question with a wave of her arm, so I had to be careful. It was hard to say what happened between them or how much pain was contained in Mother's silences. I hoped it wasn't like the situation with my father, where silence grew around loss and pain and private memories the way muscle and bone protect the heart. There was no way to open that silence without more wounding. Mother had been wounded when I began my search for my father. Silence protected her from the pain inside, and when that silence was pried open, her rage poured forth. She could be as furious as Medea and as severe as Medusa. I knew those two women well, as I had the same seeds of hurt, rage, and terror inside myself.

A woolly gray sky tucked itself around bare trees bordering Rock Creek far below the Calvert Street Bridge. I didn't want to pass this unresolved ache down to my children. The only way I knew how to begin to heal the festering wound was to open it up to the light of the present day, give it attention and space, and try to take care of whatever followed. I had to accept both Mother's need for privacy and my need to know the lost members of my family. When I told Mother about Dorothy, I wanted it to be light and easy. Conversational. "Oh Mother, by the way, I bet you thought of your sister Dorothy during 9/11, being married to a New York City policeman. Well, she's all right. She sends you her love." Stop. Wait. Breathe. Mother could respond or not, but I would have told her.

Pigeons fluttered down and pecked at crumbs on the sidewalk. I headed back to my room. Aunt Dorothy wanted to see Mother. I could imagine all of us together, but I knew that was speeding way too fast. Maybe I'd just tell Mother I had found Dorothy and then talk to Dorothy when I got home.

That was my plan. In the autumn of 2002, I was on my way to California with my daughter, Sarah, to see my youngest sister, Clare. I hadn't seen Clare since her wedding twelve years before, when my search for my father opened Mother's anguish and aroused a protective silence from the rest of the family that left me outside for several years. Sarah wanted to bring us together again and I agreed, although I was nervous.

We met in a coffee shop in Berkeley near the university, where Clare taught costume design. Clare, my little sister, came through the door with her hint of dimples, full of happiness. Sarah offered to buy us coffee or tea. Clare and I laughed as we both ordered chai. We sat and talked and I was content to be with her again and happy to end this silly estrangement. When I told her that I'd found Aunt Dorothy and asked her advice about telling Mother, Clare was adamant. "Don't. She's too fragile. It would upset her."

After leaving California, I flew to Indianapolis to see Mother and Dad. Dan, my middle brother, picked me up at the airport, looking like a younger version of his father—the same long legs and deep, dark eyes peering through his glasses. We were alone in his car when I told him about Aunt Dorothy and asked what he thought about telling Mother.

His expressive eyes widened. "Oh, you should tell her. Cousins. We have cousins. That's great."

The next day Mother and I went to lunch with Mother's friend whom I'd known since the family moved to Indianapolis, almost forty years earlier. After lunch Mother and I weren't ready to go home, so we drove to the grocery store. I used to tag along when she went grocery shopping. We talked about what to buy and ended up sharing a box of animal crackers or a bag of peanuts.

On the way to the store she told me about her friend's refusal to talk to her for two years. "I don't know why she didn't want to talk to me all that time and maybe I never will."

That was the opening I'd been waiting for. It was now or never. I'd have time to live with her reaction before leaving Sunday morning. I gripped the wheel, took a breath and began, "While you were talking about your friend, I was thinking about Aunt Dorothy. I thought of her during 9/11 and spoke to her recently. She wanted me to tell you she loves you dearly."

"Susan, I can't." Mother turned to face me. "After your father died I asked Dorothy to live with me. She had a child and I had two. I could take care of the kids and she could work. She said no. Then, when Dick and I were getting settled, she asked me for a thousand dollars for some debts. I couldn't afford to give her money and she wrote me a mean letter saying she never wanted to see me again if I couldn't help her."

I listened and simply nodded my head. This was not silence. Mother was letting me know what happened between them. I felt a deep sadness for both sisters who had no one to hold them together after their mother died—sisters who needed help and exchanged rejection.

The next morning, Mother and I were alone in the kitchen. She filled two cups with coffee and handed me one. "I didn't sleep last night. I had an unhappy childhood and don't want to dredge up the past. Don't give Dorothy my address. With what's left I just want to take care of Dick and my children and grandchildren."

Back home, I lay awake trying to understand Mother and Dorothy's estrangement. It was as if they had magnets in their hearts that had once attracted them, but then, when things built up between them, the magnets flipped over and they repelled each other. When Dorothy and I connected, she wanted to be in touch with Mother again. Her magnet flipped to attraction. Mother's magnet, though, continued to resist communicaton with Dorothy.

Oddly, I was at peace with Mother, no longer needing her help. I could talk to Dorothy whenever I wanted to and enjoy Mother without having to mention her younger sister. And I would soon have a chance to meet Dorothy in person.

— 14 —

Waiting in Brooklyn

I put off calling Aunt Dorothy for a few months after returning from Indianapolis, not sure how to handle Mother's wish not to be in touch with her. Finally I called and we planned to meet in the spring, but spring turned into summer before we talked again. We agreed to meet in early August.

The Saturday afternoon before our trip, Jack and I returned from a walk and found a message on the machine: "Hello, Susan Hadler. This is Mickey Sasko, your Aunt Dorothy's son. She's in the hospital, but she's all right. Please call me if you want to."

I was afraid and feared the worst. Mickey thought she was all right, but I wanted to know more. Had the upcoming visit played a part in sending Dorothy to the hospital?

"Well, that's it," I told Jack. "We won't be going."

"Don't be so sure," Jack said. "We can still visit her."

I called Mickey. Mickey. I loved that name. Mickey Sasko. It sounded like a tough guy and little boy all in one. Mickey told me that Aunt Dorothy would be in the hospital for a week. "They decided to put in a pacemaker. It's due to be installed on Monday. She still wants to see you."

"Maybe this meeting has added stress."

"Oh no. Your reaching out has been good for her. I can't fathom why we haven't met all these years, but that's their business."

Already I loved Mickey, my true cousin, who wanted us to meet.

"We'll drive up Wednesday, leave early to avoid traffic and be there around noon."

I e-mailed Ellen to tell her about the visit to Aunt Dorothy and about meeting Mickey. She e-mailed back:

That's great about Aunt Dorothy's family. We may never know the reasons behind their estrangement, or maybe Dorothy will tell you. I'm just glad you're doing the research. You can tell me about the visit, especially about Mickey, but please don't mention it to Mom or Dad unless they ask. That will go a long way to making my life easier!

Ai-yi-yi! What a challenge to maintain a balance between Ellen's need to care for Mother and Dad, Mother's need for peace now and privacy regarding the past, and Dorothy's desire to reconnect with Mother.

Why am I doing this? I asked myself—but with half a smile, because I knew I had to. I'd been following an inner call to find Mother's sisters. But what lurked in that inner call? Ever since first hearing about them I'd felt their absence. I was curious and I was uneasy. I wanted to know them and it worried me that I had aunts we never saw or even heard much about. If I did something awful would I, too, be banished? If I weren't able to keep things going like Elinor, would I be rejected and sent away? If Mother's sisters could be lost forever, I reasoned, I could be abandoned too—and I was already halfway down the road to orphanhood with the loss of my father.

Outside of my fifth-floor studio window, a flock of birds turned like dancers with perfect timing, wings silver in the late-afternoon sun. What does it mean to be related as family? My stepfather's family was close. Aunts and uncles and cousins had picnics, played games, gathered around the piano to sing, and shared Thanksgiving and Easter dinners. I, who had not known a true father or aunt or cousin, watched them relate. They seemed to take for granted that they belonged to each other. They included me in their family, but it was their family. I saw myself as I was then—hunched, stammering, apologizing, not knowing who I was or where I belonged, lost in a coat that didn't fit.

Dorothy and Elinor were also lost, so I was like them in ways both physical and psychological. Even though I didn't know them, we were inarguably related by blood and genes. That gave me permission to think about them, to puzzle over them, to imagine them—to stay related and live with them in my mind, and, now, to try to find them. If I could find them, I might find answers—to what it meant to be a family, what happens when we lose each other and we're cut off from the love that once was, and whether we could ever find that love again, or if it was gone forever.

I called Mickey's home and his wife, Dona, answered.

"He's at the hospital. " Before giving me his cell phone number, Dona added, "Families are so cool."

When I called Mickey, he said Dorothy was all right. "The surgery went well. Call tomorrow when you get here and I'll tell you where we can meet. If she's discharged, I'll take her to Long Beach, where she can recuperate with us for awhile, and we can meet there; or she might still be in the hospital." Then he said, "There's a whole world of cousins. We can just begin."

When I hung up, I felt elated. He wanted to meet, and he always said something original, joyful. "A whole world of cousins."

We left early to miss the traffic and I slept while Jack drove. After a stop for chai, I took the wheel, and was overcome by a feeling that Grandmother Clare, Mother's mother, another of my benevolent family ghosts, was with me. She was there if I opened my eyes and heart to find her in Dorothy, in Mickey, and in myself. What was this thread that connected us? Even with it broken, I sensed a connection with the lost pieces that once formed a whole. I never knew Grandmother Clare, and yet there she was in my thoughts as I sped to meet her other daughter, my own Aunt Dorothy.

Having missed the turnoff to Belt Parkway after the Verrazano Bridge, we drove through a corner of Brooklyn, the Brooklyn that had fascinated me as a child, knowing that Mother's sister, the little one in the polka-dotted dress, lived there. Small brick houses with enclosed porches hugged the sidewalk and flowers bloomed in every yard. Shops lined up one after the other along the wide main street—print shops, tire shops, take-outs, barbershops, donut shops, liquor shops, and grocery stores. We flew along Rockaway Boulevard and passed JFK airport. I called Dona.

"There's been no word yet whether Dorothy will be discharged or not today. Mickey's at the office. Call back in a couple of hours, Sweetie."

Back to Brooklyn, where Jack camped out in a stamp-and-coin shop and I found a bagel place. A constant flow of people came and went while the guy behind the counter called out orders and "Do You Know the Way to San Jose" played in the background. I sat back in my chair, sipped lemonade, and tried to relax. It was difficult to be patient—anything could go wrong, a car crash, a heart attack, and that would be the end of it. We'd be lost from each other forever.

When I was searching for my father there were setbacks, but his absence allowed an unrestrained openness, and nothing restricted my love for him. Longing to find him was undiluted and love kept growing. This was different. The last two years of phone calls back and forth had been a delicate dance. "We'll play it by ear," Dorothy had cautioned. And here I was, waiting in Brooklyn, playing it by ear.

I met Jack at the coin shop and called Mickey.

"She'll be in the hospital until at least tomorrow," he said. "She'd rather see you than not. She's in North Shore University Hospital in Manhasset, room 355. I won't be there until after six tonight."

"We can wait. We're flexible."

"You can go on over. She's waiting for you."

I was amazed that Dorothy still wanted to see me even when she was in the hospital.

———— ✦ ————

As Jack and I got in the elevator that took us up to Dorothy's floor, I thought about the price Mother had paid to keep her distance, not knowing her sister as an adult or her nieces and nephews. The elevator doors opened, and Jack and I walked down the corridor, past Maternity, and found room 355. I peeked into the room, and there was Aunt Dorothy lying in bed beside a window. Her eyes were closed and she looked exactly like Mother! Short, curly white hair, pink skin, and a face that was familiar. I hadn't expected that. She was different from Mother on the phone—talkative and funny, where Mother was self-contained and reserved—but I would have recognized Aunt Dorothy anywhere.

We backed away and waited in the hall. Then, holding Jack's hand, I peeked in a few more times. An orderly pushed his cart past us and when I looked in again, Dorothy's eyes were open.

She looked at me and said, "Susan."

Walking over to her, I smiled. "Aunt Dorothy." I felt an instant and deep recognition, took her hand, bent down, and kissed her. Her skin was soft and she had a big smile and dimples. Jack sat on one side of her bed and I sat on the other.

Words flowed easily from Aunt Dorothy. Whatever I said triggered something in her and she was off. We talked about her son in Sweden, and she told us about her house, what they paid for it in '73 and what it was worth now. Should she stay or sell? Her pension, her medicine. She was down-to-earth, open, and treated me as though she'd known me forever, as though we belonged to the same family.

A young nurse came in to take Dorothy's vital signs and, frowning, said that her blood pressure was way up.

"This is Susan," Dorothy said, smiling, "my sister's daughter, my niece." When the nurse left, Dorothy continued, "George, my husband, was six feet and two inches tall. My babies were big—eight to ten pounds." She told us about her operation and getting herself to the hospital. She knew exactly when she needed to go, so like Mother's and my own intuition. She was excited. We both were.

When I told Jack later that I was worried this visit was responsible for raising her blood pressure, he answered, "Well, it will go down, way down, and she'll be much healthier after we leave."

"Mickey wanted to see the pictures you sent," Dorothy told me. "When he found them, he wanted to know who everyone was." It turned out that both Mickey and I had wanted to know our cousins.

"How is Margery?" Dorothy reached for my hand.

"Mother had a difficult year with a broken arm from her fall. She was in the hospital and then in rehab for a while, but she's better now."

"And David?"

"He lives in Florida with Gloria, his wife, and they have three grown children." There was so much we didn't know about each other, about our own family.

Dorothy looked tired, and we agreed that she would take a nap and we'd return around six, when Mickey would be there. A few hours later, we walked into Dorothy's room with a basket of daisies and bluebells. Mickey, in the chair beside her bed, put out his hand and I rushed at him with a hug. Mickey talked. Dorothy talked. I talked. Mickey showed me his Laughlin chin, as long and full as Grandpa Ben's, like Clare's. Around his neck was a chain with memorial pins for the people he knew who died on 9/11. I felt close to Mickey, who openly remembered and mourned the dead.

We talked about music—Mickey's music, and the music in our family. Before getting to know Dorothy and Mickey, I had assumed the musical talent in the family I grew up with came from Dad's family. All of my siblings born to my stepfather were musically gifted. I was discovering that Mother's family was also musically talented. Dorothy confirmed this when she sat up in her hospital bed and sang a jaunty little song about Lillian Russell that she used to sing to her children. I was content to the core sitting there with Dorothy and Mickey and Jack. We had transformed the hospital room into a family room.

When Dorothy told us how proud she was to look like her mother, I reached into my bag and pulled out the presents I'd brought: framed pictures of Dorothy's mother, Mickey's and my Grandmother Clare. I gave one to Dorothy and one to Mickey. Dorothy looked at it for a while. "I have the same picture in a smaller size."

When it was time to leave, Mickey invited us to dinner at his apartment overlooking the ocean. I held Dorothy's hand, and she kissed it and then I kissed her hand. Jack and I turned to say good-bye at the door, and Dorothy blew us kisses from her bed.

Jack and I followed Mickey out of the city, across a low bridge that engulfed us in salty ocean air, and into Long Beach, where sea and sky opened wide— and wider still from from Mickey and Dona's sixth-floor apartment, where the view revealed a coast that curved into infinity. We sat on the balcony and talked between bites of pizza.

Dona was small and impressive, a teacher in the NYC schools; she'd been physically hurt several times by kids there and was spending the summer recuperating. And still she understood how it happened, how the "bad" kids find each other in their desperation to connect. She was also funny and down-to-earth, and claimed, "Mickey and I argue over whose family is the most dysfunctional."

I felt a bond kick in with Mickey as he talked about his family. "I think Mom was depressed until George died, and I hope I don't have much of my father in myself. He was mean." I laughed, but regretted it. That was Mickey being pure Mickey, with a truthfulness that reminded me of my children.

"When George died," he continued, "Dorothy found some money she didn't know he had and she fixed up the house—put in a new bathroom, a new kitchen, sanded and polished the floors, and painted. Now she can have people over. I think she's just begun to live."

I couldn't get enough of Mickey telling his stories, but it was time to leave. We hugged good-bye and Mickey told us to call them when we got home, like family.

I phoned Dorothy at the hospital the next morning.

"My blood pressure is down and I'm going to Mickey's today," she said. "I can't shower for a week. The sea breezes will take away the odor. I'll work on getting healthy—I'll live 'til 100. Are you going to be around?"

"I'll be here until Christmas."

"We'll lie low until spring, and then maybe Mickey and Dona and I will drive down to Washington. Did Jack like the visit?"

"Yes, he loved meeting you and Mickey and Dona."

We started to say good-bye several times before hanging up.

Home again, I took a cup of tea outside to sit beneath a colossal oak tree and think about the visit. It was hard to overcome my fear that the meeting was harmful for Dorothy, but encouragement helped—first Jack's, and then Mickey and Dona's. It was as if they were holding Dorothy's hand and my hand, bringing us together. Dorothy had taken a big step when she agreed to meet. She'd probably feared being rejected by me, as she'd felt rejected by Mother long ago. There was a whisper of fear in her eagerness to know if Jack thought it went well.

I felt a deep sense of kinship and love with Dorothy and Mickey, and I thought they felt it too. Dorothy would have loved to see Mother again, but I was the closest thing to Mother she had, and she accepted me without a shred of hesitation once we met. Mother and Dorothy were both orphans, having lost their mother as children, and that still lived in them, a strength that came from being on their own, and a caution, looking to others to make sure all was well. I'd have loved to listen to them talk about their lives together, but maybe that was a conversation I'd have to invent!

A sparrow landed nearby and chirped. We are so many others to each other, fluid selves, merging and shifting into each other. Dorothy called me her sister at times, and said "your mother" when she meant her mother, seeing in me, perhaps, a reincarnation of her mother, or of her sisters, Elinor or Margery. Life passes itself on through us and relationships are full of much more than we know and see, even those with people we have never before seen or known.

15

Dorothy's Cows

Gold earrings and a blue silk blouse—Dorothy was wearing her best. It was October, just a few months after we met for the first time, and Dorothy, Mickey, Dona, Jack, and I pored over old photos scattered on the round glass table in Mickey and Dona's living room, a bowl of popcorn in the middle of the table.

Mickey handed me a picture. "Here's one of Mom in days gone by."

Dorothy was gorgeous, blond hair swept up, deep dimples highlighting her smile, a cross between earth mother and movie star. She looked strong and happy gazing at the laughing baby in her arms.

I picked up a small black-and-white photo of little boy Mickey wearing a too-large policeman's cap, a twinkly-eyed smile, and missing a front tooth. Mickey laughed when I showed him the photo.

"We grew up in the projects. We'd stand at the window in our upstairs apartment and wait for Mom to come home from her job in the department store. She'd walk across the center of the projects at night, arms loaded with shopping bags. She always had a surprise for us. She had a temper, too. One time she broke my guitar over her knee. She could be tough. Never let us forget that she was a Marine."

Dorothy shuffled through the pile until she found what she was looking for: two Christmas cards, each with a photograph of my large family as we were in the late fifties and early sixties, nine of us at various ages—babies and teens, pigtails and braces, long hair, shaggy hair, short hair.

"So you were in touch with Mother over the years?"

Dorothy nodded. "She was proud of her family and sent a card at Christmas until Dad died in '64."

While the other three napped, Mickey and I headed for the boardwalk on the next street over. Sunshine and clouds came and left, waves rolled rhythmically beside us; a breeze lifted my scarf and cooled our faces. Mickey was big and solid, and he was soft. He pointed across the street. "See that art deco building over there, the pink one? That's where Dona and I lived when we were first married."

He promised to show me the projects where he grew up and I promised to guide him around the small town on Lake Winnebago where I sailed in the summer and ice-skated in the winter.

When we got back to the apartment, Dorothy, Dona, and Jack were awake, talking, and laughing. Mickey lifted his guitar out of the case and played a song he wrote for the Drips, his band at the water department where he worked. He called his music civil service rock 'n' roll. The song was witty, with a bluesy tune and a catchy title: "Leaky Drip." If Mickey and Dan and Ellen ever got together there would be no stopping the rousing, hilarious, musical fun the three cousins could create.

Dorothy sang the funny song she sang in the hospital, and Mickey supplied the chords on his guitar.

"Where did you learn that song?" Jack asked.

"My father took us out for a ride in the country one day and he started to sing this song and it just kept going on and on."

"You sang it to us when we were kids," Mickey said. "Every night we used to say, 'Sing for us!' We'd wait and we'd all laugh when you went, 'Have a smoke of Coca-Cola. Chew catsup cigarettes. Watch Lillian Russell wrestle with a box of oysterettes.'"

On the drive home I thought about our time together and how happy I was to have found them. Together we had overcome the curse of estrangement and become family. Knowing Dorothy, I could distinguish who Mother was apart from the person she'd become since she married Dad. Dorothy and Mickey's humor and their music was a part of Mother, and I could understand her love for my musical stepfather. I was less of a stranger to myself knowing what I shared with my father and what I'd inherited from my mother's side of the family.

Dorothy and Mickey and I talked and visited often. Several months after meeting, Mickey and Dona were in Washington, DC for a convention and came for dinner. The next day we stopped by the WWII Memorial, stood for a few minutes in front of the stars that marked those who had died, and remembered Mickey's Uncle David.

My sister, Amy, wanted to meet her Aunt Dorothy, so in December I drove up to Long Island and Amy flew to New York from Albuquerque and took the train to Long Island. She was waiting for me at the Massapequa train station wearing a stylish brown coat and pink wool scarf, her long white hair catching the afternoon sun.

Dorothy was sitting in her armchair when Amy and I came in. Amy hesitated, then broke into a giggle and walked over to Aunt Dorothy, who had raised her arms to Amy. We made a hearty soup for dinner, and Mickey came by the next day with his famous marinara sauce. When it was time to say good-bye, Dorothy presented us with little packages of lipsticks, powders, and lotions.

Jack and I stopped in to see Dorothy on our way north after Christmas. She gave us a queen-size blue and white afghan she had crocheted, then showed us the bright red cowboy hat and vanity license plate—it read "COWZGIRL"—that Mickey and Dona had given her. The shelves in her house were filled with cows the way mine were filled with books. Cow dolls with fur coats and boas, pitchers and spoons in the shape of cows, doorstop cows, a stuffed cow jumping over a moon, a porcelain Dorothy in Oz with a cow, a clock that mooed. Since then, every time I've seen a cow I've thought of Aunt Dorothy and sent her cards with pictures of cows and a note, "I'll love you 'til the cows come home."

16

Small Clues

Steel mills and pottery kilns once filled the air with smoke and people's pockets with money. The town's stature had faded since the boom of the early twentieth century, but in Sturgis House, a restored bed-and-breakfast with red velvet curtains, photographs from the late nineteenth century, and a pump organ in the parlor, it was easy to imagine the former glory of East Liverpool, Ohio, Mother's hometown. It was 2004 when Jack and I stopped to look around on our way to Indianapolis.

I was about to pick up a book of photos documenting the restoration of the house when a lanky man wearing a black suit sauntered into the room and sank down into the chair across from me.

"I'm Frank Dawson, the owner." He stretched out his legs. "This house has a colorful past. It was owned by Mr. Sturgis, who ran his funeral home here in the 1800s. The night Pretty Boy Floyd was killed outside of East Liverpool, his body was brought here, and my father, who was a funeral director, embalmed it in the basement. More than 10,000 people filed past the corpse of Public Enemy #1 in this very house. That was October 1934. I bought the place in 1993 and restored it for use as a B&B. Now, why have you landed in East Liverpool?"

"My mother, Margery Laughlin, grew up here, and I'm hoping to discover some family history."

"Well," said Frank, "I know more about your family than you do." He was also the director of the Dawson Funeral Home, a business his father bought from Sturgis in 1935. Frank pulled out his cell phone and made a call.

"This is Digger. Get me all of the Laughlin records." Turning back to me, he suggested that I get in touch with the local historian and gave me her phone number. "I'll have my records sent over later today."

That afternoon, when Jack and I returned from lunch, we found a thick envelope on the hall table addressed to me. It was from the local historian. I took it up to our second-story room and settled in for the afternoon while Jack set off for the antique mall around the corner.

With the kettle boiling in the little kitchen, I stepped out on the wrought iron balcony and looked across to the river beyond the rooftops. This was where my family had settled well over one hundred years earlier, and where, in 1873, my great-grandfather's cousins with the stellar names, Shakespeare and Homer, opened the pottery factory that still bore Homer Laughlin's name—the pottery that supported Mother's family throughout the Great Depression and afterwards, when her father worked as a supervisor.

I poured a cup of tea, spread the papers on the kitchen table, and read page after page until my relatives, who had died many years ago, seemed to come back to life. I read that James Johnston, my great-great-great-grandfather, came from County Derry, Ireland, and volunteered to fight the British in the summer of 1776. Fifty-six years later—in 1832, when he was ninety-four—he submitted a pension report for his service in the Revolutionary War and told the examiner, "I was taken prisoner with the rest of my fellow soldiers at Fort Washington, marched into New York, and put into prison."

In 1897, James's grandson wrote: "I was often with my grandfather when a boy, and heard him relate his severe troubles while in the army. He was taken prisoner, he said, and kept one winter in an old church, but escaped and returned again to the army and was discharged at the end of the war. Often while in the army he went without shoes for several days. He wanted to enlist in the War of 1812, but they would not take him by reason of age and rheumatism."

Doing the math, I figured out that James was then seventy-four and still eager to fight the British. Taking a sip of tea, I mused that this family's Scotch-Irish propensity for fighting had trickled down through the generations and shown up again in the standoff between the two sisters.

Wandering downstairs to look for a snack, I found another large manila envelope with my name on the hall table. "Digger" had sent funeral documents that included interment and cemetery records and newspaper clippings about the Laughlins of the past century who had lived and died in East Liverpool. I was surprised to learn that Elinor had a baby sister named Jane Clare. Born in 1916, she lived for only two months, then died of whooping cough. Mother's grandmother, Sarah Ellen, owned six gravesites in Riverview Cemetery. The sixth was marked with an X and the words, "Reserved for Laughlin daughter Elinor Del Vecchio 12/4/52."

<hr/>

When Jack came back, Carol, the Sturgis House manager, gave us directions to Riverview Cemetery. We followed the road up the hill, past McKinnon Avenue where Mother grew up. Several blocks beyond that, we turned into the cemetery and parked at the gatehouse, where we met the superintendent. An older woman with a brisk walk, Helen had lived in the superintendent's house since 1959. She knew and cared for every inch of the cemetery, and she pointed out and named various foliage and birds as she led us to the Laughlin gravesite, far above the winding river.

Trees spread their branches protectively over the graves where the Laughlin family had gathered for a century to mourn the departed. I walked to Grandmother Clare's grave, knelt, and touched her stone. That was the closest I'd ever been to my grandmother, who died at age forty-four, when her children were still young. Jane Clare, her infant daughter, was buried with her. Sarah Ellen, Grandpa Ben's mother, who lived with the family after Clare passed away, died in 1933, three years after Clare. I felt a kind of strength standing there thinking about my ancestors, those unknown people who came before me, whose genes live in me as invisible connections. There was a vacant space in the row of Laughlin graves. Elinor was not buried there with the rest of the Laughlins.

<hr/>

When I told Mother that I was planning to visit East Liverpool, she gave me the phone number and address of Bill's daughter, Ann. Because she'd grown up in East Liverpool, Ann knew Dorothy, and I was hoping she could tell me something about Elinor. She invited us to dinner at her house in Laughlin's Corners, where she taught piano. We knew we were at the right house when we saw the sign decorated with piano keys in the front yard. A roundish, smiling woman with short gray hair much like my own opened the door and welcomed us in. Bypassing the living room, where a piano took up most of the space, we entered a homey kitchen with savory aromas and a large round oak table.

After a meal of pot roast, potatoes, and carrots, Ann brought out some family photos. I picked up one of a young boy with a golf club standing in front of a house with a wide front porch. Written in blue ink on the front of the black-and-white photo were the words "Daddy Ben." I turned it over and read, "I am sending you this because it's the only small picture I have, but want you to have it. Johnnie."

"Who is Johnnie?" I asked.

"He's Elinor's child. He was born the same year I was born."

A surge of deep emotion spread through my body. This boy was Elinor's child. His words, "Daddy Ben," touched me and reminded me of my own lost father, whom I was told to call "Daddy David." I could easily project onto Johnnie the feelings of loss and longing I knew so well.

"Elinor wasn't supposed to have any more children," Ann added. "She had postpartum depression."

Believing that Elinor suffered from schizophrenia or psychotic grief, I dismissed the idea that postpartum depression could send her to a mental hospital for years.

Ann handed me a portrait of two young children. Penciled onto the side were the names David and Susan Johnson. These children were definitely not my brother and me. Who were they? Did Elinor have a daughter?

Ann left the table and returned with a blue Christmas card box. "This is for you."

Inside was a black leather Bible. I opened it and read an inscription. "Mother closed her eyes in sleep till Jesus came on Saturday, June 7th at 1:10 a.m. Mother's last message: 'Be good. Teach the children to be good and unselfish and self-reliant. I never knew so well as I know now how Jesus saves me.'" That very day, June 7, 1930, Ben gave the Bible to his son, Bill, who was twenty years old.

Tears filled my eyes as I felt Clare's presence. She was with me, helping me, leading me, and she was happy that I was trying to bring the Laughlin family together. *Dear Grandmother Clare, how your death changed the family.*

On another page Ben had recorded the names, birth dates, and birthplaces of his children. I made a note that Elinor's name in this Bible was "Sara Elinor" and that she was born on November 14, 1913—two more clues for my search.

———————

We drove on to Indianapolis to visit Mother and Dad and arrived in the late afternoon. There they stood at the front door, Dad in a plaid shirt with his arms akimbo. Mother's blue sweater matched her eyes, eyes that were even bluer now that her hair was completely white and her skin a shade more pale. On our way to the living room for a drink, we passed Mother's secretary with the two secret drawers that I was sure held all the answers. I settled into the patterned sofa beside her while Jack and Dad sank into wing chairs that belonged to my grandmother.

Jack and I told them about meeting "Digger" Dawson, and Mother listened with girlish excitement as we described our discoveries in East Liverpool. Her family, overshadowed by Dad's gregarious bunch and Mother's reticence, was seldom mentioned, and Jack's and my enthusiasm for her town seemed to awaken joy and pride in her.

"My education there has carried me this far. I go to reunions every ten years and see my friends. One, Jane, who still lives there, told me about the renovation of Sturgis House and we walked through it in '97."

I gave her the papers from Digger. She studied each page and stopped when she saw her Uncle John's obituary. The photo showed him wearing the kind of high white collar with tabs turned down that was stylish in the early part of the last century.

"Dad used to call these collars 'open gate' or 'come to Jesus' collars. I didn't know that Uncle John died in a car accident and that Aunt Kate was driving. No one ever gave me clippings like these."

"I'll make copies and send you everything I've collected." Mother, it seemed, had also experienced feeling left out of family matters.

I pointed out her mother's obituary.

She was quiet, then spoke: "Every day after school for a year after my mother died, I walked up the hill behind the house and spent time with her at the grave. In the spring, I picked violets to take to her. I had so many happy times until my mother died and Dad married Mame."

Jack and Dad carried their glasses into the den to watch a basketball game. Mother walked over to her secretary, reached into a drawer, and returned with the brown leather album I had borrowed before. While she talked about her childhood in East Liverpool, I focused on pictures of Elinor, the last mystery. In one photo she was a girl of eleven with a classically beautiful face, wearing a loose frock. There was a picture of her with a feather in her hat, pushing Dorothy in a wicker baby carriage. She looked happy and proud of herself. Four-year-old Margery walked solemnly beside the carriage. Another photo showed an older Elinor, about eighteen, her head thrown back with laughter. The picture was taken in the backyard with the three sisters surrounding their grandmother. Maybe this was when Elinor was in love with Floyd.

The pictures awakened my desire to know more about Elinor. As a child I felt connected to her, partly because, like Elinor, I was the oldest daughter with an older brother. Or maybe it was because I had an ear for the lost, a hunger for any bit of information that might help me know who they were. Having been born two months after my father died, I carried a yearning for the missing and the grief of a family who was silent about their losses.

———————— ———

We were sitting in the sun porch having coffee the next morning when Mother mentioned Ellen's unselfishness. Ellen was the one among the seven siblings, she said, who had most diligently cared for Mother during her increasingly frequent hospital visits and health crises. Her remark reminded me of the Bible Ann gave me and I ran to get it, placed it in Mother's hands, and pointed to her mother's last words.

"I know that writing," she said in a low voice. "It's so familiar." It took her a minute to understand that it was her Mother's actual last words and not something added later. She gasped feeling the immediacy of it. "I felt cheated that my mother died when I was so young. Grandpa married Mame when I was thirteen and divorced her when I was seventeen. My father and I were estranged for many years, but we had once been close."

I brought Mother a copy of the portrait of the three sisters that Dorothy sent me after we met and gave it to her. She took it with both hands and scrutinized the picture.

"Oh. Elinor had curly hair and mine was always straight."

"You were lovely, Mother, and had such a beautiful smile."

"I remember the dress I wore in the picture. I was almost eight. We were going to give it to our father for a Christmas surprise. Dad overheard me telling the postman about it and it ruined the surprise." Mother looked across the room. "Elinor was beautiful. I wonder where she is." She turned her head to look at me. "Do you know, Susan?"

"No."

"I thought maybe she was in Indianapolis, that she might be homeless and wandering the streets looking for me. I did a little research but I couldn't find her."

"Mother, do you know if Elinor had a daughter?"
Without hesitating, she answered: "Sandra."

The city rose in steps outside my studio window, gray buildings on top of red ones, stacks of them climbing into the blue sky. I sipped a mug of homemade chai. The visit was a revelation. Mother spoke more openly about her relatives and her past than ever before. She'd needed someone to take an interest in her side of the family.

Until I began my search for my father I related more to Jack's family than to my own. They provided us with stability, gathering in the summers at the beach cottage and at Christmas for ski trips. The more I found out about my father, the stronger I grew—finding my backbone was the way it felt. Jack saw that. He had supported my search and my relationship with Dorothy, and he had been behind me as I tried to find Elinor's grave.

Rows of windows in square buildings reflected the noonday sun, and behind each window was a home. I poured a second mug of chai and leaned back in my chair. There was so much pain in Mother, deep wells of pain, and there was so much joy and humor. She protected herself by not going near those painful places and not letting anyone else near them. Having walled them off, she was able to go on living, raising her children, making friends, working in the theater, teaching children to read. She was happy, but the pain was always there, ready to surface, and the old memories remained frozen in time, with no chance to change. When Jack and I took her news of East Liverpool and wanted to listen to her stories, she was able to talk more freely about her early life and more openly about herself. It was the first time I heard her say that she worried about Elinor, the first time I understood why her concern for the homeless was strong.

──── ◄ ►────

More than ever, I wanted to find out what happened to Elinor so I could tell Mother and relieve her worry. From time to time I typed "Elinor Laughlin Del Vecchio" into the computer along with her birth date: November 14, 1913. I'd try Eleanor Del Vecchio and Sara Eleanor and Sarah Elinor Laughlin Del Vecchio, not knowing which spelling of her name might have been used on a death certificate. None of the names that turned up matched Elinor's date of birth or seemed to be the right one. I tried the vast Mormon registry when we were in Salt Lake City for Jack's family reunion. No luck. Mother was haunted by Elinor and imagined her wandering homeless on the streets of Indianapolis looking for her. Maybe she had died there. The search for Ohio and Pennsylvania and Indiana death records turned up nothing.

I speculated about Elinor. She could have moved in with one of her children, been buried anywhere in the country, in the hospital burial grounds, or in an unmarked grave. I didn't want to believe that we would never know where my mother's own sister was buried. Having found so much information about my father who had no grave, I continued to search for any sign of Elinor that might remain. If I could find the hospital, maybe they would have her records, including her gravesite.

──── ◄ ►────

On a Saturday afternoon in February of 2005, I called Aunt Dorothy.
  "I'd love to find out what happened to Elinor."

"I would too, but I don't know anything that could help you. No. Wait. Elinor was in the nursing home in Massillon."

"Massillon? I've never heard of it. Where is Massillon?"

"About thirty miles from East Liverpool."

I was so grateful, I didn't think to ask Dorothy more about Massillon. The phone number for the Massillon library genealogy department was on the Internet, so I called. When a woman named Alice answered, I told her about Elinor having been sent to the mental hospital in Massillon and of my search for her grave.

"Massillon State Hospital," Alice said, "was the name of the mental hospital. They were supposed to keep records for ten years after the end of treatment, but they didn't have enough storage space, so they got permission from the government to destroy them. They had a bonfire and burned them."

"I might *never* find out where Elinor was buried," I wailed.

"She may have been buried in potter's field in Massillon." Alice paused. Her voice was softer when she spoke again. "I had a slightly retarded cousin who was placed in there and never released. She did the cooking and laundry in the hospital for the rest of her life."

Soon after the call I found an e-mail from Alice:

Susan, I was able to find that Floyd Del Vecchio died June 26, 1937. I checked the cemetery books for Elinor, but didn't find her. No stone, no record. If she died at Massillon State and was buried in their pot-ter's field, she would have been in the Massillon Cemetery record.

I am wondering if she was discharged and decided to make a new life for herself. Maybe she "disappeared" as far as the family is con-cerned. It will be awhile until the 1940 census is available. The state hospital is listed there. But since Floyd died in 1937, who knows. I checked the name in the city directory. One Del Vecchio family arrived in Massillon about 1950, but that's it. I found a John Del Vecchio—the son?

Elinor was twenty-three years old when her husband died! Her grief must have been utterly overwhelming, most likely the reason she was sent to the hospital. When Mother told me that she was schizophrenic, I assumed she went to the hospital after her mother's death. In those days, schizophrenia was a general diagnosis that would have included psychotic grief, entirely treatable now with medication. But it was Floyd's death that undid her. What a star-crossed family! Two sisters, each with two small children, both of whose husbands died way too young. Elinor was twenty-three and Mother was twenty-five. It was almost unbelievable. Their mother was dead and their father had married a woman who was less than motherly toward the sisters. Mother found support with my father's parents and then with Dad's large family. Elinor may not have had any help, and may have gone crazy with grief. *Dear Elinor. At the very least, I want to find your grave.*

I wrote back:

> *Learning when Floyd died is a great step. Did your resource for Floyd Del Vecchio's death mention anything about him? Where he was from, where he is buried, any relatives?*

Alice answered:

> *Floyd Del Vecchio died in Columbiana County, the county where East Liverpool is located. Contact the library there and ask if someone could look up his obituary in the paper. That will give a place of burial on it. It might also give you a clue as to the place of burial for Sarah.*
>
> *When I do searches, sometimes getting nosey is the only way I can get a clue. Why is it that your Mom doesn't know anything about Elinor? Was Elinor considerably older? It just seems that your Mom would have known the follow-up or at least what happened to the children.*

In April, I wrote to the Ohio Department of Health asking for their help in locating her gravesite. I included the only facts I'd discovered: her name, date, and place of birth, her husband's name and date of death, the names of their two children, and Elinor's last known residence—Massillon State Hospital. At once hopeful and doubtful, I called the number for John Del Vecchio that Alice had given me. The person who answered was friendly, but not related to Elinor. The Ohio Department of Health had no information about her burial.

Still, I was encouraged that the list of facts was growing. I reminded myself to search for Elinor with awareness that she was in my heart. The experience of searching for my father had taught me that my connection with Elinor would grow when I kept her in my thoughts. This was different from ordinary curiosity, wanting the facts of her life and death; it was more

like caring about her, wondering how she was treated, what it was like for
her, how she felt. Maybe it was closer to trying to enter into her life with a
sort of imaginative empathy. Really, it was letting myself love her.

———◄   ►———

I Googled and instantly saw pictures of Massillon State Hospital for the
Insane, now known as Massillon Psychiatric Center. The main hospital
building looked like a castle—massive, with turrets spiraling into the sky
at the center and each end. A watchtower rose over the "castle" and domi-
nated the landscape. I clicked on postcard images and found an upright
piano on a stage. The hospital complex was huge and grand, with so-called
cottages that look like manor houses. I looked up the history and found
that Massillon State Hospital for the Insane opened in 1898 in northeast-
ern Ohio, fifty miles south of Cleveland. Instead of building one immense
structure as was common in the previous era's Kirkbride plan, a variety
of brick and stone building were constructed according to the "cottage"
plan. The surrounding fields were cultivated and produced the food for the
hospital community. A trolley connected the hospital to the nearby city of
Massillon.

The Kirkbride plan was notorious for its hellacious back wards, so I was
relieved that Massillon was built in the more humane "cottage" style. Maybe
Elinor lived in one of the cottages. It sounded cozy, but knowing what I did
about mental hospitals from having visited several, I was quite sure that
"cozy" was not the right word. I copied the telephone number of Massillon
Psychiatric Center from the website.

Browsing through the various Massillon sites, I found a report dated
1915, describing the hospital's dairy, which, it said: "This should afford
some additional employment for our people and insure an abundance
of pure, unadulterated, wholesome milk. This is certainly much to be
desired in a hospital containing fifteen hundred patients, many of whom
are in delicate health.

"It seems unfortunate that while so much is being done for the health
and comfort of those of whom the Gentle Shepherd of us all has said,
'In-as-much as ye have done it unto one of the lease of these, etc.' a small
matter of expense shouldn't interfere with their further enjoyment. There
are no fly screens on any of the buildings occupied by patients, so that
swarms of flies, mosquitoes and other insects, often the bearers of dis-
ease, have access to the dining rooms, dormitories, and sick chamber. We

ask you that these unfortunates be spared further annoyance and torment by reason of these conditions.

"The charges of cruelty recently made against the attendants of some of the State institutions have led to the demand that higher prices be paid to attendants with a view to obtaining better services."

The report described a new requirement—that attendants declare any act of cruelty they'd observed during the past month when they signed for their wages.

While these snippets helped me picture Massillon, I was hungry to learn more about Elinor's life in the mental hospital. I called Massillon Hospital and was referred to Steve Moore in Records. I told him about Elinor and asked about the possibility of finding her records.

"I'd like to help you, and a thousand others, but the only records we have are stored in an attic, on 3x5 note cards in about 300 boxes. We've gone through only about thirty in three years putting them on the computer."

"Are they in alphabetical order?"

"No. There's no way to find your aunt's record, if it's there. You'd have to read every note card."

So there were records—they just weren't accessible. That was a blow. I told Steve, "I'd like to move to Massillon, sit in the attic, and go through every box and read every card until I found Elinor's."

"We'd like to have you." He laughed. "We sure could use the help."

I sucked in air between my teeth and hung up. The lives of thousands of people were reduced to 3x5 note cards and shoved away in an attic. And Aunt Elinor was one of them. I wrote Steve Moore's number in my phone book.

17

Mother's Last Breath

The plane was late. We were delayed in Chicago on the way to Indianapolis, where Mother was in the hospital, in hospice care. Would she still be breathing when I arrived? The sudden snow shower was over, and we were next in line to have our plane de-iced. The man in the seat beside me was irritated. "At least they could let us off this plane so we could get a soda."

"My mother is dying," I told him. "I only hope I get there in time."

"Well, I'm sure she's waited for you before. She'll wait for you now."

I looked at my watch again. I wanted to be there without having to get there. When the plane landed I called Dan.

"Is she still breathing?"

"Yes. She's still breathing."

My six siblings had already arrived. Dan dropped me off at the hospital and drove off to meet Clare and David at the funeral home to make arrangements. I took the elevator up to her unit, passed through the wide doors, and steadied myself with a deep breath. The thought struck me that my breath came from Mother, who had so few of her own left.

The week before, February 1, 2006, we had celebrated her eighty-sixth birthday. It wasn't the celebration that Ellen and I had planned—a luncheon for Mother and her best friends—but when I'd called Mother in January to talk about the birthday visit, she'd said, "I won't be here by then." She had been diagnosed with pulmonary fibrosis in the spring and had been using extra oxygen much of the time. A week later she'd called back to suggest that four of us—Mother, her best friend, Ellen, and I—go out for lunch.

As we passed the nurses' station, I noticed doctors and nurses standing around casually talking and smiling. The daughter in me wondered how they could be so calm when my mother was dying a few feet away. I reached an almost closed door, the door to Mother's room, and pushed it open and walked in.

She was lying on the bed, her eyes closed, a plastic oxygen mask over her nose and mouth. Her breath was deep and slow. Relief and thankfulness. I put my hand on Mother's forehead and stroked her hair. "I'm here Mother. It's Susan."

Her eyelids fluttered. I slipped my hand into hers. Her hand, like her forehead, was warm. Was that a squeeze? Did she know I was there? I sat beside the bed, held her warm hand, and watched her shoulders rise and fall with each breath. It was actually peaceful. This was the only place I wanted to be. Right there, sitting with Mother, was all of life.

My youngest and tallest brother, John, stood by the window. Amy was sitting on a chair at the foot of the bed, and Ellen was sitting on the other side of the bed holding Mother's hand. I got up and hugged them close, aware that each of us had come into life through the body of our mother, now in her last moments.

"Do you want time alone?" Amy volunteered, tucking the covers in around Mother's feet.

"Yes. Thank you, Amy."

Alone with Mother for the last time, I stroked her head and listened to her breathing, tuning my breath to hers the way I did when I was little and slept beside her. "I'm thankful for all your love and care and forgiveness and strength and spirit, for showing me everything you know about how to live, and for teaching me these past few months, through your deep generosity of letting go, how to die. You can be proud to have raised us well. I love you with my whole heart my one dear mother. I will miss you." I held her hand and breathed with her for a few minutes in silence before Amy and Ellen came back into the room.

Ellen tucked her red hair behind an ear and told me that while she was sitting with Mother the previous afternoon, Mother had asked if she was dying. "I said, 'Do you feel you are?' and she said yes. I told her we'd make her comfortable. Soon she'd be new, pure, and beautiful. That's when Mother spoke her last words, 'I know I will.'"

When Clare and Dan and David returned from the funeral home, there was tremendous sadness in their eyes as we hugged. While stroking her head we noticed that Mother was warm, and Ellen placed a cool, wet washcloth on her forehead. It was comforting to do something for Mother—stroke her head, hold her hand, and massage her feet. There was little we could give her except our complete presence—the soothing energy of love and care.

John, Clare, Dan, and Ellen left the room, and for a few minutes it was the three of us alone again: Mother, David, and me. I breathed in, knowing it was a precious moment; we had come full circle, the three of us together as we were long ago. I moved to the foot of the bed and began to rub the warm, smooth soles of her feet. During the birthday visit, when Mother was in the hospital, I had rubbed her feet, and she'd lifted her leg with a big smile and splayed her toes. She was delighted with herself and with Ellen's and my delight in that moment of girlish silliness.

"I bet you can't do *that*," she said.

———

It was Saturday, January 28, and I was at the airport, on my way to Indianapolis to celebrate Mother's eighty-sixth birthday. I'd just spilled chai on my jacket and felt like a college kid, a little scruffy and eager. Ellen picked me up and we drove to her house for a bite to eat before she dropped me off at Mother and Dad's new place, an assisted living facility.

Preparing months earlier to move into much smaller quarters, Mother had spent the fall sorting through her belongings. With Ellen's help, she'd set out one basket for each child. Into each of the seven baskets, she'd placed one item after another—things that had been part of her life and ours for the past seventy years. There were wedding presents from the 1940s, inscribed books, silverware and china we used for Sunday dinners, a little painted pitcher, the jug in the shape of a man's face that sat on the shelf in her secretary, and the silver bell we used to call her to our bedside when we were sick.

Ellen had packed the contents of each basket into boxes and mailed them. My box arrived just before Thanksgiving. Among the platters and bowls was a milk-white vase that she told me had been a wedding present when she and my father married. The vase had sat on the bookshelf beside the fireplace of every house we'd lived in. When I placed it on the bookshelf beside the fireplace in my living room, it seemed to glow in the late after-noon light.

Mother had told me that their new, one-bedroom apartment was tiny, unlike our other houses with their many bedrooms and porches and big backyards. Entering the room, I caught a glimpse of her sitting in her blue wing chair by the window, plastic tubes bringing extra oxygen into her aged body. She rose from her chair and walked toward me, her eyes sparkling, arms outstretched. She was my mother and she was beautiful in her eagerness to welcome me home, right there in her final home on earth.

We settled into chairs and caught up. Mother told me about her doctor, Dr. Byron. Lord Byron, she called him.

"When I saw him after I left rehab the last time, he said to me, 'You look like hell,'" she chuckled. Mother and her doctor shared the same dry humor. "When we moved here, I was a little appalled seeing so many of the residents traveling by wheelchair and walker to the dining room. Really I feel quite young. I decided that I would smile each time I entered the dining room." She told me about the friends she'd made and the kids from the nearby middle school she was tutoring, just as she had taught children, many with learning disabilities, the joys of reading for many years.

The next morning, when Ellen and I were having breakfast, the phone rang. Mother had had a bad night.

"The pain in my back is worse. I want you to take me to the hospital."

Ellen and I drove right over. I saw pain in her face with every movement. Ellen pulled up at the entrance to the emergency room and I grabbed a wheelchair. Slowly and painfully, Mother moved from the car to the wheelchair. Ellen drove off to park the car while Mother and I began the checking-in process. I started to tell the admitting person why we were there when Mother interrupted. "I can still speak and I will answer the questions myself, Susan."

Oops! Of course she could. Ellen would have known that, having been with Mother through many hospital visits. I stood back while Mother provided the information.

After a short wait, Dr. Byron entered the small ER room. Gray-haired and trim, he took a seat near the bed, crossed his legs, and asked Mother if she'd ever smoked.

"A little," she answered. "I was too busy raising seven children or I'd have smoked more."

Ellen and I glanced at each other and raised our eyebrows, knowing that she had always smoked lots, and often.

He asked if she'd lifted anything recently.

"I haven't lifted a finger in my entire, elegant life of leisure," she told him. She introduced me as the eldest of her four daughters.

Dr. Byron ran his hand through his hair. "I have one daughter and it's lucky that she and I are still alive."

The next morning, Dad called to tell us that Mother had a compression fracture in her spine. After hanging up Ellen turned to me. "All right, now which one of us stepped on a crack?"

It took me a minute, and then the mixture of horror and humor brought out a laugh. "Oh no. It wasn't me. It must have been Dan."

When I called Dan to tell him the news and included the joke, he came right out with, "It was Clare, Clare did it."

That was how the Henkel kids related. I was always too serious to joke around the way they did but Ellen never abandoned her efforts to include me. Since the last Mother's Day, when all seven of us were there to honor Mother, I had felt a part of the family—not exactly a "Henkel Sister," as Clare called us, but a sister nonetheless.

"We're not all Henkels," I told Clare. She stopped and thought a minute, and then, with tears in her eyes, said, "I never thought this before, but if it weren't for your father's death, I wouldn't be here."

———— ▶ ————

Wednesday, February 1, Mother's eighty-sixth birthday. Ellen and I popped over to the hospital and sang "Happy Birthday."

"I've told just one nurse," Mother said. "The last thing I want is everyone clucking over me and talking to me as if I were a two-year-old."

We left to take Dad to lunch at his favorite restaurant, The Snooty Fox, where tunes from the forties carried him back to the time he returned from war and fell in love with Mother.

After lunch we stopped at the bakery and bought four pretty little birthday cakes—no candles, because of Mother's oxygen—and headed back to the hospital. The three of us trooped in, Dad in a wheelchair, on his lap the box of cakes, a bag of cards, and presents. When Mother informed us that she was being discharged in a few minutes, Ellen and I looked at each other wondering how we'd manage to take care of her while she was still in a considerable amount of pain. Ellen rolled Mother's wheelchair and I rolled Dad's back down the hall, out the door, and into the car. Home again, Mother settled into her blue wing chair by the window and opened her birthday cards.

Early the next morning, Ellen dropped me off so I could have time with Mother before leaving for the airport. While she slept, I sat in her blue chair, so content to be there that I forgot I was leaving soon. She woke and asked me to put socks on her chilly feet. Just then Ellen came to pick me up. Time to go. I kissed her, told her that I loved her, and then I was out the door.

———————

Five days later I was back with Mother and my siblings in the hospital. Clare had found a disc player and a CD with Celtic music she knew Mother liked. One or the other of us stroked her head and talked softly to her. We told her not to worry. We were all right. Dad would be well taken care of. She'd done everything she needed to do and she'd done it well. She could rest. She was loved beyond measure, and we would remember her as long as we breathed.

I listened to the conversations floating in the air—small things families talk about. Amy passed around a bag of almonds. I took a handful and concentrated on the words of the hospice nurse who came in and quietly alerted us to new signs that death was approaching. Dan stood by Mother's bed, watching her every breath and I was drawn back to Mother, knowing that she was still alive but there was little time left. Her feet were warm and soft. It was comforting to slip my hand in hers and feel connected. Sometimes she moved, squeezed a finger, her eyes fluttered or her forehead moved. She was there and she was fading.

Amy readjusted the plastic oxygen mask when it slipped down and seemed to cut into her chin. Mother's chin carried part of her history. Embedded there were a few gray specks, pieces of gravel that were never removed when she had a bicycle accident after her mother died. She borrowed a bike and when she fell, there was no one to notice the burn on her chin and wash out the gravel. She was sensitive about those gray specks, but to me they were part of her, like her blue eyes.

The hospice nurse entered the room and suggested that we might want to remove the mask. No one objected and the nurse took it off, leaving the two plastic tubes that sent Mother extra oxygen. Her shoulders rose to help her pull air into her lungs. Ellen wet her lips with a sponge on a stick soaked with water and we saw her sucking the water. She was thirsty. We took turns wetting her dry lips.

A few minutes later, as I massaged Mother's feet, I noticed that her left toe was a little cold and that she was losing color.

Ellen had just come into the room, and she heard us talking about it. "Let's gather everyone in a circle around her."

We put our arms around each other. Ellen turned to me and said, "Susan, pray!"

Gratitude for Mother began to flow out of me—gratitude for her love and care, for her support of our creativity, for her no-nonsense humor, for her spiritual center, for her love of hymns and poetry and writing. Then, one by one, each of us joined in with something we loved about Mother—her love of words and language, her patience with our troubles, teaching us to read and teaching others to read, being a friend to our friends and teaching us about friendship, giving us dance lessons, music lessons, acting lessons, picnics, good food, and honesty. The room was filled with love and gratitude for Mother.

As we became quiet again, Mother's breath was the only sound in the room. It was shallower, her skin was pale, and she rested longer after each breath. Ellen left the circle to pick up a book and began reading, "Yea though I walk through the valley of the shadow of death, I shall fear no evil for thou art with me." We remembered the words and joined in. "Thy rod and thy staff shall comfort me. Thou preparest a table before me in presence of mine enemies. Thou annointest my head with oil, my cup runneth over." We watched Mother's shoulders rise and fall as she took a labored breath. "Surely, goodness and mercy shall follow me all the days of my life, and I shall dwell in the house of the Lord forever."

We looked at Mother. She was gone. We said it in a whisper, "She's gone." We looked at her and we listened and we saw—there was not another breath. We whispered to each other again and again, "She's gone. She's gone."

We hugged each other and tears flowed freely. How could the death of our beloved mother bring this feeling of peaceful completion and deep connection? Mother helped us accept her death as she was learning to accept it, not by giving up but by seeing what was happening in her body. She used her spiritual and her intuitive wisdom to accept what was happening and to help us accept it. She did that with generosity and grace so that we were ready to come home and stay with her until the end. Mother waited for all of us. We were as one in our love and presence with her through the moment when she left her body. She had taught us to live and she had taught us to die. She'd brought us into the world, and she'd let us help her leave it.

We each would feel loss in our own way; at moments we wanted to tell her something about our lives, something she would enjoy, at other moments we'd miss her with the full force of realizing that she was not beside us anymore. She'd taken her secrets with her and I was all right with that; I'd found what I'd needed, and Mother and I had made our peace. She was no longer sitting in the blue wing chair by the window ready to answer the phone when we called. She was inside of us and we were filled with the light of knowing that all of us, together, had entered the natural flow of life that included death. Mother wasn't afraid, and we followed her into this bright place of natural and peaceful death.

"Yea though I walk through the valley of the shadow of death I shall fear no evil, for thou art with me." Mother was not alone. None of us was alone. We walked through this place together, holding hands, singing, praying, breathing, and accepting with full awareness that our Mother was taking her last breaths. There was nothing blocking our love. What we experienced was the complete wonder and peace of being with her, with ourselves, and with each other as we stayed with her through the last breath of her life.

18

A Note From the Past

Five months after Mother's passing, I was shocked to find out that my brother, David, had liver cancer. My big brother was dying. David was my last living connection with my father. As it became clear that he was growing weaker, I flew to Florida at the end of January and stayed with him to the end.

The day before he died, in March 2007, wearing his Harley Davidson bandana and T-shirt, he took a spin around the block in the electric wheelchair his friends had given him. He was off on a set of wheels, which is where he loved to be. The next morning, his wife, Gloria, who knew he was close to the end, called me into the bedroom. Without opening his eyes, he said, "They know when to come."

"Who, David?" we asked, "Who knows when to come?"

"God," he answered.

Mother had joined the family ancestors, and now David had. Because I knew Mother and David and was there when they died, they were not ghosts like my father once was, like Elinor was, but ancestors who lived in me.

———————

The next January, Dorothy and I celebrated our birthdays together. I boarded the train bound for Long Island in DC, and got off in New York City to view an exhibit about people who spent their adult lives in a New York State mental hospital. The exhibit, *The Lives They Left Behind: Suitcases from a*

State Hospital Attic, was being shown at the New York Public Library for one more week. The authors had discovered hundreds of suitcases in the attic of a mental hospital—the very suitcases brought to the hospital on arrival and left there.

The exhibit immediately drew me into the lives of people who were mostly unlucky, not necessarily mentally ill. Many were sent to the hospital when their reactions to stressful situations threatened the people around them. Way too many were left in the hospital for years and years and died, forgotten by family. Many of those in the exhibit were immigrants whose families, like Elinor's, lived just miles down the road from the hospital.

Among the saddest objects left in a suitcase were a white, hand-knitted baby bonnet with pink ribbons and roses, a delicate, handmade christening gown, and tiny baby booties. They belonged to a woman named Ethel who had lost two of her four children as infants. Packing for what she thought would be a short stay in the hospital, she filled her suitcase with baby clothes and quilts she had made, stitch by stitch. The exhibit led me to wonder what Elinor had taken with her the day she was sent to the hospital. Was there anything left that might give me a sense of who she was?

I stopped at Macy's department store on the way back to the train and chose a set of rose-colored Homer Laughlin dishes for Aunt Dorothy. On the evening of our birthday celebration, Mickey arrived with dinner, a birthday cake, and his guitar. We sat around the table and sang the evening away, just as we did in my family, just as Mother, Dorothy, Elinor, and Bill did when they were growing up.

Over breakfast, I asked Dorothy about Elinor. She picked up her coffee mug, looked into it, then put it down. "Elinor took care of me after my mother died. She was like a mother to me, a refuge. Later, she and Floyd lived at the country club. He was the greenskeeper, the golf pro, and Elinor was in charge of the events—you know, the luncheons and things like that. I went with Grandpa to visit her in the mental hospital. She called him Mr. Laughlin and didn't even recognize me. I couldn't go back."

The next morning, just before leaving, I checked my cell phone for messages and found one from Ellen. "Dad is in his last days. Come to Indianapolis as soon as you can."

I called her. "Is he still . . . ?"

"Yes, but you'd better come today."

Mickey arrived to drive me to the train station; instead, he took me to the airport. My siblings were already there when I walked into Dad's room at the hospice care center. We kept a vigil for him and were with him as he turned his eyes to heaven. On the morning of Mother's birthday, February 1, Dad took his last breath.

After the funeral, we gathered in our parents' final home. Only their most necessary and valued possessions were left. We knew what each other wanted and sounded like a chorus of encouragement.

"Mother's blue wing chair is for you, Amy."

"You have that pitcher, Clare. You've always liked it."

"John, here's Dad's watch."

"Ellen, the statue of the Holy Family is for you."

Dan lifted a Bible off the bookshelf. "This was Grandpa's Bible." He leafed through the wing-thin pages.

"You should have it, Dan," we said in unison.

Mother had given me one of Grandpa's Bibles several years before. Tucked between the pages were things precious to Grandpa—a letter from eight-year-old Margery and a poem written by grandmother Clare. Mother had kept the Bible Dan was holding, and it had still been in her desk when she'd died two years earlier.

A scrap of paper fell out and Dan picked it up. "Elinor to Massillon 12/7/36. Floyd died June 1937."

I let out a piercing yell. No words, just sound. Everyone stopped talking and looked at me. Smiling, Dan handed me the paper. "Here it is. The very day Elinor was taken to the mental hospital." That was a tremendous gift, a note from the past opening the way to Elinor.

Jack and I decided to return to East Liverpool in March. We could visit Massillon Hospital to get a sense of the place, see if we could find out where Elinor had lived, where she might be buried, and look for doctors, nurses, or anyone who might be able to give us an idea of what it was like when Elinor was there. We could look around East Liverpool—the country club, the high school, and the church—and we'd check county records for the birth dates of John and Sandra.

The week before we left home, I sat at my desk and thought about life and death and Elinor. Since Mother's and Dad's passing and David's last days, I'd been missing what once was, although at the time it was so ordinary, just us with our flaws.

Looking up at the portrait of the three sisters above my desk, I noticed that Elinor, who was sixteen, had covered five-year-old Dorothy's hand with her own. I was moved by that gesture and addressed her as if she could hear me: "Elinor, my mother's sister, older by seven years, what happened to you? You were so young, just twenty-three, when they took you to the state mental hospital. You had two children, babies, and you were working, managing the events at the country club. Your mother had died six years earlier, and you took good care of Mother and Dorothy, especially when your father married a woman who didn't like Grandpa's girls. I'm pretty sure no one in my family was there for you before or after you were sent away. Where are your children now, my cousins? Do they know where you're buried? I'm about to enter wholeheartedly into your life, whatever is left of it. Help me, Elinor. Help me find you."

———————

I called Steve Moore in the Records department of Massillon State Hospital in early March to tell him the date that Elinor was taken to Massillon. I told him everything I knew about her, wanting to change her in Steve's mind from a note card to a person with a history and a family. I asked him again about her records and where she might be buried.

Steve listened until I finish. "Hospital patients were buried in the local cemeteries. The county health department might be able to locate your aunt's grave, or you could call the cemeteries." He gave me the number of the county health department and the names and numbers of the local cemeteries. "There's a man here named Nate Carey. Give him a call. I'll let him tell you what he has."

When I called the health department, a woman answered and began searching for information while I waited. After a while, she asked me to call back in ten minutes. When I did, she was still searching.

I dialed the number for Mr. Carey and told him about Elinor.

"There's a place here," he said, "called McKinley Mansion, where old records are kept—dates of admission, diagnosis, all of it." We agreed to meet in his office on the hospital grounds when we were in Ohio at the end of March.

That was closer to Elinor than I'd ever been. It was also ironically romantic, a mansion on the grounds of the hospital with the lives of so many stashed away in old records, the lives of people who had little say about their lives. If Elinor's records were there, I'd be able to find out what happened to her.

I called the health department back.

"I probably won't find anything today as it's the end of the day, but I'll let you know if and when I do," the woman said.

I went for a walk and checked messages when I got home. There was a new message.

"Susan, hi. I'm calling from Massillon City Health Department. I checked with my local genealogist here in town and she said that Elinor is still living. She's staying at the Colonial Nursing Home on Market Avenue in Camden. I can give you a phone number for the Colonial Nursing Home to make sure she's the right person. We believe she is."

"Elinor is alive!" I shouted out loud. "She's alive! Elinor is ninety-four years old and she is alive! We can visit her!"

I called the woman right back to thank her. "How in the world did you find her?"

"She wasn't listed in any of the cemeteries around here, so I called my friend who is a genealogist at the Massillon Library. Alice found that in 1994, according to the Stark County Probate Court records, Elinor was assigned a guardian.

"I am enormously grateful to you, and to Alice."

I looked up Camden in the atlas. It was on the west side of Ohio. I'd take Elinor a picture of her mother and the one of the three sisters. I called the nursing home and asked for Elinor Del Vecchio. "I am the niece of Elinor Del Vecchio, who is my mother's sister. I've been told Elinor is there."

"This is an unusual call," said the person at the other end of the line. "Just a minute." After a few minutes she returned. "We can't give out information due to privacy, but the social worker will call you tomorrow morning. Betty Jennings is her name."

Elinor was alive! And we could visit her, hopefully. Jack said she might be in Camden because it was near her children. I didn't care why she was there, I was just happy we'd finally found her. I located a John Del Vecchio living at Lake Milton, which was between Massillon and East Liverpool, but decided against calling for fear her children might not want me to see her. There were so many hurdles, and yet she was right where they left her, where she'd always been. How could anyone survive living in a mental hospital for seventy-two years, especially a mother who had lost her entire family and everyone she'd ever known? No wonder we'd all thought she was dead. What a lesson in believing the perception rather than remaining open to reality, even if we think it could never be true.

I decided to stay home the next day to take the call from the social worker at the nursing home. Finding it hard to wait, I sat at the table and made lists—grocery lists, to-do lists, lists of birth dates and presents to buy, lists of books to read, lists of people to call. I waited until I couldn't wait any longer, then dialed the number. No answer. I tried again. Still no answer. I checked with 411 and they said they didn't have a Colonial Nursing Home listed for Camden, Ohio. I listened again to the message with the number of the nursing home. Sure enough, I had miscopied the number. I called the right number and got through. It was in Canton, not Camden, and it was just forty miles down the road from East Liverpool, quite near Massillon.

The woman who answered put me on hold. I waited. She checked to see if I was still waiting and put me on hold again. She came back to the phone and asked, "Betty didn't answer?" A bit later, she returned and asked, "Still waiting for Betty? I'll go back and look. She's probably with one of the residents." She put me on hold again and I waited some more.

Betty finally came to the phone. "Oh honey, I can't give you information. She has a legal guardian."

Thinking that one of Elinor's children was the guardian, I asked her about them.

"Well, I know she had two children, but I haven't seen them. I'll have to talk to the legal guardian. What is your goal?"

"My mother passed away in '06, but I've always wanted to know what happened to Elinor. I was trying to find out where she was buried, as I didn't want her to be forgotten and just yesterday learned that she was still alive. This is just incredible."

"She's okay. I can tell you that. I'll call her legal guardian and see what she says."

"We're coming to East Liverpool next week. If we can, we'd love to visit Elinor."

"What a sweet person you are. Many don't want to know, for reasons who knows. After I talk to her, hopefully today or tomorrow, I'll call you."

Betty called back later that day. "I have permission to talk with you. Elinor's legal guardian gave me permission."

"Wonderful." I exhaled.

"Elinor was admitted here in 1994," Betty continued. "She lived at Massillon State Hospital, diagnosed with schizophrenia, from 1936 until the mid-seventies, when Governor Rhodes ordered all except the most psychotic discharged. Social workers had to scramble to find places for them—3,600 people were suddenly out on the streets or put into group homes. They tore down all the cottages and sent her to a group home, not the best of circumstances. In the days when Elinor went to Massillon, people were signed in and never signed out, and the treatment was pretty awful.

"When she got to us she had a case manager and our doctor was able to manage her meds. She wasn't ambulating. She had fallen in the group home and broken a hip and it had been left untreated. One leg is shorter than the other now. She uses a walker. She's not on meds.

"When they came in from the hospital we didn't get much information. Wait. Here's something she wrote while she was here: 'I'm expecting a baby and if anything I need help in taking care of it.'"

I shake my head knowingly when I heard that. Surely, she had postpartum trouble.

"She spells very well," Betty continued. "She had to have education. I knew she came from somewhere. She mentions Bill and Susan B. Anthony."

"Bill. That was her brother's name, Bill Laughlin."

"Oh. She calls herself Laughlin. When she came here she was bright and played the piano beautifully. She's pleasantly confused and calls everyone Dorothy. We call her Mother—she wants to be called Mother. She likes to wear hats with flowers. She tells jokes, little things that make us laugh. She can be ornery—she speaks her mind. And she's cute. She has white hair that's wavy and curly, and when it's cut right, it falls into place. We love her."

Betty began to cry. She'd be sixty-five in July and she didn't know who her parents were. She was adopted. "It was during WWII. I saw my birth certificate but haven't been able to find them. My mother was sixteen and unwed; my father was probably a soldier. My son wants to know his medical history, for himself and his daughter. Seldom does a family want to find their people unless they read in the paper there's money. I wish this were me."

"The American WWII War Orphans Network might be able to help." I told her about my father and that the network helped me find information and offered support during my search. "I'll bring what I have when we come on Sunday to see Elinor. Will it be okay to give her some family pictures?"

"Bring the photos. They may spark something. The nurse's aides are close to the residents, enjoy buying them clothes, but it's difficult work. They want to see if you resemble her."

I was ecstatic! Elinor still played the piano, or had until several years ago, and sounded enchantingly eccentric—wearing hats with flowers, joking and calling everyone Dorothy. Everyone was her little sister Dorothy, and she was everyone's mother. My heart and mind traveled in different directions— joy knowing that she was alive and well, sorrow and regret about all that had happened, sadness not to have known her earlier, and horror that she was left, abandoned to the state.

Shopping for a gift for Elinor, I found a soft wool shawl with a design of musical swirls. I made an album with pictures from her childhood and framed the portraits of her mother and the one of the three sisters. Would she recognize anyone in the pictures?

I was beginning to understand why Mother had found it so difficult to be with her family. The truth of Elinor's life in an institution was there along with the memories—guilt, shame, wondering, worrying.

———— ▶ ————

I called Dorothy that afternoon and she immediately began to talk about her big sister. "She and Floyd lived in back of us—around the corner and down the alley, first house on the right, upstairs. Every day after school, I'd walk over there and stay with Elinor until Dad came home. Floyd worked at the country club. Elinor and I were together most of the time. We were very, very close."

I could almost see Elinor as a young woman busy in the kitchen when Dorothy came in the back door. Dorothy would have been nine when Elinor was twenty in 1933.

"She may not recognize me." Dorothy sounded worried. "I don't want to get her confused, make things worse. If she's happy, I don't want to change that. I have my memories. I can live with those. I don't need to see her.

"She was pretty, slim, even with children. Different things happen. Floyd died and his sister adopted the children."

Dorothy thought that Mame, the woman Grandpa married after their mother died, wouldn't let Grandpa bring Elinor home. "He never stood up to Mame," she said. "I'm angry with myself for not staying in touch with my family. Your mother and I could have, and should have, stayed with each other."

Later, Mickey called with some revealing and disturbing information. "I spoke with Mom last night after you called and she told me that while she was still living at home, before she joined the Marines, she overheard her father tell Mame that Elinor was better and he'd like to bring her home. Mom said she heard Mame shout that she didn't want that crazy girl in the house."

My heart raced. I felt hot, then cold. Elinor was just twenty-nine when Mame walked out in 1942, and still Elinor was left at Massillon. How could he leave her there?

We started out early Saturday morning of Easter weekend and took the scenic route across Western Maryland. Carol at Sturgis House welcomed us back. That night we met Ann for dinner. The restaurant in downtown East Liverpool was a simple, friendly place with blue-and-white-checked table-cloths and home-style cooking. Ann, already seated in a booth, saw us and waved. We ate and talked for two hours.

Between bites of spaghetti and garlic bread, Ann talked about the family. "My mother knew Elinor in school. She took me to visit her in the hospital in the forties when I was about ten years old. We gave her lipstick, the one thing she was allowed to have, and she loved it. She was scattered. Mother told me that Elinor had postpartum psychosis and that she had treatment and it helped. The hospital thought she could live normally, but the family didn't take her. Then, during the mid-seventies, we got a letter saying they were releasing Elinor. My parents couldn't deal with it. Dad had cancer and died in 1977. Sometimes Mother said that I was like Elinor. What she meant is that I, like Elinor, had great ups and downs."

Ann was surprised to hear that Elinor played the piano. "My dad played by ear. He could hear a piece of music once, remember it, and then play it perfectly. He played in a jazz group."

We walked Ann to her car and Jack offered to let her know about Elinor.

"Only if it's good." She smiled.

Walking back to Sturgis House, I gripped Jack's hand. "Elinor recovered. She could have lived a normal life, and not one of us came to help her or take her home. The whole family left her there. I cannot bear that, and yet Elinor has borne it alone all these years and survived."

19

Stay With Me

The sixty miles of flat country roads between East Liverpool and Canton wound through farmland and small towns. Jack and I had no trouble locating the nursing home on the main street, a turn-of-the-century converted mansion painted white. Four pillars surrounded what was once a grand entrance, and several large oak trees shaded a small green lawn. We entered through a side door that was part of an add-on and found ourselves in front of a long counter where several nurses conversed. One of them noticed us and came over.

"We're here to see my aunt, Elinor Del Vecchio."

"Oh, you're Elinor's niece. Betty told us you'd be coming. Elinor is over there in the day room. Stay as long as you like." She pointed to the dayroom just beyond the nurses' station.

I peeked in and scanned the room. It was easy to tell the residents from the staff: the old ones sat at tables or shuffled along in walkers, the younger ones came and went briskly, setting down trays or taking them away.

"There she is. There's Elinor!" I whispered to Jack and pointed to a woman with short, snow-white hair in a wheelchair beside the far wall.

Jack nodded. "Let's go."

We walked around tables, avoided aides with trays, and moved toward her. She was eating, dipping her spoon into a cup of yogurt. Jack sat beside her and I pulled up a chair facing her. She looked like Aunt Dorothy, with her strong chin, and had Mother's sharp blue eyes.

She scrutinized me for a few seconds, filled her spoon, and offered me a bite.

I smiled. "Oh, thank you, Elinor, but I've already eaten."

A bib tied around her neck caught the liquid that spilled from her spoon. She had no teeth and it was difficult to understand her words, so I bent my head toward her and listened closely.

"I'm embarrassed." She took off her bib and pulled her blue sweatshirt up from the collar to hide her head for what I imagined was a moment of privacy in a world where privacy didn't exist. Minutes later she continued to eat, spilling a few drops on her sweatshirt. When she finished she rested her head on her chest and fell asleep.

Jack and I exchanged smiles.

The dayroom was crowded and noisy, yet surprisingly cheerful. Aides helped many of the residents eat, and they dispensed medicine, chatting over the noise of the TV. Visitors wandered through and a man with hollow cheeks pushed his walker past. Another resident had her radio tuned to music of the fifties. I caught the Big Bopper singing "Chantilly Lace" as I watched an ancient-looking woman in a chair at the far end of Elinor's table, sleeping soundly, oblivious of the noise. Alarms sounded regularly. Each wheelchair had one attached by a string to the resident's clothes so that when the person tried to stand, the alarm sent out a piercing, beeping sound until a staff member rushed over to turn it off. There were no luxuries here, but the old building was clean and the staff was friendly.

An aide with a dimpled grin walked over. She winked at me as she turned to Elinor and shouted, "Mother, you've got company. Your niece is here to see you. Wake up, Mother. Mother!"

Elinor opened her eyes, lifted the edges of her bib from the table, and folded it carefully. Her hands were elegant, with long fingers and graceful movements. She looked at me with penetrating eyes, trying to figure out who we were and why we were there.

"I'm your sister Margery's daughter, Susan, and this is Jack, my husband. We've come to see you."

Elinor took me in and studied Jack. I gave her the photographs and the album, a book of her life before. She put them on the table; a full five minutes passed before she picked up the album. "This is a book." She looked, paused, and then looked again at the pictures.

"Do you know who this is?" I pointed to a picture of her brother taken long ago.

"A boy," she replied matter-of-factly. She studied the pictures and put the album down.

She said nothing, and I couldn't tell if she recognized any of the people.

Turning her attention to the framed picture of her mother, she looked at it closely for a long time, put it down, and then examined the photo of the three sisters. She returned that one to the table with the others and rested her soft, warm hand on top of mine.

I couldn't restrain myself. "I love you, Elinor."

"What did you say? You left me?"

"No. I love you."

"Oh. You love me. How much?"

"As much as the world and with my whole heart."

"Your poor heart?"

"Yes. With my poor heart."

"My mother loved me and she acted like she did."

I was a stranger to Elinor and took her warning seriously.

The aide looked at the photos and printed the name of each sister on the glass. "The staff will want to know her sisters' names so we can talk to Elinor about them. She sings 'You Are My Sunshine' every night, all three verses." She turned to Elinor and shook her shoulder gently. "Mother, sing 'You Are My Sunshine.'"

Elinor sang the entire song in a well-timed, on-key voice. Sitting beside her, I heard the familiar words as Elinor might have heard them with her many losses: "The other night, dear, as I lay sleeping, I dreamed I held you in my arms. But when I awoke, dear, I was mistaken and I hung my head and I cried."

———◆———

A man in a black suit with several strands of dark hair combed over an almost bald head marched into the center of room, opened his satchel, and pulled out a hymnal. "Let us join our voices," the preacher shouted, "and sing our praises to the Lord on this blessed Easter day." He raised his arms to include everyone in the room and beyond. Chairs scraped the floor as people turned around to face him. A blind woman with a long white braid trailing down her bent back tapped her way to an empty chair in front of the preacher. Elinor and I sang along and touched our hands together to the rhythm of the hymns—"Rock of Ages," "I Come to the Garden Alone," "Blessed Assurance." After more hymns the minister began to preach. "Mmm-hmmms" and "Yes, sirs" punctuated his words. The preaching grew progressively gruesome as the minister ranted about blood, nails, and sinners.

Suddenly Elinor's voice boomed out over the preacher's, "Shut up!"

Jack and I looked at each other and grinned. That was exactly what we had wanted to say.

After the preacher left, Elinor reached over and took Jack's hand. He beamed. She kissed the back of his hand and he was radiant. He kissed the back of her hand and she kissed his hand and he kissed her hand.

A lady in a pink dress, looking quite prim sitting in her wheelchair, watched them, then hollered out, "Are you available?"

Chuckling, the aide called back, "He's already taken, Margaret."

I gave Elinor a present wrapped in pink paper with a white ribbon.

"Thank you." She patted the gift and let it sit on the table in front of her. Silence was part of being with Elinor. When she was ready, she pushed up the sleeves of her sweatshirt and began to open it. Slowly, she unwrapped the shawl and left it folded on the table. Taking a Kleenex from the box beside her she carefully covered the shawl, as if to hide and protect it.

Her fingers, I noticed, could reach octaves on the piano.

"I heard you play the piano,"

"Yes, I do play the piano." Elinor drummed the table with her fingers as if touching keys. After a period of silence she shouted, "Take me to bed!"

I realized that we'd been with her for two hours. It was time to go. But having never seen my father, I appreciated the tremendous miracle it was to be there with Elinor, and I didn't want to leave. I kissed her cheek and told her we'd be back.

On the way out, a nurse invited us to stop by Elinor's bedroom. Her bed was in the middle of a long, narrow room with four beds. An oxygen tank stood on the floor beside her bed, and there was paraphernalia for treatments on a little end table. Two lone cards were tacked to the bulletin board above her bed, both dated 1991.

The nurse stopped to talk with us. "Elinor stays up late. She doesn't like to go to bed. When she first came to the nursing home from a group home, she walked over to the piano after dinner and played. Now she's in a wheelchair due to an untreated hip fracture that happened some time ago, probably when she was at Massillon. I wish you could have known her when she first came here."

The next day we returned to Canton for a meeting with the social worker. Betty greeted us at the nurses' station. A hint of lavender hung in the air as we followed her upstairs to her office. Jack and I sat across the desk facing her, the top of an oak tree visible through the front window.

Betty opened a file and began to read while I took notes. "Elinor was admitted to the Colonial Nursing Home on March 4, 1994 from the Princess Stone Group Home in Canton. Her diagnosis was schizophrenia. She was not depressed or anxious, and she wasn't on any medication. She had no coherent history. Wasn't homicidal or suicidal. She was alert and pleasant and talked on different topics."

Betty put down the file and explained, "The Princess Stone Group Home was African American and Pentecostal and Elinor came here singing gospel and preaching. She would have had to be independent to have lived there. Her health was good, but she was becoming incontinent. I wish you could have known her then, when she could talk more. The staff are attached to Elinor and take good care of her."

"It sounds as if there were times when Elinor was all right. It's hard for me to come to terms with my family who didn't take her."

"Yes. You're right. There were times when she could have left, but she didn't, and you have to accept that. Her diagnosis was schizophrenia, but she had postpartum depression. Nowadays that's treatable with anti-depressive medication. That's enough to make you go crazy. And to be put some place where you couldn't get out. You had to be signed out to be released from the mental hospital. Like jail."

On our way back to East Liverpool, Jack suggested we stop at the county courthouse to check for records. We stood at the counter and filled out a request for the record of the hearing that sent Elinor to Massillon and handed it to the clerk, a heavyset man wearing aviator glasses. He returned with the Probate Court Record from December 7, 1936. Together Jack and I held the document and read the unnerving title: "Insanity of Eleanor Del Vecchio: Inquest of Lunacy."

> 1936. Dec. 7. Affidavit filed. Inquest held, Doctors Certificate filed. Patient adjudged insane.
> 1936. Dec. 7. Application made for admission to Massillon State Hospital.
> 1936. Dec. 7. Admission granted. Warrant to convey issued to J. Floyd Del Vecchio.
> 1936. Dec. 9. Warrant to convey returned and filed.

"Lunacy." "Insane." The language reflected the attitude of the era when Elinor was committed to the institution—a time when people were labeled and locked away for untold reasons, including illnesses that were seen as mysterious, frightening, or dangerous, a time when diagnoses were non-specific and treatment was generalized,

Jack suggested that we try to find the dates that Elinor's children were born, so we headed back to East Liverpool. The Health Department closed at 3:00 p.m. and it was already 2:45 when we asked for John and Sandra Del Vecchio's birth certificates. We guessed that the children were born somewhere between 1933 and 1936. Lo and behold, the woman came back with both birth certificates: John Floyd Del Vecchio, born on August 10, 1934 to Floyd Del Vecchio, thirty, a superintendent of greens at the East Liverpool Country Club for nine years, and Elinor Del Vecchio, twenty, a housewife for seven months. Address: 316 Jackson Street. Sandra Lou Del Vecchio, born on July 20, 1936 to John Floyd Del Vecchio, thirty-two, superintendent of greens at the East Liverpool Country Club for ten years, and Sara Elinor Del Vecchio, twenty-two, manager for three years of the clubhouse.

———————————

The next day we had an appointment with Nate Carey at Massillon State Hospital. On the drive over I felt sick and irritable thinking about the years Elinor had spent there. I'd never know what it was like for her, but driving that road I thought of all of us, the Laughlins and the Del Vecchios, who had been affected by Elinor's institutionalization, a sad heritage of mystery, loss, and guilt.

Elinor was twenty-three when the court ordered her to the state mental hospital. When I was twenty-three, I had just finished college and was full of vitality and plans. I thought about the rest of my life, the effort and wonder of raising two children, a boy and a girl two years apart, just like Elinor's children. I thought of the years we lived abroad, of graduate school, and my professional life, the things I'd learned, mistakes, adventures, and the ways I'd grown. Elinor spent those years confined to a mental hospital for an episode of postpartum psychosis from which she no doubt recovered within three or four years. She was in her sixties, my age, when she left Massillon for a group home. I was about to visit the hospital to which she was abandoned, the mental hospital where she lived in who knows what kinds of circumstances for more than forty years. Like Mechernich, I feared the place. I didn't want to be there and yet I did want to enter Elinor's life in the ways that I could. I could never make up for the years my family had ignored her, but I could try to lift the veil that separated her from the rest of us and begin to relate to her life.

The directions were excellent, and we soon drove into the hospital grounds. A few of the old buildings still stood, but the land was open now, with slightly rolling hills—different from the way it had looked in 1936, when Elinor arrived. Old photographs showed stately trees arching over the long approach to the hospital complex, which resembled a village of manor houses. Our appointment with Mr. Carey was in a new building. Architecturally, the new, lower, more simply designed buildings gave an impression of informality quite different from the massive red-brick buildings of the last century. The sign outside the new main building informed us that Massillon State Hospital was now called Heartland Behavioral Healthcare.

Mr. Carey, amiable and casual in jeans and a plaid shirt, welcomed us into his office and gave us a quick history. "Massillon State was one of the first hospitals for the mentally ill to be built on the cottage plan. It opened in 1898 and eventually included forty-nine buildings that housed 3,000 residents on 1,226 acres. Gargoyles topped several of the buildings; they were meant to keep out evil spirits, a sure sign that things were different then, when we knew less about mental illness. Demolition of many of the old buildings began in 1976 to make way for the new. Now there are just 130 beds, although the hospital serves thirty-six counties."

He had something special to show us in the old superintendent's cottage. On the walk over, he told us about life at the hospital when Elinor lived there. "For many years the residents worked the farms on the hospital grounds. They had meaningful work and the food was fresh. Those who were able walked to the cafeteria. There was a trolley that connected the hospital to the town, and many of the residents were free to come and go. Hospital workers lived on the premises, so the hospital community was like a small village."

"It sounds as if those who built it had a vision that today might be considered healthy," Jack volunteered. That thought, it turned out, was a bit hasty.

"In the 1970s," Mr. Carey explained, "many of the residents claimed they were being abused by a system that used them as cheap labor, so all of that stopped and the residents were left with little to do."

We approached the superintendent's cottage, although "cottage" was not quite the word to describe the gabled Victorian mansion in front of us. The house was furnished in art nouveau style—a couch with curving back, cabinets carved with flowers and vines, chairs upholstered in floral fabrics. All of it looked as it had when the last occupants vacated years earlier. The kitchen was huge and spare. A sizable porch with wicker furniture surrounded the back of the house.

Mr. Carey led the way upstairs. "Massillon had a school for nurses on the grounds, which, I believe, added positively to the treatment of the residents. The good news is that, fortunately, no doctor at Massillon performed lobotomies, which did happen in the state hospital at Athens and many other mental hospitals."

All in all, it seemed Elinor was lucky to have been sent to Massillon, where the environment was probably more humane than it was at most hospitals in those days.

We were standing in the upstairs hall, where Mr. Carey showed us a heavy, white, cotton shirt with extra-long arms—a straightjacket designed to keep the patient's arms tied to the body, a very different way to restrain a person than the drugs we use today. We examined a wooden box with wires for electroshock treatments.

"What was the date Elinor was admitted to Massillon?" Mr. Carey opened the door to a closet.

"December 7, 1936."

He disappeared into the closet and returned with a large leather book bearing the title GENERAL RECORD OF MASSILLON STATE HOSPITAL. "This has the admittance records." He opened the cover and turned large pages with columns of information. "Here it is. Right here. Take a look."

About a quarter of the way down page 267, scripted in black ink across the columns of the page, I read: *Eleanor Del Vecchio – Columbiana County – 23 – Married – Two children – Housewife – Protestant – Duration of Attack – 2 months.*

In the column labeled "Diagnosis," a different hand had penned *Dementia Praecox – Paranoid 12/7/1936.*

Every diagnosis of "Dementia Praecox" on the page and surrounding pages was written in the same handwriting, as though the same doctor had given the same diagnosis to everyone he examined. In those days, they seldom distinguished between different kinds of mental illnesses. Later Elinor's diagnosis was changed to schizophrenia, a term first used in 1911, which revealed the more accurate observation that psychosis, unlike dementia, did not always result in mental deterioration.

Unlike most of the others whose admissions were recorded on the page, there was no discharge date for Elinor. I looked through the rest of the book and saw that many of those admitted at the end of 1936 were set free, as evidenced by the conclusive words "improved," "recovered," or "released." Mr. Carey explained that in order to be released, patients needed a place to go.

Gratitude and sorrow overwhelmed me as I closed the book, heavy with the suffering of so many lives. Gratitude for the opportunity to touch a concrete moment of Elinor's life, and sorrow that she was not released even though she improved and probably recovered. Massillon State Hospital was not the same place it had been when Elinor lived there, and yet it was the ground she'd walked for forty years. I was beginning to mesh her life with mine, just a bit, by allowing it space to live inside of me, as I had with my father's unknown life.

Jack and I returned to the nursing center and found Elinor in her wheelchair at the end of the table. We pulled up chairs and sat beside her. The TV was blaring forth the evening news, and the resident at the table behind us had her radio turned up, playing tunes from the fifties.

"Do you like this music?" I asked Elinor.

She glared. "I *have* to like it."

The staff was curious about Elinor's family, and nurses and aides stopped by to look at the pictures of Elinor as a girl with her sisters, her brother, and her parents. After hearing everyone mention that she played the piano, I asked her about it.

"Would you like to play the piano now, Elinor?"

"Mmm-hmm." She blinked and looked around.

We wheeled her into the front room and placed her in front of the worn keys.

She lifted her arms and gently touched them. "I need shoes to play the pedals." Socks, but no shoes, covered her long, thin feet. There was a bold ring to her voice: she deserved shoes, and she now had witnesses.

A young aide rushed off to find some shoes and came back with soft slippers that had no soles. "These are the only ones I could find."

Elinor was silent. We sat for a few minutes and then began to talk. I wanted to talk about her past, the people with whom we shared a history, those no one around her knew, people she might not have spoken of for years.

I leaned forward. "Did your father teach you to play the piano, Elinor?"

"No. Mary Headley was my piano teacher." She rested her chin on her chest.

I put my hand on the back of her wheelchair. "Did you teach Dorothy to play the piano?"

"No. I didn't teach Dorothy." Her voice was low; her eyes were on the keys.

"Did you take care of your sisters after your mother died?" I held my breath and waited for her to answer.

"Margery and Dorothy took care of themselves." She raised her head and turned to look at us. "Take me home."

"Where is home, Elinor?" Jack's voice was tender.

"East Liverpool," she answered in a singsong sort of way.

I asked her about Floyd and her voice was soft with a hint of possessiveness. "*Floyd* loved me. He put his arm around my shoulder and touched my neck." She tilted her head as if Floyd was beside her.

The young nurse came to tell us it was time to take her back for supper. In the dayroom, I asked Elinor if she wanted us to stay or leave.

"Stay with me. "

We sat with her while she slowly spooned up bite after bite, and then we left. The next morning we'd head back to Washington. It was hard to leave. The shadowy past, when I'd imagined her as a demented and unreachable lost soul, was gone. I'd fallen in love with Elinor—her warmth, her spunk, her quiet ways of relating with her hands, her kisses, and her words.

———— ▸ ————

On the drive home, I thought about Elinor. How she had survived without family, without her children, without a home of her own or even a scrap of privacy. Without medical and dental care or the essential things I take for granted. Her mother had loved her and Floyd had loved her, of that she was certain, and she'd remembered their love all those years through who knew what kinds of conditions. But the rest, everyone else in the family, had abandoned her. I would have understood if she had turned her back on me, a representative of everyone who rejected her. Instead she had put her hand on mine and I'd felt her warmth, still alive.

I saw how deeply Mother's fear, sadness, worry, shame, and guilt about Elinor had affected me. How, in a sense, I'd inherited an unfinished part of Mother's life when she wordlessly communicated her desire to help Elinor. As a child, I knew there was a world of pain in mother when she told me that her sister was in a mental hospital. With few other details, the particulars of who Elinor was, what happened to her, and why she was missing were left to me to figure out. As a teenager, I was drawn to books about people in mental hospitals that could help me understand what she might be like. Later, I volunteered in a house for runaways, many of them rejected by parents. After that, I worked with teenage mothers—young women who, like Elinor, had trouble beginning their lives as mothers. Then, in graduate school, I studied psychology and became a psychotherapist. I found many "Elinors" in the people I saw, and they helped me understand and imagine my unknown aunt as a real person.

The other thing I thought about on the drive home was that we are all so deeply interconnected, what happens to one of us in a family affects the rest of us, on down through the generations. What mattered to me now was that I was able to open the silence, find out as much as possible about those who were missing from my life, free myself from inherited troubles and judgments, and fill myself with what remained. I was lucky to have found Elinor alive, and maybe when we sat together she'd felt a little more connected to her early life and to her family—and, like me, a little less lonely.

20

Speechless

When I was with Elinor I snapped a photo and e-mailed it to Mickey. He e-mailed me back.

I framed the photo of Aunt Elinor and took it to Mom this afternoon. She was a little surprised, or maybe forgot that I told her I was bringing it. I asked her if she was okay with seeing it, and she said she was. She opened the photo and stared at it for a few moments. Then she raised it to her lips and started to cry. (At this point I already had two major teeth marks on my tongue.)

I heard the excitement in Dorothy's voice when she called to say she'd found a picture of herself wearing a blue top like the one Elinor wore in the picture. "I look just like my sister, the same white hair and blue eyes. I told my girlfriends about her and they couldn't believe it. We figure she didn't think about the past, just hung on to what was around her." Dorothy spoke more slowly. "I couldn't see her. Her brother, the same. Dad remarried and didn't go. None of us ever investigated what happened to her."

Elinor was left to the miniscule and dicey world of the mental hospital for the rest of her life, separated from our world by walls and distance far greater than miles. No one went to see how she was doing or to investigate what happened to her. No one brought her home when they were told she could "live normally." She was a person without family or history or home. She was forgotten, yet forgotten is too simple a word to describe what we did to Elinor. I looked "forgotten" up in the dictionary and found the words "out of mind," "left behind," and the ominous phrase "consigned to oblivion." Elinor had survived our faults and was still able to receive with affection an unknown relative who waltzed in seventy years late.

On a July morning in 2008, I packed the car for a visit with Elinor. After an easy drive to Canton, I pulled up to a sizable brick house with a sloping roofline, the B&B I'd found on the Internet that was within walking distance of the nursing home. A woman with smiling brown eyes opened the door and invited me to tea and freshly baked cookies. Kathy's warmth suffused the large kitchen. Her husband, Randy, a sprightly man with clear blue eyes, appeared, and the aura of congeniality grew. They were intrigued about Elinor and said they might know someone who worked at Massillon.

After settling into my room, I walked down the street to visit Elinor. There she was, in the same place I last saw her, sitting in her wheelchair at the end of the table beside the wall. I sat beside her and took her hand.

"I like you," she told me, and confided, "I am old. I'm almost finished." She seemed tired and vulnerable, almost childlike, when she turned to rest her head on her neck.

Before leaving DC I'd gone to a shop in my neighborhood to find something beautiful to bring Elinor. I told the owner about her and he picked out a colorful pin. "Tell her it's from a fan of hers," he said.

When I put the box with the pin and the new book of family photos in front of her, she touched and patted them from time to time, like they were precious things that had their own life. When she opened the book and looked at the photos, she was silent for awhile, then she said softly, "Elinor, Margery, Dorothy, and William." She had a terrible cough and almost choked. When she recovered, she said, "I am bad."

"No, Elinor, you're good."

Perhaps looking at photos of herself and her family from around the time she was sent away reawakened a sense that others, like her father and her stepmother, may have instilled in her when she was overwrought and vulnerable from postpartum illness. I put my hand near her shoulder, and she flinched as if she expected to be hit. All those years she lived unprotected by family, she'd had experiences we knew nothing about, and she carried them in her body and her heart.

She looked at me and asked, "Do you like me?"

"Yes, I do. I love you."

"How much?"

"As much as the whole world and forever."

"I'm in heaven," was Elinor's reply.

I wheeled her outside and we sat under the trees in the patch of grass. She began to talk: "John is a smart boy, tall and thin. He lives in a church and has a small box of crayons. They have all different colors. I tried to fatten him, but I didn't do a very good job of it."

I was attentive as Elinor talked about her son. He was still her little boy in her mind, and I heard her motherly pride and her regret.

Her back hurt. She told me where to rub and I massaged it. Distracted by a car that pulled into the driveway, I watched a woman wearing high heels and a dressy coat walk into the nursing home.

Elinor reached over and touched my trousers. "Why do you cross your legs?"

She tried to cross her legs, but they slid back down. Her slipper fell off and I put it on again. She looked up at the treetops and musingly spoke to the sky: "I've searched the world over for what I want and I don't know what it is."

I told Elinor that I was happy being there with her, and she smiled a big smile. The afternoon passed peacefully, sitting together under the trees. It was time to take her back inside.

"Good-bye, Elinor. I'll see you again soon."

"I love you, too," she replied.

Walking back to the B&B, I thought about trying to find the group home where Elinor had lived for seventeen years—from 1977 to 1994, from the time she was sixty-four until she was eighty-one. When I got back to my room I checked my notes until I found the name. There was no listing for a Princess Stone Group Home in the phone book, so I decided to give Princess a try. No luck. Just to be thorough, I checked under "S" for Stone. There it was: "Stone, Princess." I dialed the number and a woman answered.

"Yes. This is a group home."

I explained who I was.

"My mother is out. Call back around two. My mother will remember."

Returning to the coffee shop I'd noticed when I drove downtown the day before, I ordered a salad, sat outside across from the quiet town square, and waited to call the group home again. Pigeons landed on the sidewalk and pecked at crumbs until two boys whizzed by on skateboards and the pigeons scattered. A group of women in short dresses and flip-flops walked into the coffee shop chattering and giggling. Around 2 p.m., I called the Princess Stone Group Home and a woman answered, "This is Princess Stone."

So Princess Stone was the name of the lady who ran it. She said I could come over right away.

The house, situated in an industrial area, was blue with white trim. Baskets of red and white flowers hung from the wide front porch, and white hydrangeas bloomed in the yard. A stout, cheerful man rose from his chair on the front porch and called his mother. Mrs. Stone, wearing round glasses and dangling earrings, invited me to sit beside her on the flowered sofa in the front room.

I plunged right in. "Do you remember my aunt, Elinor Del Vecchio, who lived here some time ago? She must have been in her sixties."

"Of course I remember Elinor. She was beautiful. The day she came here she walked up the front steps and when I opened the door she held out her arms and called me Mother. She endeared herself to me."

Her granddaughter, a pretty girl, about eleven years old, came into the room and snuggled up beside her grandmother. Mrs. Stone continued, "Every night she wet the bed and the next morning I would wash the sheets. I didn't get paid any extra, but she was so loving I didn't mind. Sometimes she'd forget who I was and I had to remind her. She sat on the porch and she'd walk to the corner and back every day. She could sing—we liked to sing, and she kept right up with us. We were family, the five residents, my own children, and my husband."

Mrs. Stone called out to one of her daughters, "Crystal, do you remember that old white woman?"

"Wasn't she in that room upstairs with another white lady?" Crystal sort of remembered. "She was nice."

Mrs. Stone was surprised that Elinor was still living. "I thought she'd have passed on by now. I'll have to get over there and see her."

I drove back to the B&B, parked the car, and walked to the nursing center. Elinor and I were sitting under the oak tree enjoying the shade when something urged me to ask her about her children.

"Elinor, do you have children?"

"Yes. Two. John and Sandra, and I love them very much. John's a good boy. He goes to church." She looked as if she had tears, but I wasn't sure. "I don't like to be lonesome. I like to have company. I'm trying to be good."

"Oh, Elinor, I really like sitting here with you."

She reached around to pat and rub her back, which set off the alarm attached to her clothes. I reattached the alarm, sat down, and listened closely as she continued.

"I have two lives to live. It'll be better next time."

Elinor had no teeth and I couldn't always make out her exact words, but I heard her say, "Clare McConnell."

"Yes! You remember your mother's name."

She looked pleased. "Take me home! Please take me home! I feel like a foreigner. I don't understand. I have trouble understanding."

Sitting on the bed in the yellow and blue room, thinking about Elinor and her children, I again questioned my intense need to find out all I could about the lost people in my family, which now included Elinor's children. The answer always began with Mother. Her adult life was built on the ruins of fatal illness, war, insanity, and feuds. She went forward by never looking back, at least not out loud. She and my stepfather built a solid, loving family centered on artistic expression, scholarship, and religion. You would never know the devastation she survived, and yet you could sometimes catch a glimpse of the wisdom that came from surviving. "Save your tears for something worth crying over," she often told me. It was more a warning than a prohibition: sad times will come and you'll need your tears. She held life in perspective. One night when I was about nine, Mother and Dad had friends over to play bridge. I watched from my lookout on the stairs as the game became increasingly competitive. The pressure was high when I saw cards fly through the air and rain down on the table and the carpet. Dad, who was in the game to win, looked stricken. Then I heard Mother laughing. "It's only a game."

Mother couldn't do both—raise her family and tend to her past. I was a remnant from that uneasy past, and I was both disturbed and captivated by the unknown people in my family. Like Elinor, I had trouble understanding what had happened, and I, too, often felt like a foreigner. Maybe I could give her a bit of the sense of wholeness I'd come to know with each discovery. I couldn't take Elinor home, but I could be with her and I could try to find her children.

Jumping up from the bed, I knew that this was what I'd needed:

permission from Elinor to find her children. Before that, I couldn't imagine finding them; I had so little to go on, and was unsure about what would happen if I did find them. Now it felt like an urgent obligation.

Kathy was in the kitchen and poured us each a glass of lemonade. Sitting at the counter, I told her about my desire to find Elinor's children.

"What do you know about her husband, Floyd?"

"He was the golf pro at the East Liverpool Country Club."

The next morning Kathy told me she had Googled "John Del Vecchio – golf" and found someone who looked promising, a golf director at ABC.

After breakfast, I walked the ten blocks back to the nursing center to visit Elinor. She was alert, wearing glasses, and looking bright.

"How are you Elinor?"

"I've been waiting for company."

I returned her smile. "Would you like to sit outside?"

She nodded and I wheeled her outside, where we sat under the oak tree.

After some silence, Elinor spoke. "My mother died." She talked about the Queen of England and about making chocolate cake and angel food cake. I listened, catching only several words here and there until she said quite clearly, "I played tennis with my friend. We said, 'We are very lucky!'" She laughed and I joined in. We laughed and laughed, feeling very lucky to enjoy a light moment together.

"But I didn't play golf. It's too hard," she confessed. "I worked in the pottery. I painted lines on the plates and pink roses in the center."

When I scratched her back too vigorously a moment later, she jumped. "That's awful!"

It was pleasant sitting there side by side, chatting like friends on a lazy day. She put one hand in each pocket of her pink flowered dress and declared, "My mother is on this side. That's where they left her. And my father is here."

"You know so much, Elinor."

"So much I don't know. Do you think I'm intelligent?"

"Yes! I do."

"They said I was crazy. I'm not crazy!"

She smiled when I told her that I liked to hear what she had to say.

"Mother was a good cook. She got down on her knees and prayed. She read the Bible. William played the piano better than I do."

We sat in silence feeling a breeze and listening to the birds. After awhile I asked if she'd like to write a letter. She dictated: "Dear Mother, How have you been since you've been away from me? Today is a nice day. Help wanted: Male and Female. How many children do you have? My grandmother lost her shoe in the year of '82. Found it hanging on the line in 9089 AMEN!"

I wrote "2008 – 1913 = 94 years old" And asked, "Aren't you proud?"

"No," said Elinor, "I'm ashamed. I have no clothes to wear. I'm naked. Floyd asked me to sleep with him and I said I wouldn't wake up and he said he'd get me an alarm clock."

The nurse brought her a cup of orange juice with meds. Elinor turned to me. "You want some? Here, you have some." I held the orange juice and she said, "Dorothy, Margery, William, Elinor. If I do the ironing, I'm a good girl and I can go home."

"Elinor, you've put up with a lot."

"Yes, I have."

I left Elinor at about ten thirty and drove to Massillon hoping to see Alice Watson, the librarian genealogist who'd found Elinor. I had intended to go to East Liverpool to do some research, but when Elinor responded to my question about her children with such clarity, I decided to look for Alice at the Massillon Library instead.

Alice had offered to try to find John when we were there in the spring, and she had given me a list of possibilities, all John Del Vecchios who lived in Ohio. Not knowing how her children might react, I wasn't ready to share Elinor with them yet. What if they didn't want me to see her again? More out of duty than desire, I called several of the names on the list. The numbers were either disconnected or it was the wrong family, and I was relieved.

By the time I arrived in Massillon it was 11 a.m. and I was told that Alice wouldn't be in until one o'clock. I was exhausted and wanted to go back to the B&B and sleep but walked to a coffee house instead, hoping to find a cup of soothing chai. I was lucky again: they had chai. I ordered a big mug of it and a cinnamon bagel.

When I finished, it was noon. Too early to find Alice. Still sleepy, I walked back up the hill to my car and fell asleep. When I woke it was almost one. The receptionist pointed me toward Alice's desk on the second floor.

Alice, with a bright red–lipsticked smile, was at her desk. I told her that Kathy had Googled "John Del Vecchio – golf," and what we'd found. Alice quickly began playing around on her computer, trying Delvecchio, Del Vecchio, adding Pennsylvania and Ohio. I remembered that I had the date of John's birth in a folder in my car and ran to get it. Jack and I had carefully recorded the dates we'd found, but I couldn't find the right folder. I felt light-headed knowing we were close to finding Elinor's children. What had John and Sandra been told about their mother? How would they react to the news and to the messenger? Was I doing something terrifyingly horrible, something everyone would rather have left undone? Or was this something that could be good for all of us?

Aware of the healing that came from knowing about my father and making him part of my life, I wanted to give John and Sandra the opportunity to do that, and I wanted to give Elinor the chance to be with her children again. Finally I remembered that the dates of John and Sandra's births were recorded in Jack's notes. I flipped to that page and there they were: John Floyd Del Vecchio, August 10, 1934. Sandra Lou Del Vecchio, July 20, 1936.

I wrote the date of John's birth on a piece of paper and handed it to Alice, who added the information to her search. We sat together playing with possibilities for an hour and a half.

Alice tapped her pencil. "In Ohio, golfers go to Florida when they retire." She typed in "John F. Del Vecchio – 73 – Florida." A list came back on her screen with John Del Vecchio, 73, Havana, Florida at the top. We both knew this was our John.

I felt surprisingly calm with the phone number in my notebook, and I walked around the block before going into the B&B to make the call. I plugged in my cell phone to make sure there was enough juice to last, then sat on the bed and dialed the number.

When a man answered, I said, "I'm looking for John Floyd Del Vecchio who was born August 10, 1934 in East Liverpool, Ohio."

"Yes. That's me."

"I'm your cousin. Our mothers are sisters. I've been here in Canton, Ohio visiting your mother, who is living in a nursing home."

"It's not my reputation not to talk. I retired ten years ago as a marketing executive. I can talk the back legs off a damn billy goat—but right now I'm speechless. Some time ago my sister Sandra and I tried to track down Mother. Sandra called the institution and they told her she'd passed away. How did you find her?"

"A local genealogist found your mother through probate court records that dated from the time she was assigned a guardian in 1994."

"What is her diagnosis?"

I told him about finding the book with the diagnosis "Dementia Praecox" and the diagnosis of schizophrenia. "But it's my belief that your mother suffered from postpartum psychosis."

"I was raised by my father's sister and we wondered about that, my sister and me. We were raised in western Pennsylvania. How are we related?"

"I am your cousin. My mother, Margery, was Elinor's younger sister."

When I asked John what his sister's married name was, he answered sharply, "I won't give you that. You know everything already. You don't know that? My sister, Sandra, is all right. She has a good family. I have to digest this."

After we hung up I waited by the phone without moving for about twenty minutes, except for a quick call to Jack to tell him that I'd found John.

The phone rang. "What did you have in mind to call me?"

"It's your right to know that your mother is alive, and I thought that you might want to see her."

"I'm not in good health. I can't fly."

"I hope I didn't upset you."

"No, you didn't." Click.

A few minutes later the phone rang again. "There is no Elinor Laughlin in the nursing home. This is a scam. You'll hear from the state's attorney about this."

End of call.

Knowing the immensity of this discovery and that John may have needed to push it, and me away, I took a few deep breaths before calling back and leaving a message: "Here's the number of the Colonial Nursing Center, where your mother lives. Ask for Elinor Del Vecchio. I won't contact you again."

After a few minutes the phone rang. "I apologize profusely," John said. "Mother is there. I can't come to see her. I have some health problems—respiratory and heart. "

"I can be a bridge with your mother. Even having talked will bring you into the relationship with your mother."

"What is your relationship with the Laughlin family?"

I told him a little about our family, and Dorothy's and Bill's. "I'll send you copies of what I have and pictures of Elinor as a girl that came from Mother's album."

"I don't have anything."

He remembered Elinor's father, our Grandpa Ben. "I spent summers at the home place. We went to the pottery, rode the trains there where the trains go into the showers. I'd hitch a ride. I was yanked away from that family so quickly. The few times I visited, Daddy Ben's new wife Mamie was strong. I was three or four."

John told me about his family. "I have two children and six grandchildren. They're all athletes. One is a dancer and two grandsons are into baseball and have been scouted for pro teams. One may be drafted. Not one is a golfer."

I heard love and pride in his voice.

"I thought I had no family. Now I've got more than I can handle. I'm grateful that you contacted me. Thank you, dear. I'll be calling my sister tomorrow morning."

21

Sandra is Coming

The morning after the talk with John, I stayed in my room to be close to the phone in case Sandra called. At about 10:00 a.m., the phone rang.

"This is Sandra. My brother John called me this morning and told me about my mother."

We spent a confusing moment figuring out the members of the family, then Sandra continued, "I want to see her while you're there. I'll call the airline and arrange tickets and call you back with the details."

Several hours later she called. "I'll arrive tomorrow night at six fifteen." Before ending the call, she told me some of her history. "No one talked about it. I always thought I'd see Mother, if not in this life, then the next. Clara, my father's sister, the one who adopted us, never liked her and told us that she was bad, terrible, but Martha, Floyd's mother, loved Elinor and said that she was intelligent, talented, and beautiful.

"I was told that my mother was dead, or I thought she was until I was twelve and we went to visit our father's grave. I noticed there was no grave for my mother. Clara said, 'You don't want to know about that.' The implication was that my mother, or what happened to her, was unspeakable. The ladies in the garden club told me she was mentally ill.

"John wanted to see Mother when he was in his twenties. When he asked Grandpa Ben about her he was told, 'The pages of that book are better left unturned,' and John never took it further. I also wanted to search for Mother, but I was afraid I'd worry if it were schizophrenia. Someone else might have it, a child or a grandchild."

Sandra's husband wanted their daughter Amy to go with her, but Sandra didn't want to disrupt Amy's life. She told me about the upcoming reunion with her four children and their children. Elinor was a grandmother and a great-grandmother!

"There's a lot of mystery," Sandra said. "This is as big as marriage or childbirth. It's been missing my whole life and now I can see her. Thank you."

Feeling protective of Sandra, I told her a little about her mother and mentioned that Elinor might not recognize her. "Not recognizing family is vintage Elinor," I explained. "It may be her way of letting us know how insignificant she's felt since being sent away. Sometimes she's talkative and sometimes we sit without talking."

Sandra agreed. "With my nursing background, I understand that."

Sandra was coming. She would see her mother for the first time since she was five months old, Elinor would see her daughter for the first time in seventy-two years, and I would meet my cousin. Luckily, Kathy had another room free, so Sandra could stay there. The third floor with the two bedrooms and a sitting room would be ideal for the two of us.

The next morning, I raced over to the nursing home. The staff gathered at the nurses' station to hear about Elinor's daughter, and everyone was excited. Some had tears. They remembered Elinor when she came in 1994, how she had kept them entertained. There was a feeling of joy when they spoke of her.

"Elinor knew all the songs when someone came to play the piano."

"When we told one of the patients to sit down, Elinor would say, 'Sit down.' She loved children."

One of the nurses, smiling, said, "Elinor thinks all the time. One day she called me over. 'Nurse, Nurse,' she said, 'did your mother give you another name besides Nurse?' I'll never forget that."

The nurses were going to give her a shower and dress her up. That morning, they told me, she was unusually alert, and they took her to the piano and she played!

Having been invited to eat with Elinor, I returned at noon. A young aide took me to a private room and set the table with a pink tablecloth and a vase of pink plastic roses. The TV was turned to a music station, and while I waited for Elinor, I heard the Beatles singing "When I'm Sixty-Four." Thoughts about Elinor's life and my life ran together as I remembered hearing the song for the first time when I was in college, almost the same age Elinor was when she was sent away. I thought sixty-four was very old then, that I had years and years before I'd be sixty-four. I couldn't imagine living all those years in a mental hospital with an incessant gaggle of people, never being able to go to my room and close the door or go out to wander and browse and meet friends for lunch or a movie.

An aide wheeled Elinor down the ramp into the room. She looked beautiful. A pretty blue blouse highlighted her very blue eyes, and a string of pearls added a dash of fashion on that auspicious day. As soon as the nurse left, Elinor fell asleep. A few minutes later, a nurse with a bumptious manner brought Elinor's tray and poked her shoulder. "Wake up. Wake up, you. Here's your ginger ale."

Elinor opened her eyes. "Root beer?"

"No. We don't have root beer."

Elinor closed her eyes.

The nurse scooped up a bite of food with a plastic spoon and Elinor pushed her hand away. "Elinor, did you do that?" Elinor went back to sleep.

She opened her eyes after the nurse was gone and announced to the table, the TV, and me, "My mother had silverware." Then she tilted her head to one side and closed her eyes again.

Ah, Elinor, I thought to myself, *there's still a brazen young girl alive in you!*

The TV had been turned low, but the Beatles caught my ear again as they sang "Yesterday." An aide with a soft voice came in to see if Elinor was eating. She'd known her for the eight years she had worked here. We chatted while Elinor slept. "Elinor told me about her family, her mother and her father, that they always went to church. She knows all the old hymns and she used to play them for us on the piano in the front room." The aide stood up. "Since she's still sleeping, I'll take her back to her room."

———————

At about three o'clock I received a phone call from Sandra's daughter, Amy, who told me she was driving from Chicago to surprise her mom. She hoped to arrive around five. Before setting off for the airport in Akron, I checked my messages and found two. Sandra's plane was delayed in Chicago, and Amy's trip was taking longer than she'd planned.

I drove over to the nursing home to tell them that Sandra would be late and sat with Elinor, who was eating dinner.

"Are you all right? Did you have a fall?" she asked.

"I'm okay, Elinor. I'm excited because your daughter Sandra is coming to see you. Do you know you are a grandmother?"

Elinor pointed to her chest. "Me?"

The dayroom buzzed with alarms and arguments.

"I bring you vitamins every day. Take them."

"No. I won't."

Two women residents were shouting.

"Shut up."

"No. I will not shut up."

"I said shut up."

"You can't make me. Who the hell do you think you are?"

Elinor was watching me. "Quite a chorus," she said, and drew me back to the two of us. "Do you cook? I make spaghetti."

Earlier, she had tried on my beaded bracelet. I asked if she liked it and when she said yes, I put it on her wrist. She was still wearing it.

"I have a green bracelet," she told me.

"Who gave it to you?"

"I bought it. I went to the store and bought it."

Elinor's response challenged my assumption that she couldn't have gone shopping, but she let me know that she had and she'd bought herself something pretty.

"They said I'm crazy. I'm not crazy."

"No, Elinor. I *know* you are not crazy."

When I implied that she could not have bought the bracelet herself, Elinor probably detected my perception of her as a mental patient, an attitude held by most of the people she had come in contact with the past seventy years. How tiresome for her. She was skillful with relationships and able to disabuse me of my arrogant attitude and return us to a relationship of friends, of family, simply chatting.

———————— ◆ ▶ ————————

I left Elinor and walked back to the B&B. Kathy invited me into the kitchen while she made dinner. She knew that I was about ready to jump out of my skin with anticipation, and she asked me about Elinor's family. Before I could answer, my cell phone rang.

Amy was close, but lost.

Kathy figured out where she was and directed her to the airport. Sandra's plane was still delayed, now due to arrive after nine. A few minutes later, Amy called to say she was at the airport, and I headed out to meet her.

I recognized Amy immediately. She was lean with blond hair and blue eyes, like my daughter Sarah, and like Sarah, Amy was enthusiastic and related easily. I felt an immediate connection. We settled into comfortable chairs near the gate and Amy told me about her family.

"I'm the oldest of four children, two girls and two boys. Mom's sad that she never knew her mother. This is huge for her and I needed to be here to share it with her and also to make sure she's all right. I've always felt a connection with my grandmother even though I never heard much about her. What is she like?"

I told Amy everything I knew about Elinor and the Laughlins.

She put her hand on my arm. "In just one hour I've learned more about my mother's family than I've ever known."

Looking up, we saw Sandra walking toward us. She was petite, with blond hair and Elinor's blue eyes. Sandra burst into tears when she saw Amy. She was too tired after the long delay to visit Elinor that night and wanted to be fresh when she saw her mother, so we decided to go together in the morning. I called the nursing home and found out that Elinor was still awake, sitting in the day room in her nightclothes.

When we arrived at the B&B, Kathy took us upstairs to the third floor, where we had our own little apartment. Sandra and Amy chose the room with twin beds and I took the one with the queen-sized bed.

———

I woke early and nestled into an easy chair in the sitting room. A few minutes later, Sandra appeared.

"Amy's sleeping. She's tired after her long drive. I brought you a photograph of Mother with Johnnie."

The first thing I noticed was the similarity between Elinor and her mother—both women, in pictures taken a generation apart, gazed at the babies in their arms rather than at the camera. Elinor was an elegant young mother, wearing a wool dress with a matching coat and a fancy hat. Johnnie was about a year old, a pudgy toddler turning in his mother's arms to look at the photographer.

Sandra talked about her life without her mother. "I've never known a

mother's love. Our stepfather loved us. He was good to us, but Clara, our stepmother, was cold. The Del Vecchios told me that after her mother died, Elinor had a breakdown. One reason they did not like the Laughlins was that the Laughlins never told them that Elinor was unstable.

"When our father, Floyd, was in the hospital, he said that when he got out, he would take the children and drive west. He died several days later. Perry, Floyd's brother, was supposed to send money, but rarely did. The Laughlins didn't help at all, which the Del Vecchios resented. When we were children, we were tricked into signing away property that was ours."

At about nine thirty, I mentioned that I usually went to visit Elinor about that time. When Sandra said that she wanted to stop for flowers, Kathy offered to cut some white hydrangeas from her garden.

We drove down the road and turned in at the Colonial Nursing Center. This was a once-in-a-lifetime moment. In another minute, we'd be inside, and Sandra would see her mother for the first time since she was five months old.

The nurses were smiling as we stood at the entrance to the dayroom.

"Do you know which one is your mother?" I asked Sandra.

"No. Show me."

I pointed to Elinor, sitting in her wheelchair, head down, finishing breakfast, thankfully awake and alert.

Sandra walked over and I followed a little behind. The nurses stood off to the side. Sandra gave Elinor the bouquet of hydrangeas tied with a trailing scarlet ribbon.

"I like roses," Elinor said to no one in particular.

Sandra knelt beside her mother and tilted her head. Elinor leaned toward Sandra and their heads touched. "I'm Sandra, your daughter."

Elinor was quiet before she spoke. "You're a stranger."

My heart sank. *Oh Elinor, you are so completely Elinor, so true to who you are, unaffected by what you should say. You don't betray yourself even as the rest of us are hoping that you will recognize your daughter and take her into your arms, like a fairy tale. But your life is no fairy tale, and this moment is nonetheless a holy moment when the two of you are alive together in the same place once again in this life.*

Elinor sat for a minute, then turned to look at Sandra. "I like you very much."

Elinor spoke the truth when she said that Sandra was a stranger, just as Elinor was a stranger to Sandra. We came too late for Elinor to become familiar with her daughter, too late for Sandra to know her mother well. Still, Sandra gave her mother what no one else could. She gave the comfort of her presence as Elinor's daughter, even as Elinor ruined Sandra's hope for recognition as her mother's daughter. And still Sandra knelt beside her mother without turning away as everyone in the family had turned away. In that moment I saw Elinor's courage and great heart in Sandra.

———————

Sandra later wrote her own version of learning that her mother was alive, and of seeing her in the nursing home for the first time.

She's Alive . . .

I only had one picture of my mother, which I kept tucked away in the top dresser drawer. She was elegantly dressed in a woolen suit, holding my brother, John, who faced the camera, smiling, while she looked at him. He was wearing a knitted outfit with short pants and a cap to match.

I loved this picture because my mother looked the way my Grandmother Del Vecchio described her—tall, beautiful, and talented. I wanted to be just like her. But after finding out that she was mentally ill, something about the picture bothered me. My brother's baby shoes were very dirty, they hadn't been polished, and the shoelaces were also very dirty. I wondered if this was a sign that my mother hadn't noticed because she was becoming ill. Was she pregnant with me at the time, beginning to feel overwhelmed with the thought of another baby? I kept the picture tucked away, just like the thoughts of her in a mental institution were tucked away in the far corners of my mind.

I was about twelve or thirteen when I found out that she had not died when our father did, but was living in a mental institution somewhere in Ohio. It was a very dark and sad day for me. I was angry at Aunt Clara for telling the women who worked at the country club before telling my brother and me. They were talking about my own mother, whom I wanted to know and love.

When I approached Aunt Clara about it, she said, "We took you to see her and she just let you fall off her lap. The doctor said you wouldn't inherit her illness, but might inherit her low stress-tolerance level." I didn't understand at the time what that meant.

When Aunt Clara became angry with me, she said, "You are going to grow up to be just like Elinor." Did she mean that I might be mentally ill someday? I wanted to ask her if she could love me like I was her own daughter, but she never did.

From that day forward I didn't tell anyone about my mother until I began dating my husband, and when I did, his response was, "Your family troubles are nothing compared to mine." I knew I wanted to marry him someday!

I became a nurse, got married, and had four lovely children. I thought that my mother's family was looking after her, that maybe someday I would see her, but I never tried to find her. The thought that she was mentally ill and living in the back ward of a hospital was just too overwhelming. When the children asked what she died of, I said I didn't know.

About thirty years ago, my brother, John, called to say that our mother had died. I began to cry. I never got to see her. What did she die of and why didn't we know that she was ill enough to die? John was more courageous than I, for at least he had tried to find her.

When the phone call came in July of 2008, from a cousin I didn't even know I had, telling John and me that she had found our mother alive at age ninety-four, living in a nursing home, it was a miracle. Finally, I could see the mother I never knew. I remember thinking that being in a nursing home at age ninety-four seemed rather normal. It wasn't going to be the back ward of a psychiatric hospital, and maybe she wasn't very psychotic, if at all. I wanted to touch her and know that we were once part of each other.

After hanging up, I ran to the computer room where my husband was working and said, "She's alive. My mother is alive." He looked up with tears in his eyes and said, "That is so amazing."

And so with great anticipation, I boarded a plane for Akron, Ohio. The flight from Chicago was several hours late and I began to panic. Each time I called my cousin, Susan, she said, "Everything is going to be just fine." Her voice was calming. I could not wait to meet her.

The plane finally arrived in Akron at nine. I was totally exhausted. While walking to baggage claim I saw two young women coming toward me. They looked alike. As they got closer I realized that one was Amy and burst into tears. She drove all the way from Chicago to see the grandmother she never knew. I knew I could do this now, and so we drove to a cozy B&B.

The next morning, before going to the nursing home, Susan and I talked. I never knew that my mother had two sisters and a brother, or that she was a concert pianist. From all of Susan's research, it seems that she had suffered a postpartum psychosis after giving birth to me. She probably did recover, but her husband had died and no one else would take her. This was most distressing. We all abandoned her.

The nursing home was clean and neat, but not one bit fancy. I couldn't identify my mother and Susan pointed her out dozing in a wheelchair. Her hair was white, cut short and wavy. I went over to her, knelt down, put my arms around her, and said "I am Sandra, your daughter." She looked at me and said, "I think you're a stranger, but I like you." She was soft and her skin was flawless. Her eyes were bright blue. Mine are, too. She was not one bit angry or agitated. She didn't seem psychotic, just a little confused.

She was my mother and she had survived living in confinement for seventy-two years. I had no idea how she did it, but she was lovely as she talked about her children who she loved and the husband who loved her. Her heart seemed filled with love and music.

We returned to the B&B and sat down to breakfast with Amy. Kathy had made a feast of French toast, strawberries, and cream.

"My mother is amazingly bright for a ninety-four-year-old woman," Sandra told her daughter. "She doesn't look or act schizophrenic. In fact, she's more aware, alert, intelligent, communicative, and affectionate than many ninety-four-year-olds, and quite a few younger people.

"The Del Vecchios told us that Grandpa Ben wanted Elinor committed so he could marry Mame. My father, Floyd, was handsome and dated a lot. Floyd's sister, Myra, the one who liked Elinor, warned him that he'd get someone in trouble. Elinor was pregnant with John when they were married. Another time I was told that my mother threatened to harm me."

The three of us agreed that it was good to open the secret and find out the truth, to end a needless, frightening mystery. Putting all of our information together, we were sure that Elinor suffered from postpartum psychosis. Amy voiced what we were feeling when she said, "I am so thankful that you can no longer send people away and forget about them and leave them there forever."

That afternoon we went back to the nursing home. It was Amy's first visit with Elinor and she was unsure about meeting her grandmother, who had been a specter in her life. How would she react to Amy?

Elinor loved Amy! She commented on her full-length, pretty blue skirt. In fact, Amy was beautiful in every way, and who knows but Elinor may have seen her young self in Amy. We took Elinor outside and parked her in her wheelchair beneath the tall, thick oak tree. Sandra reminded her mother again that she was truly her daughter. Amy followed with, "Who am I?"

"An Indian, " Elinor quipped. We raised our brows and smiled.

Elinor was alert and generous and good-hearted and funny. She sang "You Are My Sunshine," then held one arm up to Sandra and reached for Amy with her other arm. That was a moment for all eternity. I didn't know whether to laugh or cry as I stood there with the three of them looking like the family they were and had always been without ever having had the chance to exist on the same spot of earth. When Amy showed Elinor a picture of her

eight-year-old son, Jack, Elinor looked at her grandson with great care and her face brightened. She turned to Amy.

"Take me home."

Sandra later wrote her version of the visit:

In the afternoon we took her over to the piano but she said she couldn't play right then. She sang "You are my Sunshine." She was funny at times. She put her arms out as if to hug me. I think she knew I was her daughter at some level, but it was too hard for her to express. Now I know my brother and I missed a life of music, love, and laughter by losing both of our parents, but especially by losing her.

We stayed for several hours and took her outside to sit under the trees. She seemed happy to be with us. This was her family. She loved Amy, her granddaughter, and touched her skirt asking if we thought she was pretty. I am sure Amy's beauty reminded her of her own self when she was young. At one point while sitting under the tree my mother leaned forward in her wheelchair and said, "The wind is very piercing." Now when I walk on the beach and feel the wind I think of her and those wonderful hours I had with her.

———— ◆ ————

Later that evening, after a good meal at a downtown restaurant, Amy and I took a walk. I asked her how her mother was doing.

"Mom feels bad that her mother was abandoned, and thinks Elinor could have made a life outside the hospital, but who knows? She said her stepfather and stepmother did their best. My dad thought maybe Elinor's father provided a trust fund for her and she had good care. Mom's basically all right, relieved that Elinor isn't very sick. She'll have a good cry, then go on."

Happiness enveloped me as I left Sandra and Amy the next morning. Elinor had seen her daughter and she had met her granddaughter. Sandra had seen her mother alive and the ghost that was Elinor had turned into a funny, endearing grandmother. Sandra and Amy were now a part of my life. One by one, my family was restoring itself.

22

Shoes for Elinor

After meeting Sandra, I called Aunt Dorothy and told her that Grandpa discouraged John from finding his mother.

"What I want to know," she said, "is why my father said Elinor passed away. I never went there again. My father didn't talk much about anything. You had to drag it out of him. He was a good man, but he wanted us to leave it alone."

I looked at the floor and shook my head. It was hard to hear that Grandpa discouraged the family from having anything to do with Elinor and even more disturbing to learn that he had pronounced her dead.

"Elinor took over after our mother died," Dorothy continued. "She was the backbone of the family. Your mother left and it was Elinor and me. We were very close. I want to go and see her, but I can't. She's with me."

―――――――

The year had been extremely busy, beginning with my visit to Aunt Dorothy and my stepfather's passing. In May I attended a conference in Hanoi studying ways to bring the Buddha's message of peace and interbeing to the problems of war, violence, and poverty. Jack and I flew to Beijing in August to see his brother and his wife who lived there, and I was scheduled to go to India in October. But when I returned from China, all I wanted to do was go to Canton and sit with Elinor. I canceled the trip to India, and Jack and I drove to Canton on Columbus Day weekend. Before we left home, my sister, Ellen, called to say that she'd been in touch with Mother's childhood friend, June, who now lived in California. Ellen gave me June's phone number and I called her that evening.

"Elinor was pretty," June remembered, "but soon after her daughter was born, she put the baby in the driveway. That's when they sent her to the hospital."

Then it was true, I thought to myself. Elinor, who had taken care of the family after her mother's death, had suffered from a serious form of postpartum illness that included symptoms of confusion, insomnia, delusions, hallucinations, and thoughts of harming herself or her baby. I thanked June for speaking openly about Elinor.

"Call Jane," she said. "She was one of your mother's closest childhood friends. Jane still lives in East Liverpool. She'll remember Elinor."

I poured some tea and called the number June gave me, and Jane and I talked as if we'd known each other forever. "I knew Margery from three years old, when we moved in across the street. Elinor, Margery, and Dorothy shared a room on the second floor in a glassed-in porch. You had to walk past the grandmother's room to get there. I remember sitting with your mother teaching Dorothy to read and write.

"Your mother's mother was a wonderful mother," Jane continued. "There were hollyhocks in the backyard where she hung out the clothes. We'd pick the hollyhocks, turn them over, and make little dolls with big skirts. When she invited me to dinner it was like a party. Before her mother died, Margery took me to a Christmas pageant at the church where her mother and dad were in the play."

I sipped my tea, relishing the conversation.

"Your mother was ten when her mother died. Elinor was sixteen and took it hard, went to stay with her Aunt Allie in Cincinnati for a month. When she came home, she showed us what she had learned to do there, to sew and make bracelets and things. Elinor was a pretty girl. Married Floyd Del Vecchio, the golf pro. One time your mother and I went out to the country club to go sledding. After that, Elinor became mentally troubled. I remember when they took her.

"Your parents were engaged and your dad's family came to East Liverpool to meet your mother's family. Mame wanted to take Elinor home from the hospital to show your father's parents that Margery came from a family with mental illness, and Margery didn't need that. Your mother was happy to be in love and that sounded terrible. They talked Mame out of it."

While her words gave me a sense of that long ago time when Mother was young and in love, I shivered to hear again how Elinor was used by the family and abandoned.

Jane turned her attention to me. "Your mother brought you and your brother David to East Liverpool in 1946 after your father died. You took your first steps here."

Bringing the conversation back to Elinor, I asserted, "You know, it's amazing that I found Elinor alive and well after all that time."

"Well, maybe it's not so good," Jane said. "They closed the institution and let people into the town. I heard that Elinor was a housekeeper for somebody."

Jane's husband, Will, had gone to Sunday School with my mother. We agreed to meet at the church on the Sunday of our visit and have brunch afterward.

On our way into Canton, Jack and I stopped at the nursing home to see Elinor. The nurses, aides, and residents waved and smiled and I was happy to be back. Elinor was asleep, so we settled into our room at the B&B and returned after dinner. Elinor was still asleep when a nurse tried to wake her. "Margery's here." Elinor swatted her away and we left for the night.

In the morning Elinor was at her place at the table eating oatmeal the way I learned to eat at Plum Village: slowly, mindful of each bite.

The first thing Elinor said to us was, "I'm the king."

"You're my aunt," I replied, and it sounded like "ant." Conversations with Elinor sometimes began with nonsense, and I wondered if she believed nonsense was expected of her as a "crazy" person. Or if she was in a sort of dream state, having little other than food to ground her thoughts and sensations. Was it the result of dementia, or was Elinor being playful, hoping to get a lighthearted response from us? Maybe it was the way Grandpa joked with her or the way her brother teased her. If I were her doctor, I would guess that her remark was a sign of mental illness, but as her newly discovered niece, I decided not to be too sure about what her remark meant and save myself and Elinor from easy judgments.

The first time Jack and I met Elinor, when we took her into the front room to play the piano, she refused, saying that she had no shoes and couldn't work the pedals. I had wanted to get her shoes then, but didn't know her shoe size. I noticed now that every other resident had shoes. Jack and I decided that getting them for Elinor was our mission. It was the only thing she had let us know that she wanted, other than for us to take her home.

After sitting with Elinor awhile, Jack walked over to the nurses' station. "One thing we wanted to do here was to buy Elinor a pair of shoes. What kind do you think would be best, and where can we find a shoe store?"

A nurse informed him that Elinor needed shoes with lifts. "One leg is shorter than the other."

"I'm all for it." Another, older nurse, joined the conversation. "You can try Payless up on Route 62."

I glanced at Elinor in her rickety wheelchair with the broken back, then turned my attention to Jack, knowing that Payless was the last place he'd like to be—but he loved Elinor, so he set off on foot to get the car we'd left at the B&B.

While Jack was gone, the nurses took Elinor to her room to get ready for the shopping trip. They brought her back in purple pants, a white jacket, and socks, and, to my relief, transferred her to a smaller, collapsible wheelchair.

As we waited by the front door for Jack to bring the car, the older nurse said she'd tried to figure out Elinor's shoe size by trying different shoes on her. "Eights are too small and my eight-and-a-halves were too short. She has long, narrow feet."

We guessed maybe nines as we watched Elinor, uncomfortable in the smaller, narrower, slippery wheelchair, fidget, slide down, and push herself back up. The nurse explained that she didn't like to put her feet on the footrest.

Possibly, I thought to myself, *because she has no shoes.* I leaned over. "Elinor, do you want to go shopping for shoes?"

"Uh-huh."

"What color would you like?"

"White."

The nurse added, "Maybe slippers would be good, or tennis shoes, but not athletic shoes." Then she realized that Elinor needed shoes to keep from bumping her toes and left to find some. She returned with purple shoe bags. "It's all I can find." She shrugged.

———————◆▶———————

Our red Toyota pulled up outside the door and the nurses maneuvered Elinor into the front seat and the wheelchair into the trunk. It was a warm October day, and the car had been sitting in the sun. As we pulled out of the driveway and headed down Market Street, Elinor fanned the air in front of her face. "It's hot!" Jack turned on the air conditioner. At the stoplight Elinor cried out and extended her arms to brace herself. "I'm scared!"

I reached over from the backseat, put my arm around her shoulder, and said soothing things in her ear while she looked out the window. I wondered if she had been in a car since Floyd drove her to the hospital in 1936.

Ten minutes later, we turned in and parked at the Payless store. Jack brought the wheelchair around to Elinor's side while I explained what we were about to do. I remembered watching my nephew, Davey—tenderly, sadly, and because it had to be done—lift his father, my brother, David, out of his chair at the end of his life when he didn't have the strength to stand. I helped Elinor swing her feet out the door.

"You're hurting me!" she yelled.

I put my arms around her, then lifted her up, and all of a sudden she was in the wheelchair. "Are you okay, Elinor?"

"No!"

Entering the store, I tried to imagine how this cavernous, steely place looked to her. We told the clerk what we were looking for and she brought us a tan moccasin with a blue rawhide bow.

"Do you like this one, Elinor?"

"No!"

Jack hunted for white shoes and came back with various tennis shoes. Size nine and a half was too small. All of the shoes we'd chosen were too small. Elinor wasn't comfortable, but she cooperated and let us try shoes on her very long, very narrow feet. When she slid down in the chair, she pushed herself back up, said she was tired, felt sick, and wanted to go home. Jack talked to her gently and helped her look at other shoes.

As she slid her foot into a size ten moccasin, Jack chuckled.

"Don't laugh at me!" she scolded.

"Sorry, Elinor. I wasn't laughing at you, just happy to find the right size. "How do they fit?"

"All right."

"Shall we take them off and pay for them?"

"No. Leave them on."

I lifted her into the car and we drove back to the nursing home. She seemed exhausted, but perked up when we sat under the trees. She moved her legs up and down as if she were dancing in her new shoes.

"Did you like to dance, Elinor?" I asked.

"Floyd danced with me. And then I played the piano. I played 'Let Me Call You Sweetheart.'" Elinor sang, and I imagined her at the piano, Floyd beside her, the two of them singing:

Let me call you Sweetheart, I'm in love with you.
Let me hear you whisper that you love me too.
Keep the love-light glowing in your eyes so true.
Let me call you Sweetheart, I'm in love with you.

She looked at me with wide, blue eyes, spread her hands on her lap, and almost smiled. "Sharps and flats and notes." She turned to Jack. "I'll tell you a secret. Floyd thought I was afraid, but I wasn't, and a baby came."

"What was the baby's name?" Jack asked.

"Jack Frost. He was a good boy, just asleep, not dead. He wet himself."

Elinor's experience as a young mother was still with her. Maybe like all young mothers she was daunted by the enormous responsibility of caring for new life, or maybe her fear that the baby had died was evoked by the memory of her baby sister's death at two months, a fear that worried her still when her baby was little.

The aide called Elinor to lunch and Jack told her we'd come back later.

"When you come I'll give you a kiss."

———— ▪ ▸ ————

That evening, Elinor was alert, the day room was quiet, and we talked.

"I'm looking for Mother," Elinor said. "She loves me. Take me home."

Jack stroked his beard. "To McKinnon Street or to the country club?"

"Yes. To the country club."

"What will we do there?"

"We'll play cards. We'll put up the card table. I have the king." She patted Jack's hand and touched his arm and he covered her hand with his own.

After some silence, I decided to ask Elinor about her life in the hospital. Taking a long breath, I plunged in. "Elinor, what did you do in the hospital?"

"I folded napkins. If I don't finish they don't pay me, but they don't pay me anyway." Her voice was almost inaudible.

"Did you have friends?" I leaned toward her.

"Yes."

"What did you do at Princess Stone's?" I knew as soon as I asked that it was the wrong question.

"I wasn't there," Elinor snapped back and looked up. "Do you like jazz?"

"Yes, I do. How about you?"

"I'm crazy about it. It's nice music." Elinor drummed her fingers on the table.

"What else do you like?" I continued to fish for details about her life.

"I like to read."

"What do you like to read?" The chair creaked as I sat back.

"A book," she said matter-of-factly.

"About what?"

"About life and love and children."

I smiled thinking of Elinor hiding herself away in a small corner of the hospital or under a tree on the grounds, a book in her hands and a story growing in her mind, forgetting for a time where she was, entering a life with romance and warmth and children. "You have a lot of memories."

"Like an elephant, and one mind."

"What do you remember?"

"The elephant's nose turns up like this." She stretched out her arm to make a trunk in the air.

I looked over at Jack, his chin in his hand, smiling.

Elinor shifted in her chair and chatted on about somebody who confused an apple and a pear. I could almost understand, and then the words were garbled until she began to talk about her mother.

"My mother taught me how to cook and left me in the kitchen and went upstairs. I made the salad with lettuce and tomatoes. I made scrambled eggs and bacon."

That reminded me to give Elinor the family photographs I had enlarged thinking that maybe she was not able to see the smaller ones clearly.

"Here's Margery," I pointed out. "And who's this?"

"Ida Clare McConnell."

"Yes, that's your mother." I smiled and Elinor beamed. "And this is a picture of you, Elinor."

"That's who I am."

She talked about babies wetting themselves and being a lot of work. Jack asked if the baby was John. She stopped speaking and put her head down until the silence was broken by loud moans coming from a room behind us.

"It's noisy in here. Does it bother you?" I asked.

"Yes, it makes me feel cheap." She leaned over and the buzzer went off. After I shut it off she continued, "My birthday is November 14th."

"How old will you be?"

"Forty-five?" She pushed herself up in her chair.

"We'll send you a card."

"You will?"

When Jack told her we were going to leave, she replied, "I'll call for you in the morning."

——————

That night we drove out to Laughlin's Corners to pick up Ann and take her to her father's favorite restaurant, on the grounds of a golf course. Looking out over gently rolling hills, I told her about finding Elinor's children, our mutual cousins. She was moved to hear that I'd found John, born the same year that she was, and warmed to Elinor when I told her about Sandra's visit, seeing her mother for the first time since she was five months old.

Ann asked to keep the photo of Elinor, Sandra, and Amy to show to her children. "Our family does not communicate, but I'm glad you're doing this. Grandpa Ben was ashamed about Elinor."

"What a telling statement," I mentioned to Jack on the drive back to town. "With Grandpa's shame, the love in this family got stuck, slowed to a trickle, and almost stopped. We've finally begun to open the flow and get things moving. We're becoming family again."

——————

Jack and I met Jane and Will at the church on Sunday. Will, looking grand-fatherly with silver hair and kind eyes, was waiting for us at the door. Inside, we met Jane, who was wearing high heels with tiny straps.

"Don't tell my orthopedist." She was elegant and warm, a small woman with twinkly eyes and a bright smile.

After the service we went to brunch and talked about the family. The town was still interested in Elinor years after she was sent away.

"I heard from your cousin Ann's mother that Elinor had died. That was in the fifties. I said, 'No, I don't think so.' When your mother called, I told her and she said, 'Elinor has not died. I would have heard.'

We filled our plates from the buffet and returned to the table. Jane continued, "Margery's dad and mother posted a Bible verse by the front door and the children had to learn a new one each week. Clare, your mother's mother, was stately, wholesome. My own mother was insecure, but she was there for your mother after her mother died. Your grandfather was not good to your mother. He taught Mame's daughter, Martha, to drive, but he wouldn't teach your mother and she was furious about that."

After brunch they drove us through the old neighborhood, pointing out Mother's house and Jane's house on opposite corners. Before we left, Jane gave me a picture of a recent reunion, Mother among them, of the girlfriends who were friends for life.

When we saw Elinor in the morning before heading home, she greeted us with a command. "Take me to the potteries. I want to go to the potteries in West Virginia."

I wish we could have taken her back to the time before the tragedies when her mother was alive and the family flourished, to the time when Ben went off to work and Bill, Elinor, and Margery walked down the hill to school, to the time when Clare cooked and wrote poems and looked after baby Dorothy, to the time when Elinor was growing into a talented, bright, and beautiful young woman.

And yet there was another side to the family even before Grandmother Clare's death. While the church gave them a sense of community and esteem, it may have also played a part in the shame Ben felt when Elinor was pregnant and unmarried. The people in the community where Ben had been raised and where he was a respected elder knew that his daughter had gone astray, *sinned*. They would have used that word. It was easy to imagine that he was humiliated by her condition and even more so when she began to act strange and fell into postpartum psychosis. Most likely, he saw her behavior as a moral problem rather than a medical one. He was raised with a strict sense of right and wrong, of good and bad, and Elinor, in Ben's eyes, was undoubtedly irredeemably bad.

While the hymns and Bible verses she learned as a girl gave Elinor an inner strength, she probably took to heart her family's religious notions and the church's teachings of good and bad; seventy-two years later, she still, in part, saw herself as bad. Fortunately, it wasn't the only way she saw herself. She was also "Mother" and the "Queen," and in spite of a touch of dementia, she knew that she was not "crazy."

23

Home Sweet Home

In early December, while Christmas shopping, I spotted wooden music boxes and bought one for Elinor. After wrapping it and addressing the package I waited a few days before mailing it, wanting it to arrive close to Christmas. Suddenly and miraculously my schedule cleared and I could take Elinor the music box. Kathy said she would have my room at the B&B ready, so I packed the car and headed west.

Clouds darkened the sky and it started raining lightly, but, thankfully, the temperature was above freezing. There were many mountains to cross, huge, long mountains, beautiful in summer but treacherous in winter storms. I popped a CD into the player and Kate Wolf, a favorite folk singer, serenaded me up and down the mountains. One of her songs, "Give Yourself to Love," touched a chord and I sang out loud as I drove. "I always knew I'd find you, though I never did know how and like sunshine on a cloudy day, you stand before me now."

After arriving in Canton that afternoon, I went straight to the nursing center. Betty was at the front desk. I gave her a red tin of Christmas cookies and a card for the staff. She ordered dinner for me so I could eat with Elinor. There she was, sitting in her place at the far table, in a new wheelchair.

Never sure that she knew who I was, I looked into her blue eyes and said, "Hello, Elinor, I'm Margery's daughter Susan."

"Margery," she said, "is my sister."

"Yes." I smiled. "And did you know she has children?"

"Yes, two," Elinor affirmed.

"You're right! And I'm one of them." So Elinor and Margery were in touch until at least 1945, when I was born, nine years after Elinor was sent to Massillon.

"How is Margery?" she asked.

I was caught off guard by her entirely normal and direct question. Still carrying fears of her fragility, I failed to tell her that Margery had passed away. "She loves you. And so does Dorothy."

"We played tennis. We put our heads together, then got our tennis rackets and played doubles. Margery . . ." She seemed about to cry. "Margery was a good girl."

"She didn't get into trouble?"

"Well, she fell down and we left her on the floor," Elinor said playfully.

She tried crossing her legs, as girlfriends do when they sit and talk to each other, but her leg slid down every time she tried. I uncrossed my legs and scooted to the edge of my chair. "How would you like to go for a spin? It's too cold to go outside like we did last summer, but we could go into the front room and take a look at the Christmas tree."

"All right."

Elinor studied the little golden bell I took from the tree and gave her. A younger resident walked over and stood with us. Elinor patted her hand and the woman told her to stop. Elinor was silent. "She's your friend," I told the woman.

"I know she is, but she's patting me and I don't like it."

I wheeled Elinor across the room to the fireplace, where she could see the crèche on the mantle. When I gave her the baby Jesus, she began to sing. There in her wheelchair, cradling the figurine in her veined hands, she sang every verse of "Away in a Manger," and it sounded like a lullaby.

When she was finished, I placed a small statue of an angel in her hand. "Who is this?"

"Margery."

"Oh, Margery is an angel?"

"She's good."

"Was she smart?" I bent down to hear.

"No," her voice was loud and clear. "She's dumb." Elinor did not suffer fools.

An aide called us to eat. Elinor's dinner was served mashed up, food for a toothless mouth. After serving Elinor, the aide set a tray in front of me: chicken nuggets, potato fries, beets, and a brownie. Elinor took her time eating. She seemed to relish her food, especially the potatoes, spooning up bite after bite, scraping the dish clean. Others in the dayroom were arguing, refusing to eat, and calling for help. A stocky, bald-headed man with a grin passed by our table guiding his wife, who looked straight ahead with big eyes and a rigid expression. His eye caught mine, "Here we go again." Thankfully, the television was turned off. Elinor tugged at her clothes and I reached over to help.

"Get your hands off me," she yelled, "and keep them off!"

Hearing echoes of what may have been threatening encounters, I was heartened that she spoke up for herself. After dinner I stood up and told her I was going to leave.

"I thought we were going to talk."

I sat down. "So what should we talk about?"

"School." She took the napkin from her lap, carefully folded it and placed it on the table. "There were four or five in school."

"What did you study?"

"Math. Reading. History."

Two little girls skipped by on their way to see the tree. I watched Elinor watching them and then I asked if she liked school.

She looked at me with her piercing blue eyes. "No. I liked to stay home. I am a little girl. I am tall and thin. My mother's dead."

I picked up the new album I'd brought and we paged through it and stopped at the picture of her mother. Elinor looked at the photo for a time without speaking, and then turned the page. When she came to a picture of her grandmother, she pointed. "That's a patient in the hospital." Closing the book, she patted the table, "This table needs a tablecloth."

"You are all right," I told Elinor, enjoying her company.

"I love you."

"And I love you."

"That's the way it should be."

———— ▶ ————

Over breakfast I told Kathy about Elinor singing "Away in a Manger" while holding the little Jesus.

"Elinor could come here," Kathy offered. "We could invite Elinor to the house. There's a tree and a wreath over the mantle with lights and lots of Christmas decorations. It's old-fashioned and may seem like home to her. You could give her the music box and I could play Christmas carols on the piano." Randy, who had just entered the room, suggested that we could carry her up the front steps.

He left to sweep away the dusting of snow on the walk and Kathy and I began to imagine bringing Elinor to a place that looked home.

When I arrived at the nursing center Elinor was taking a nap in her room. "You can go and see her there," the nurse suggested.

She was in a new room with plenty of space and more privacy. A corkboard hung over her bed, bright with birthday cards, including one from Sandra and one from Clare. Framed pictures of her mother, her sisters, and her daughter decorated the top of her dresser. Elinor was almost asleep when I bent down and asked, "How are you?" She looked older and more frail.

"Fair."

"It's almost Christmas," I told her.

"Then you give me a kiss."

I did. "And now you give me a kiss."

She did and then she went to sleep.

On the way out I asked the nurse about taking Elinor to Kathy's house. She checked the calendar and noticed that there were no appointments the next day, so they could take her in the van. Remembering how difficult it was to get Elinor in and out of the car when we took her to buy shoes, I was grateful for her offer.

———————————

When I returned, Elinor was eating and I sat with her. "I'm back and happy to see you."

"Well, clap your hands," she mimicked, parodying my enthusiasm.

"How do you feel, Elinor?"

"I feel like talking. My mother brought a tray of food and she said to drink the milk and I said, 'I'm not a cow!'" Elinor laughed and laughed. We both laughed, maybe the way Elinor laughed with her mother over silly, nonsensical jokes.

Feeling tired, she rested her head on her arm and hugged herself. Her eyes closed. Her lips said, "Mother.'"

An aide at the other end of the table, feeding a very old lady who would rather sleep, told me that Elinor used to sing and play the piano. "She talked about Uncle Raymond and Aunt Mabel."

"Raymond was her mother's brother and Mabel was her father's sister."

Another aide, with straight black hair falling over her shoulders, stopped to talk. "My grandmother's Indian, she's ninety-six and talks about things she remembers back to 1914. I think about Elinor all the time. She's amazing.

She knows three languages and can tell you what they mean. One day I asked her to speak French and when she did, Elinor told me what she had said. I asked her to say something in Italian and the same thing happened."

When Elinor woke up, the aide looked at me and winked. "Elinor, speak French."

"*Merci beaucoup.*"

Elinor looked uncomfortable, and I asked if she was all right.

"I have pain in my bottom. It doesn't feel good. I might not be here tomorrow."

"Where will you be?"

"Home, in East Liverpool. I was in an accident and got killed. God was with me."

"When?" I asked.

"A little while ago."

She talked about menstruation, or as she referred to it, 'falling off the roof,' when she was with Floyd. "He said, 'Don't put the Kotex on.' And then you have to take care of the baby." Elinor stopped talking and I let her words sink in, aware that much of the rest of her life had turned on that one delicate moment.

Not wanting to pepper her with questions, I worked on the blue sweater I was knitting while she rested with her head on her shoulder. It was oddly peaceful sitting there among people of all ages, colors, and backgrounds. Nurses and aides came and went with meds and trays. Residents wandered in and out, guests arrived and left, calling out greetings as they passed.

The aide who would drive Elinor in the van the next day stopped to make plans and I mentioned the visit to Elinor who was awake. "Would you like to go to my friend's home tomorrow?"

"Uh-huh."

When the aide left Elinor looked at me and said in a clear, low voice, "You're a good girl. You have to keep everything you've got. All I've got is a son and a daughter. I'm their mother."

Time stopped when I heard her say that. It was her meaning and her fortune. She had kept it to the end, and now she was sharing it with me. I opened the album and showed her the photograph of John and Sandra.

She took it in both hands and looked intently at the picture. "John peed on the floor and Sandra left too soon."

John was a toddler and Sandra a baby when she was taken from them; Elinor's memories were bitter few, but she was still and always would be their mother.

Awhile later I took out my notebook and asked Elinor if she wanted to write.

She nodded her head. "I don't have anything to write with. Write your name and then my name and then 'Norbert Johnson.' I forget how to spell my name."

"Would you like to write a letter to Dorothy?"

"Yes, I would."

"What do you want to write Dorothy?"

Elinor coughed and cleared her throat. "Dear Dorothy, I'm very nervous and high-strung. Write me a letter. Elinor."

"Have you always been nervous and high-strung?"

"They put me in the hospital to make me well. I'm sick."

"Is there anything else you would like me to write to Dorothy?

"You have a mind of your own, you figure out what to write."

A chair alarm shrieked out a warning for the eleventh time. "It's noisy in here. It hurts my ears," I complained.

"Get a hat," Elinor advised.

After jotting down a few notes, I spoke. "Elinor, I went to your church in East Liverpool and they have the most beautiful stained glass windows."

She looked at me and squinted. "You think so? Dorothy went there."

"She sang in the choir, did you sing in the choir, too?"

"Yes, I fell down and got hurt."

Noting another reference to falling, I looked up from my notebook.

"And you keep writing," she told me. "Mr. Laughlin said I couldn't go there anymore or he'd have me arrested. I have the old key. God gave it to me. And then Mr. Laughlin had the key."

I wrote down her words just as she wished me to—cryptic, notable words that told her story.

"They put us in a room and gave the clothes back and I didn't have to beg or steal."

I didn't understand the meaning of her disclosure, but I sensed cruelty behind it and felt a mixture of outrage and sorrow. I thanked her for telling me.

"I told you the truth," she responded.

A middle-aged, gray-haired woman wearing a plaid overcoat walked toward us. She took off her coat and introduced herself as Elinor's new guardian, Pat McConnell.

"McConnell was Elinor's mother's maiden name," I told her, and we began to speculate about a link between our families. It was time for me to leave and let Mrs. Del Vecchio and Mrs. McConnell get to know each other.

Writing this in my studio months later, I feel immense sadness for Elinor and utter abhorrence for my grandfather. What villainous blood had I inherited from this man who deserted his own? What should I do with the crimes of cruelty and abandonment sitting in my heart? Now that I knew what my family had done to Elinor, how could I keep from accusing them and perpetuating the cycle of judgment and bitterness?

Birds flew past the window. Black against the blue sky they soared and plunged and turned to silver when their wings caught the morning sun. My father's words appeared in my mind, the advice he sent me in the V-Mail letter days before he died. *For me, adhere to a belief in tolerance, a genuine liking for others, and always give to life to the fullest.* My wise, young father was still with me. His words changed my mood from blame to tolerance, an attempt to understand. There had been times when I was filled with more pain than I could bear and I'd turned away—rejected, renounced, dismissed—and bowed out from circumstances far less urgent and way more removed than a psychotic child or sibling.

Grandpa must have been completely defeated with what he could neither tolerate nor understand. The idea of seeing Elinor after having abandoned her when she was better must have filled them all, Ben, Bill, Margery, and Dorothy, with dread, shame, and helplessness, with guilt and grief so deep they couldn't bring themselves to see her again, much less take her home. In those days, less was known and society was all but closed to people with mental illness. Psychotherapy was rare; there was too little support for and too much judgment toward families of the mentally ill. Knowing the severe suffering Elinor's illness brought to the family, I wanted to hold all of them in my heart as Elinor told me in words, few and shadowy, the truths of her sad life.

I returned to the B&B early the day of the visit and waited. No one was home. The house was ready: a wreath with twinkling lights hung above the mantle, and a Christmas tree sparkled in the front window. The aide was bringing Elinor at one o'clock and it was quarter of. We'd need Randy to help us bring the wheelchair up the steps. Kathy arrived, and a few minutes later Randy walked in, home from his work as a chaplain at nearby Malone University.

The front door was open when the blue van pulled up, and I rushed outside to greet Elinor. She sat like royalty in her wheelchair inside the van wearing the purple hat and white jacket Sandra had sent her mother for her ninety-fifth birthday. I saw her looking through the window in the van and waved, and she waved back. We lifted her up the front steps and took her into the house.

It was bitter cold outside, and Elinor let us know that she was freezing. Kathy brought a blanket to wrap around her legs and draped a quilt over her red sweatshirt.

When Randy took a few pictures, the flash annoyed her. "What was that?"

"That's a light from the camera," he explained, "so we can take pictures indoors."

I pointed out the lighted wreath above the mantle and the Christmas tree by the window.

"I can't see very well. I'm going blind." Her hat had fallen over her forehead and Kathy asked if she'd like to take it off.

"Yeah."

Kathy leaned toward Elinor. "Where did you get your beautiful blue eyes?"

"God gave them to me," Elinor said in a proud, singsong way.

I noticed Randy smiling at Elinor. We wheeled her into the living room and Randy offered to move her to a chair, but she wanted to stay in her wheelchair. Like a kid who couldn't wait, I gave her my present. When she didn't open it I asked if she'd like help.

"Yes."

I took the off paper, slid the box out of a velvet bag, opened the lid, and music twinkled out.

Elinor held it and listened. She picked up the bracelet I'd placed inside and I fastened it around her wrist.

Kathy had a present for her but Elinor shook her head. "I don't want it now. I want to go to sleep." She tilted her head and closed her eyes.

Kathy brought glasses of eggnog and the three of us talked quietly.

When Elinor woke up, Kathy sat down at the piano and began to play "O Come All Ye Faithful."

Elinor sang along until Kathy switched to "Away in a Manger." Elinor looked surprised. "Where is the piano?"

"Over there, right in this room." Randy pointed to the piano behind her. "Would you like to play? I'd love to hear you play, Elinor."

"All right."

We wheeled her up to the piano and Kathy tucked Elinor's legs under the keyboard so she could touch the keys. She reached out her long, slender fingers, played the melody with her right hand, searched for the chords with her left hand, and the familiar tune filled the room. Time slipped away, and for a moment the past caught up with the present.

A little later Kathy asked, "Would you like to play something else? How about 'You Are My Sunshine'?"

Elinor picked it out note by note and slid back into "Away in a Manger." Wanting to preserve this moment, I took a picture, but when the flash went off, Elinor stopped playing. I suggested she play "Let Me Call You Sweetheart." She began to play the melody from her youth and once again slid into "Away In a Manger." After a few stanzas she lifted her hands from the keys.

"Is there anything else you'd like to play?" Kathy asked.

"House! I like to play house. Home sweet home."

Kathy put her arm around Elinor's shoulder. "How about if I play 'Let Me Call You Sweetheart'?"

Elinor dropped her hands into her lap. "I'm finished playing the piano. You go ahead and play."

Kathy played and Randy sang. As I watched Elinor observing Randy I wondered if she saw, in her dimmed vision, a likeness to her father, both men having the same build. Like Ben's, Randy's voice was strong and true.

I heard Elinor speak, addressing Randy. "Where do you work? Do you work in the pottery?"

Randy realized Elinor was talking to him and turned his attention to her.

She told Randy something about her dad having the keys and then I heard her say, "I love my dad. I always will."

Aware of her history with her father, I felt an inner jolt. Elinor had overcome what no one should endure and she'd done it with a heart still able to love even the one who destroyed most of her life.

A minute later she asked Randy to take the bracelet off her wrist.

Randy bent down and unclasped it. "Shall I put it in your music box?"

"Don't ask me!"

Randy and Kathy gave her their gift and he helped her untie the package. Elinor yawned. "I wish I could go to sleep."

Kathy noticed it was three o'clock, time for the aide to pick her up, and we helped Elinor into her coat and retrieved her purple hat for the trip back to the nursing center.

Kathy held out her arms. "Can I have a hug?"

"No!" Elinor replied emphatically.

"Can Randy have a hug?" Kathy asked.

Elinor reached for Randy and gave him a hug. He kissed her on the cheek. We took a few last pictures and Randy gave Elinor his hand.

Elinor took it and, with her other hand, rapped him on the knuckles. "That was ten," she said. She had begun to even the score with her dad.

Randy enjoyed bantering with this ninety-five-year-old woman who was still fetching and feisty. He invited Elinor to come back again and she accepted.

"This is nice," she said.

The aide arrived and we carried Elinor down the steps and into the blue van.

I returned to the nursing center that evening to see how Elinor survived the Christmas party. She was sitting at a table in the middle of the room with several women residents—Nancy, Rosalind, and Margaret. Every few minutes Elinor moved and the buzzer attached to her chair pierced the room. There were no attendants around and the alarm didn't seem to bother anyone except me. Each time it sounded, I reconnected the magnet to silence it.

Rosalind talked about her sister who didn't come to visit and her mother who left her alone forever. Margaret, who was often ornery and argumentative, stuck out her fist at Rosalind. I suggested she might feel better if she gave Rosalind a smile instead.

"I don't know how to smile," she said.

I asked her to give me a smile and she laughed. "That's it!" I said. "Now give one to Rosalind." And she did.

Elinor took the music box out of the bag. We listened and then she put it back in and shoved the bag away from her. She told us about the country club. "We played cards and there were dances and people spent money, even when that was nearly all they had. I lived there a short time, about a month." Elinor's mind was clear and her speech direct, and I got a sense of how it might have been to be part of her life through the years. But all I had was that moment and I was enjoying sitting there with Elinor and the women gathered around the table. When it was time to go, I kissed Elinor good-bye and told her I loved her. I shook hands all around, talked to the nurse, punched in the code that opened the door, and left.

24

The Fall

The day before my birthday in January 2009, I stopped by my home long enough to check the mail. Ellen had told me to be sure and watch for a package. The box arrived and I opened it as I listened to the messages on my answering machine. I stopped opening the package when I heard Sandra's voice.

"Elinor passed away on January 19th."

Oh no! I walked over to the machine and hit replay.

"Elinor passed away on January 19th. The social worker at the nursing home tried but wasn't able to reach either of us."

Sandra answered my call right away. "This is so hard, not knowing her for seventy-two years, seeing her once, and now she is gone."

We shared memories of our time together with Elinor and talked about arrangements for her body and a memorial service.

Betty, at the nursing center, was vague about Elinor's death. "She was taken to the hospital on December 31st and spent the last four days in hospice. I called you and left messages, but never heard back."

I asked her what number she'd used and found out she had the wrong one. She'd read a four as a nine.

When I hung up with Betty, I felt bereft. I would have gone. I would have liked to have stroked her hair and held her hand to the end. I was so happy to have found her alive and to have had the chance to be with her, to know a little bit about Aunt Elinor, my mother's sister who had survived abandonment, neglect, and loss with her heart and mind and spirit intact.

There was so much more I wanted to ask her—especially about her years in the hospital. Did anyone in the family visit her? What were her days like? When did she fall and hurt her hip? Who cared for her and made her life bearable? What kept her going? There were so many things I'd never know, and yet it was all right. I really didn't need to know more. It was enough that we were together in this life. Strangely, I noticed myself feeling connected to Elinor in this grief, a tiny speck of the loneliness she must have often experienced.

With Elinor it was somewhat the way I felt with my children: every act, every word, was important to me. She was truly Elinor and she was also a little bit my child, my missing father, and my grandmother, my father's mother who lost her only child. I loved my grandmother with my child's heart, and when she became deeply depressed with overwhelming losses and sickness and ended her life, I was devastated. When I found Elinor, that deep, pure love I'd once felt toward my grandmother returned. It was there all along somewhere inside, asleep but not dead, ready to wake up and suffuse a new relationship. The flow of love may become blocked but the source survives storm after storm, as it had for Elinor and for me.

I was glad I'd gone to see her before Christmas, and understanding what it was like to not have memories of my father, I was grateful to have memories of Elinor. That morning during meditation, I felt her presence. It was golden and warm. She was part of the universe now, and she was with me as I sat on my cushion watching snowflakes softly fall to earth.

———————

I called Pat McConnell, Elinor's guardian, and she expressed her sadness at not having been able to speak with me sooner, as she too had the wrong number.

"I left Elinor just a half hour before she passed away. The hospice nurse had suggested putting the phone to her ear and calling you so you could have one final connection with Elinor, tell her of your love and say good-bye, but the phone number was the wrong one. Elinor passed away peacefully. I said good-bye to her. The day you left, when I was sitting with her, I asked her to sing 'Silent Night' and she sang it all the way through."

"What happened? Was she sick?"

"Elinor fell on Christmas Eve. She was agitated in her chair and fell forward and hurt her head badly."

Fury flashed through me as I remembered being with Elinor that last night. Her chair alarm had gone off and I was the only non-resident in the room. Where was the staff when she fell? I didn't want this to have happened and I wanted to blame the nursing home, yet they were the ones who had taken care of her all those years and my family never had. She talked often about falling when I was with her during the last visit; I think she may have had a premonition, but that's something else I'll never know.

"I saw her in the emergency room and spoke with the doctors," Pat continued. "She was conscious in the emergency room, and very aware when she was in the hospital; she would argue about eating. Then she got pneumonia and a urinary tract infection. They put her in hospice and she was drugged somewhat so she wouldn't hurt herself. Before the end, when she was still alert, her hands were mittened and she had the oxygen tube that she didn't like and she was batting at me. I saw that as a sign that she was getting better; she had more energy. I looked at her feet and there were no sores, and her skin in the nursing home was so smooth. She had good care there too. The orders with the doctor were to make her comfortable. She looked comfortable. We had an eleventh-hour volunteer signed up to come and sit with her, but she passed away that afternoon around two fifteen. I talked to her, and my husband went with me to visit her."

I was relieved to hear that Pat was with her and that her husband had come to see Elinor. Elinor liked men. When I expressed my appreciation to Pat, she told me, "I wasn't able to have hospice for my mother, so I'm glad I could be there with Elinor."

———

At our weekly gathering on Sunday night, I told the sangha, the Buddhist group I belonged to, about Elinor. "She was twenty-three in 1936 when she was taken to the mental hospital with what we now know was postpartum psychosis. She spent the rest of her life in the mental health system because the family abandoned her. I found her last year, ninety-four years old, alive and living in a nursing home in Canton, Ohio, and visited her four times during the year. She didn't see her children grow up. She owned nothing. She seldom, if ever, walked down the street for a cup of tea. She had no private space, and yet she was expressive, affectionate, and feisty. Every evening she sang 'You Are My Sunshine.' I found out that she passed away on January 19th."

I asked the sangha to sing "No Coming, No Going."

No coming. No going.
No after. No before.
I hold you close to me.
I release you to be so free
Because I am in you and you are in me.

They sang in harmony so heavenly I'm sure that Elinor was lifted even higher. After the meditation, I walked up to several of them to thank them and they burst into "You Are My Sunshine" in four-part harmony.

When I met Elinor I simply loved her. It wasn't based on appearances or experiences or memories and wasn't related to pity; her spunk disabused me of that. Elinor, as I came to know her, was beyond categories. She was neither young nor old, sane nor insane. When I sat with her I could be anybody: Mother, Margery, Dorothy, nurse. She had no preconceived ideas of who I was or should be and no expectations of me. I felt no pressure to entertain her or to take care of her. I went only to sit with her, to be as present with her and with myself as I possibly could. The space between us was open, uncluttered. The fact that she was alive, that we were alive together at those moments, was all that mattered. Free of my usual worries, needs, and responsibilities, I felt an inner spaciousness. Maybe that was partly why I felt so much love when I was with her. There was room for love to thrive.

———◆———

Love was also returning to this family that had been shattered by shame and fear and the silence that followed. Many of us planned to gather in East Liverpool in March for Elinor's Memorial Service. In addition to wanting to honor her, we were curious about each other, cousins we'd never met. Mickey hoped to bring Aunt Dorothy. I talked with Ann, who would be there and had agreed to play the piano. Sandra and her husband, her two daughters, and Elinor's great-grandson were planning to go, as were four of my siblings. That meant that for the first time since 1936, people from each of Mother's siblings' families would be together. We'd travel from New Mexico, Colorado, Chicago, Massachusetts, Indiana, New York, and Washington, DC to celebrate and honor Elinor. Would Mother have come? And David? What a grand reunion that would have been. I cradled my mug of warm chai and thought of Mother and David. They felt close, Mother looking into my eyes, letting me know that all was well, and David thoughtful, quietly noticing everything.

Putting down my mug, I picked up a pen and wrote Elinor's obituary. The picture I'd taken of her when Sandra and Amy were visiting would do. She looked sharp and alert. Unfortunately, I'd forgotten to take her bib off, but her face showed her fierce spirit.

Elinor Laughlin Del Vecchio, formerly of East Liverpool, passed away on January 19, 2009, at the age of ninety-five, in the care of hospice. She was born Sara Elinor Laughlin on November 14, 1913 in Cambridge Springs, Pennsylvania to Clare McConnell Laughlin and Benjamin Fisher Laughlin. In her youth Elinor sang in the United Presbyterian Church choir and she played the piano on radio station KDKA in Pittsburgh, PA.

Mrs. Del Vecchio was the widow of Floyd Del Vecchio. She is survived by her two children, John Del Vecchio (Jeanne) of Havana, Florida, and Sandra Berkley (Edward) of West Falmouth, Massachusetts. She has six grandchildren and ten great-grandchildren. She is also survived by her sister, Dorothy Laughlin Sasko of Massapequa, NY, and many nieces and nephews.

Mrs. Del Vecchio loved children, fancy hats, and jazz. She sang and played the piano until the end. She was affectionate, funny, talented, and related to everyone around her as family.

On that snowy day in January it was time to make calls to the superintendent of the cemetery, and to Sturgis House, to arrange for our stay. I was hoping we could rent the entire B&B for a grand Laughlin family reunion—or rather *union*, as this would be our first gathering.

The B&B was ours, the whole house. There were exactly enough rooms for all of us who were coming from out of town. The superintendent of Riverview Cemetery informed me that they didn't bury on Sundays, so Saturday would be the day we'd bury Elinor's ashes. I called Reverend Mark Dunn, pastor of the Presbyterian Church where Elinor sang in the choir, to ask if we could have the memorial service there. In good Irish fashion, Reverend Dunn expressed sympathy for our troubles and said he'd have to check with the elders.

The elders were part of my childhood and no doubt part of Elinor's. They marched down the aisle to take up the collection, beginning with the front pew. Dressed alike, in dark suits and white shirts, their shoes clanked on the bare floor as they walked in unison to the front of the church, sounding like soldiers. They were a source of solidity and stability, representing the men who were missing in my life, men who upheld the way of the ancestors, the "faith of our fathers living still, in spite of dungeon, fire, and sword," in the words of the hymn Mother sang with a touch of love in her voice. They were upright and anonymous, and always there, respected and staunch, handing out programs before the service and bidding us good-bye with a slight nod.

———— ◄ ►————

My cousin Sandra and I were getting to know each other as we called back and forth with news and questions. One day she said she thought her mother had waited for her. "It's been hard for Johnnie, having been told by the hospital that she had died and believing that she was dead, and yet she kept going on. He said that he'd be thinking of us. I wish you knew Johnnie. He's funny and always joking, a happy person." Sandra continued, "The Del Vecchios tainted our attitude toward our mother. Floyd's sister who raised us said that Elinor thought she was better than everyone else. How could we not in our heart condemn her? They said those things early on and then they didn't talk about Elinor."

Having inherited negative feelings toward the Laughlins, Sandra was as eager as I was to connect and to ease the woes of the past generation. In fact, all of us had experienced the subtle effects of a family that had deserted its own—degrees of stoic self-reliance, detachment, secretiveness, foreboding, fragility, shutting down and shutting out. While we were moving from estrangement toward connection, I approached the weekend with a measure of caution. Mother seldom mentioned her Laughlin sisters, and we had learned not to ask about them. I felt quite sure she would have loved this gathering, but I knew the reluctance of my siblings to do anything that might distress her and reopen painful wounds. Even after death old fears could hover. I also knew the strength of my sisters' and brothers' identification as Henkels. We grew up with our Henkel cousins as our only cousins in a close-knit family. I wondered if my younger brothers and sisters might feel a sense of betrayal of Mother and of the Henkel family in meeting our Laughlin cousins. They may not have the hunger for family that I did, having known no "blood" cousins. Yet my siblings, who had also inherited the old wounds, were not paralyzed. They were willing to meet their Laughlin cousins.

The next morning, while meditating, I felt Mother's presence—her essence of lightness, excitement, and eagerness. I heard her mention the Laughlin gathering. "I'll take care of it," she told me, and I felt relieved. All I had to do was be there and not get in the way.

25

Cousins

After maneuvering through DC morning rush hour traffic, the road was open and Jack and I were on our way to Elinor's memorial service and the first Laughlin family gathering. All of us except Dorothy, Mickey, and Dona would be there. Mickey had been diagnosed with cancer and the treatments were wearing him down. Jack slept while I drove over the blue hills of western Maryland, feeling sad that I wouldn't see Elinor sitting in her chair at the table beside the wall, sad that I wouldn't slip in beside her or wheel her outside to sit under the trees and talk.

Suddenly gratitude for all that had led us to that weekend sprang up like mayflowers: for Mother, who kept her helpless love for Elinor alive and transmitted it to me; for the people who had helped me find her; and for each person who had treated her kindly and helped her survive. Elinor's suffering was real and beyond anything I could ever imagine, yet I was tremendously happy that I'd been able to sit with her and see that despite all the horrors she'd faced, she was still able to sing and laugh and love. The abandonment and rejection had not ended her life or her joy. I'd felt her love and I had seen her joy when she reached for Sandra and Amy on that summer day outside the nursing home. The memorial service would be a time to remember all of it—the awfulness of what we did to her, Elinor's years of imprisonment, the wonderfulness of finding her alive—and then reunite our broken family.

While driving, I slipped a CD into the player and listened to a cowboy poet sing "You Are My Sunshine." Before I left home I'd looked up the words to the song and found that it wasn't published until 1939. Elinor had been in the hospital for about two years by then, and Floyd had died. I'd always thought that he was Elinor's sunshine, but as I listened to the words while driving I begin to think that it could have also been a link to her father and his disastrous marriage to Mame. Elinor likely heard the song on the radio or from someone at the hospital and she made it her own. All those years she sang "You Are My Sunshine," she may have been keeping Floyd and her father alive in her heart—not romanticized, but in a way that she could remain true to herself, the girl whose dreams were shattered when her father remarried, the girl who wanted to remain her father's darling, full of music and promise, the young wife who lost her husband, the woman who forgave her father.

Music was Elinor's métier. Betty had told me that Elinor arrived from the group home singing gospel music. Nursing home records from that time listed her religion as Pentecostal. She was a child of serious Calvinist Presbyterian parents and yet she sang gospel. Gospel was the music of survival, with its stories of the ways to heal wounds and darkness, stories of the faith Elinor grew up with. Music seemed to have been a bridge for Elinor, connecting her with what she'd lost and at the same time creating a bond with the people around her.

Jack and I drove into Pittsburgh and made our way to the airport, where we waited for my sisters' planes. Both were on time. Ellen was looking like a movie star in a bright yellow coat, rolling her fancy luggage. As my white-haired sister Amy arrived, I spotted Sandra's daughter, Amy, and rushed over to her. I introduced sister Amy to cousin Amy and then I noticed Ellen standing alone and walked back to take her over to meet Amy. The momentous, historical weekend had begun.

Ellen, Amy, Jack, and I trooped out of the airport and climbed into our red Corolla. On the way to East Liverpool, less than an hour's drive, we passed through Beaver County, the area our ancestors settled more than two hundred years ago. The two-lane road wound around hills and cut through the same forests that were there when the first Scotch-Irish Laughlins arrived from Ireland with their Bibles and their dreams. We passed Laughlin's Corners and I pointed out our cousin Ann's house.

Through my sisters' eyes, East Liverpool, this town I'd grown to love because it held my family's history, looked bleak. Quite a few of the buildings were vacant, debris scattered about as if the owners were too tired to finish moving out. Victorian houses and shops built in the late 1800s and early 1900s seemed neglected and worn out. Yet a closer look revealed their former glory, still visible in turrets, garrets, and carved pillars.

When Mother was growing up, the potteries and steel mills bellowed smoke and jobs were plenty. The town buzzed with business and prosperity. The steel mills closed in the early 1980s and a highway was built between the upper town and the lower part that hugged the river.

"If you can imagine the town before the freeway chopped through it," I tell my sisters, "you can see the beauty in this hilly town overlooking the bend in the Ohio River as it was in Mother's day." We drove by the Travelers Hotel, a river town hotel where Paul Whiteman and Marion Anderson stayed when they played the Ceramic Theater across the street. In those days, Highway 30 passed by the front door and the hotel sign beckoned river travelers to spend the night. The hotel looked dark as we drove past, as did much of the town.

We pulled up in front of Sturgis House, our home for the weekend. The front porch with white wicker furniture and a swing at the far end welcomed us to the four-story Victorian house. Ellen and Amy relaxed as we explored the tastefully restored parlor and dining room. We climbed the stairs to the second floor, where the Del Vecchios would stay, then more stairs to the third floor. Amy, Ellen, and Clare would stay together in a room with a double bed and two twin beds, and Jack and I would be next door in the room with eaves. Dan had the downstairs bedroom, where he could practice his guitar in peace.

Our hostess, Carol, showed us the kitchen and explained that there were snacks available at all hours. We poked around, thrilled to find cheese and yogurt, red licorice, pretzels, biscotti, granola bars, soda, bowls of candies, and a freezer still full of Klondike bars.

Clare wouldn't arrive until eight o'clock and had asked us to wait so we could go to dinner together. Ellen and Jack settled in for a nap while Amy and I set out to scout restaurants. Thankfully, the coffeehouse was still in business. After sipping chai and catching up we asked the grandmotherly woman behind the counter to recommend restaurants. There were just two choices if we wanted to stay in the downtown area and walk to dinner, which was what we decided to do. Not knowing if Sandra and her family would want to come with us, we chose the Coachman's Inn, a bit seedy and quite charming—just my taste. The waitress promised to keep the restaurant open for us.

When Amy and I got back to Sturgis House, everyone had arrived. I'd been looking forward to meeting Sandra's daughter, Annie, and there she was—short, dark hair, the slim body of a runner, smiling and friendly. Dan emerged from his first-floor room, the room in which the citizens of East Liverpool crowded to view the corpse of Pretty Boy Floyd. I followed Dan downstairs to the basement, a small museum where Pretty Boy Floyd's body had been embalmed. Photographs and newspaper articles covered the walls; artifacts and a death mask sat on the counter. It was like stepping back into history to the time when Elinor lived in the town with her husband and new baby, the time when East Liverpool was ablaze with news of the death of Public Enemy #1.

Coming up from the basement, we met Amy, her husband, and their eight-year-old son, Jack, on their way out for an early dinner. Sandra, her husband, and Annie would join us for dinner. Clare phoned to say she'd gotten lost. It was getting late, so Jack offered to wait for her while the rest of us walked over to the restaurant, a good choice with basic fare, modest prices, and comforting retro charm. Clare and Jack arrived and talk flowed easily. We got along surprisingly well, like family.

The next morning we fixed our own breakfast and took it into the dining room. I slipped into a chair beside Sandra, mesmerized by her stories of the Del Vecchios. Floyd's father, Joseph, had come over from Naples, Italy and had worked as a stonemason. He grew wealthy and married Martha Clark, an American of English descent. Troubles multiplied when Joseph became an alcoholic, and the couple divorced. Clara, Floyd's sister who raised Sandra and John, was depressed and unhappy.

"Joe had money," Sandra told us, "but he left it to the sons and not to his daughters, so Clara received nothing. Floyd's brother Perry was supposed to give Floyd's share to John and me, but he never did, so John and I inherited nothing from our father."

She showed us pictures of her family, which prompted Ellen to bring out the family album she'd brought. When Sandra saw a picture of our brother David, she shouted, "That's just like Johnnie! They look so alike!" I was thrilled to hear that and only wished that David were still alive to be there with us. I wondered if he knew about Elinor and John and Sandra. There was much we didn't talk about, and often we didn't talk for long stretches, but I knew his secret suffering of having lost two fathers by the age of six, when our father-like grandfather followed our father to the grave. None of it was talked about, but I knew. David was like my left hand, as close as I could get to my father.

By now it was time for Jack and me to pick up the pies for the reception after the service. Walking in the front door of the bakery, we met old East

Liverpool. The décor hadn't changed since the forties, maybe since Elinor lived in town. It was a combination bakery, grocery store, soda fountain, and diner selling homemade macaroni and cheese and hand-made chocolates. I saw from the menu boards that hot dogs cost 85 cents. We chose apple caramel, lemon-meringue, cherry, and black raspberry pies, and ordered dinner to be delivered that night at six.

The day was colder than we'd expected. Ellen, Dan, and I bundled up and left for the church, but it was locked. Just as we called, the man in charge showed up to let us into the round sanctuary filled with morning light shining through exquisite stained glass windows. The church was ready for us. The heat had been turned on and there were flowers, a vase of long-stemmed white roses from Dorothy, Mickey, and Dona, a huge basket of pink and white flowers from Sandra and her husband and a colorful bouquet from their children. Sandra placed the framed photograph of her mother holding Johnnie on the table beside the basket of flowers, and Clare added a purple hat with pink silk flowers for Elinor. Ann arrived with her music, and she and Ellen arranged for Ellen's solo. Dan tuned his guitar and I handed out programs. Jane arrived in fur, a fedora, and high heels, her husband, Will, beside her.

Mark Dunn, the minister, began the service in a lilting Irish brogue. After prayers we sang "Amazing Grace," the hymn we had sung for each one we'd buried those last three years: Mother, David, Dad, and now Elinor. Sandra's daughter Amy read a passage from Ecclesiastes—*a time to be born and a time to die*—and we sang the hymn that Sandra chose, "The Summons," a traditional Scottish melody. The words seemed to come from Elinor:

Will you come and follow me if I but call your name?
Will you go where you don't know and never be the same?
Will you let my love be shown, will you let my name be known?
Will you let my life be grown in you and you in me?

I walked slowly to the lectern and began to read the thirteenth chapter of Corinthians, the passage on love. When I read the part that said love bears all things, hopes all things, endures all things, I knew I was reading about Elinor, who bore and endured all things, and tears filled my eyes.

Ellen sang "His Eye is on the Sparrow" as only she could in a voice that I'm sure reached Elinor when she sang, "I sing because I'm happy. I sing because I'm free." After Annie read the Beatitudes, Dan played two Celtic pieces on his guitar. As he played, I saw Ann smiling in pure delight. Later she told Dan that her jazzman father and Grandpa Ben, who strummed mandolin and banjo, would have loved to hear Dan play. No one will ever hear the music that all of them—Ben, Bill, Elinor, Ann, Dan, Ellen, and Mickey—and that all of us, could have made together, but the beauty of what remained was there in that moment.

Sandra read the poem she wrote after her mother died.

A Tribute to my Mother, Elinor

We had so little time together
You and I
Just the first six months of my life,
And only a few hours in the last six months of yours.

Once young and fair
With eyes so blue,
And auburn hair,
I did not see your lovely face
Or hear your music playing in the air.

In all those years we were apart
My heart cried out
To know the mother you must be.

And now in death as you are truly gone
This crying heart has come to understand

That perhaps it was just meant to be
That I would find you and your loveliness
In the children of this family.

Rest easy now and be in peace
For just as God loves you
We love you too.

Jack stepped up to the lectern and we relived the story of Elinor's life, as much of it as we knew. "Through the long years of institutionalization, she kept love alive by relating to everyone around her as family."

As Jack spoke, I watched Reverend Dunn taking notes. When it was his turn in the pulpit, he compared Elinor to the Biblical Joseph, who was reviled and rejected by his family and sold into slavery. Elinor, like Joseph, persevered, and in the end it was Elinor, like Joseph, who lived through hard times and brought the family back together.

Driving up St. Clair Avenue, the road that Mother and Elinor and Dorothy walked every day to and from high school, we passed their street and turned into Riverview Cemetery. Two gravediggers met us at the site of the Laughlin family plot. Gangly and bedraggled, they looked as if they'd stepped from the pages of *Hamlet*. One of them took Jane's arm and kept her steady when her heels sank into the soft earth.

After reciting together the 23rd psalm, as we had at Mother's bedside, Jack invited us to offer stories and songs. Sandra spoke for all of us when she declared, "Elinor has come home! After all these years, Elinor is finally home." Dan picked up his guitar and began to play "You Are My Sunshine" and we all joined in, serenading Elinor as we laid her to rest beside her mother and father.

Elinor was with all of her family, the living and the dead, at that one glorious moment. We knew who she was and we knew where she was buried.

———————

When we returned to Sturgis House, Carol had the pies cut and the coffee ready. Afterwards, I walked Will out to his car. He stopped on the sidewalk and let Ellen and Jane go on ahead. I sensed that he wanted to tell me something. I waited, and after a few minutes he began to speak. "You know, I remember when Elinor was sent away—the whole town was talking about that." He walked away, his body shifting from side to side with every step. Will wanted me to know how it was back then, when what happened to Elinor was more than the family, more than the church, more than the town could handle. It was a time when you hid your secrets, especially shameful ones, but when Elinor was taken away, the whole town knew.

Looking down the street past the Elks Club, where Grandpa lived in his later years, I watched Jane and Will drive away. If Elinor had been released from the hospital when she was still young, her mental troubles would have hounded her, followed her like a mad dog the rest of her days in that small town. People would have remembered, as Mother's friend, June, remembered, that she had left the baby in the driveway. Or maybe they would have eventually forgotten that when she gave a concert at the Ceramic Theater, or maybe they would have forgiven her when they saw her with her children, a good mother after all. Maybe Floyd, had he survived, would have taken Elinor and the children to California, where they could have started over. As it was, no one helped her, fought for her, or took her part; they even stopped visiting and killed her off in their heads, in their conversations, in their lives.

Will and Jane were witnesses to that time, and they had trusted us enough to come to the service for Elinor, despite the gossip and their memories. They remembered the Elinor of the past, and because she disappeared, they'd had no chance to revise their view of her. At the memorial service, however, they'd seen her as a great human being who'd lasted through all the years of neglect with a strong heart and irrepressible spirit. They'd heard Sandra's sorrow and they'd seen how happy we were to know her and how proud to be related to her. What a relief to know that we didn't have to be silenced or paralyzed by past wounds, that we could change the present outcome of past troubles.

Some of us took a nap, some took a walk, and some visited the antique mall around the corner with its assortment of Homer Laughlin china. We all went back to the house for dinner. Afterward, several of the adults played a game with young Jack and the rest of us gathered in the parlor, where Dan played guitar while we sang along. As we said good-bye the next morning, we were already planning to meet again in October.

26

Last Words

The year after Elinor died, Jack and I decided to return to Massillon in hopes of finding people who had worked in the hospital when Elinor lived there and could tell me what it was like back then. Or maybe I was missing her and wanted to return to the people and places she knew. Before leaving for Ohio, I called Sandra to ask if there was anything she wanted me to find out.

"I was never able to call her 'Mother' until I met her. Now it's easy to call her 'Mother.' I think about her hip that was left untreated. It would be difficult to hear that she was mistreated in any way."

The day we left I called Kathy at the B&B to tell her that we were getting a late start.

"I have someone for you to see," Kathy told me. "A friend of mine worked at Massillon State Hospital. Mabel is eighty-six. Her recent memory isn't too good, but I'll bet she remembers Massillon."

Jack and I had an easy drive to Canton. Over tea and freshly baked oatmeal cookies, Jack and Kathy and I talked about Elinor, and Kathy mentioned her friend. "I spoke with Mabel's daughter, who said she remembers her mother bringing patients from the hospital home for Sunday dinner."

Her words went straight to my heart. I hoped Elinor was one of the lucky ones.

The next morning, Kathy and I set off to visit Mabel Owens. She lived in a nursing home about ten miles outside of Canton. As we drove, Kathy cautioned, "When I called Mabel this morning to ask if we could visit her today, she didn't remember speaking with me yesterday."

"You know," I responded, "she'll be the first person I've met who worked at Massillon and is a link to Elinor's time there."

We signed in at the office, pinned nametags onto our sweaters, and took the elevator to the fourth floor. Mabel was sitting in her easy chair looking out over blue hills. Setting a tin of oatmeal cookies on the table, Kathy asked her to tell us about the state mental hospital at Massillon.

"Oh my land, that was so long ago." Mabel patted her knee. "I have a lot of time to think. Some memories are wonderful and some not so good. You choose and pick what you think about. Diane, my daughter, knew some ladies at Massillon and Diane would take them out to lunch. That meant a lot to Diane and it meant a lot to the women."

"What was it like to live in the hospital?" Kathy asked.

"They were called cottages"—Mabel threw her arms wide—"but they were big houses."

Kathy opened the tin and passed it to Mabel. "What did you do there?"

Glancing into the tin, Mabel smiled. "I visited with the women."

"Did they cook the meals?" I reached for a cookie.

"No, we took them to the dining room, or delivered food if they couldn't get there."

"Did you do the laundry?" The room was warm, and Kathy unbuttoned her cardigan.

Mabel shook her head. "No! They did their own laundry."

"Did the women come and go," I asked, "or did they stay in the house?"

Mabel looked out the window. "They'd come and go, had different activities like sewing and knitting, things to what their ability was. We'd take them for walks or to the commissary, where they'd buy little things like ice cream, or into town, where they could buy what they wanted. What they wanted was birds or hamsters to bring back. They were supposed to take care of them, but nine out of ten didn't, so the nurses had to. If they behaved we went to a restaurant, and at Christmas we'd take them shopping. We enjoyed each other. It was regular living."

Birds and hamsters, I thought to myself. *What they wanted was a regular life with their children.*

Jack was in the room when I got back, and I told him about Mabel and her stories of Massillon, how her broad accent and unassuming manner plunked me back into my midwestern childhood. "Salt of the earth. Doesn't that come from the Bible?"

"It's from the Sermon on the Mount." He reached for the Bible on the bookshelf behind his chair. "Here it is. 'You are the salt of the earth; and if salt has lost its taste, how shall it be restored? It is no longer good for anything except to be thrown out and trodden under foot by men.'"

Suddenly indignant, I bellowed, "That's just what Elinor faced after she was better—sanctimonious judgment that allowed her to be seen as worthless so she could be locked away forever."

Jack closed the Bible and laid it on the table. "Benevolence may have been lost when it clashed with social norms, but it lived on in people like Mabel and her daughter."

The next afternoon, despite predictions of a major snowstorm, Jack and I drove to Heartland Behavioral Healthcare, which used to be Massillon State Hospital. We decided to explore the area on foot. Walking the grounds that Elinor knew well, I could almost imagine her there. Many of the buildings she would have seen were gone, but a few remained. The most accessible was the church, so we headed for that.

The receptionist told us it was the Shrine of Saint Dymphna, dedicated on May 15, 1938. I made a mental note that Elinor was twenty-five years old and had been living in the hospital for a year and a half at that point. Her husband had died a little less than a year before. We followed the receptionist into the spacious sanctuary, where wooden beams crisscrossed high above the pews. Stained glass windows along the sides pictured Jesus healing women. A statue of St. Dymphna, a young woman holding a book in her left hand and a sword in her right hand, stood in a niche beside the altar. I read the plaque beneath the statue. "Patroness of those afflicted with mental and nervous disorders."

The receptionist invited us to stay for prayers. We accepted and sat with several others toward the front of the sanctuary. Elinor grew old at Massillon State Hospital. I imagined her sitting right there when she was twenty-five, when she was forty, then fifty, and when she was sixty-four, just before she left the hospital. It was as close as I'd ever be to the place where Elinor had spent so much of her life.

Before leaving I bought a book about St. Dymphna, born in Northern Ireland around 600. Her father was the local king and Dymphna was his only child. Dymphna's mother died when she was young, and her father went insane with grief. After searching the kingdom for a woman who looked like his wife, he determined to marry his daughter. Dymphna refused and fled. Her father hunted her down and when she rejected him again, he cut off her head. Miracles happened at her grave—sick people were cured, especially those with mental illnesses.

Elinor's story contained striking parallels with Dymphna's story—her mother's death, her father's devastating grief, his deadly abandonment and cutting her off from everyone she had known. And like Dymphna, miraculously, Elinor endured and lived long enough to heal our shattered family.

Before I left DC, Kathy suggested I contact her friend Charita Goshay at *The Canton Repository* to see if she'd write an article about Elinor as a way of finding people who worked at the state hospital when Elinor was there. Kathy's suggestion ignited a spark of fear. Until I found her, Elinor had belonged to Mother. Mother had lost Elinor to the hospital and I had lost Elinor to Mother's silence. I worried that if I told Elinor's story to Charita and she wrote the story, it would belong to her. When I noticed fear inhibiting my ability to act, I asked an acquaintance at *The Washington Post* for advice. He encouraged me to work with Charita.

Charita, comfortably dressed and with curly, dark hair and an attentive manner, met me at the door to her office. "I've been looking forward to this all week." I felt an instant connection, lost my fear, and talked. Charita's perceptive curiosity stirred thoughts about Mother, Elinor, and me. Opening my notebook at a coffee shop after the interview, I picked up my pen and wrote a letter to my mother who passed away four years ago. I had things I wanted to tell her.

Dear Mother,

When I was younger I wanted you to be different from the way you were. I wanted you to be more open about where you came from and what happened to you. I desperately wanted to know who my father was and later I wanted to know your sisters. They were alive for you and I needed you to tell me who they were so they could live in me too. I wanted the intimacy that comes from heart-to-heart talks.

My search has given me a deeper understanding of what formed you and hence, what formed me. I feel close to you as a sixteen-year-old girl who was alone with frightening events you didn't understand and who was afraid and ashamed to tell anyone, who felt bereft losing your big sister so soon after losing your mother. You talked about losing your mother, but you rarely spoke of losing Elinor. I didn't know enough about Elinor to understand what her institutionalization might have meant for you. It must have been an even deeper wound. And then war and the horror of your husband's death far away on enemy soil without even a body to bury—unspeakable catastrophes in your young life. When we placed roses on his marker at Arlington, you told me that you couldn't have done that and I now believe you. It took all you had to keep going. That was what you had to do and that was what you did.

The next step, finding the missing and bringing them back into the family, was what I had to do and you prepared me well. You taught me to go beyond what we can see and hold, to trust the unknown, that even though there's fear and sorrow, there's also light and love. It has taken me until now to untangle this knot and see you more clearly. I almost lost you to the fear. I could have lost my father, Dorothy, and Elinor forever, but the love in your silence was my guide into mysteries of life and death.

My father is part of the family now, as are Elinor and Dorothy and their offspring. I finally feel that I belong and no longer need to defend the missing ones. Knowing my father, I know myself as his daughter, and knowing your sisters, I know myself as a sister to my younger siblings, something you and Dad wanted for all of us. Dear Mother, the more I discover about our family, the closer I feel to you. My love for you grows even after death.

And what would you tell me about silence and fear and love?

Dear Susan,

I never wanted to hurt you. The things that happened to me when I was young were too terrible to handle. No one was there to help me and all I could do was keep them inside. I didn't know how to help you without falling into a place so dark I was afraid I'd never find my way out, and the rest of the family needed me. They were fine with not knowing and I thought and hoped you would be, too.

Your questions disturbed me but they also brought a little light. Somewhere deep inside I was pleased, even thankful, that you wanted to know Dave and my sisters. I sometimes felt alone, separated from my earlier life, from my family and Dave. I thought about them especially in church, where I had a few minutes of silence and the hymns

brought back those earlier times. I think you may have sensed that
and that's why you worked so hard to find them.

I wanted to give Dave a memorial marker, but I couldn't get past
the shock and pain of his death. I worried about Elinor but I didn't
know what to do. I couldn't take her when I had seven children of
my own to raise, and I didn't know how she was, if she was still so
disturbed. I couldn't have her drag my life down again, so I left her
there and worried about her. Dorothy infuriated me. I tried to stay in
touch with her, but I never heard back so I stopped trying. I needed
my family. I needed my sisters. I missed them but they weren't there
and I couldn't rely on them. I missed Dave, but I made a new family
and love returned.

Be fierce, Susan, hold on to what keeps you going. Tell your story if
you must; your story is our story so tell it true. You know more than
you think you know. Stay in touch with everyone and be there when
they need you. Get together now and then to sing and play and have
fun. Read to the children. Listen to the ancestors. Keep learning your
whole life and when your time comes, let go slowly. I'm here in the old
hymns and whenever you think of me. Mother

That night I dreamed about Mother and Elinor. They were wearing floor-
length prairie dresses and they were joyous, kicking up their heels, clapping
their hands together in the air, hugging and singing. "We lived through our
whole lives!" they were saying, "*We lived our whole lives!*" It was a victory
celebration. I woke feeling happy.

Snowflakes began to fall as we headed back to East Liverpool. The next day
we woke to well over a foot of snow, a white and silent town. Jack and I
stepped into our boots and walked down the street to see what was open.
There were no cars on the road. Shops and restaurants were closed. Every
step we took was a new mark on the windless, immaculate earth. Back at
the house, Carol called to tell us that no one was able to navigate the snowy
roads and hills, so Jack and I had the place to ourselves. Luckily the pantry
was filled with cereal and raisin bread, the refrigerator with yogurt and fruit,
and the freezer still held four boxes of Klondike bars. DC was also snowed
in, so, with more snow expected that night, we stayed over, curled up with
popcorn, and watched the Super Bowl.

On February 8th, the fourth anniversary of Mother's death, two more feet of snow covered the town. Standing at the upstairs window looking out over white rooftops, I thought of the poem tucked into Mother's Bible, the one Grandmother Clare wrote one snowy morning long ago.

> *How beautiful earth is this morning*
> *wrapped in a mantle of white;*
> *how softly the beautiful snowflakes*
> *came down through the darkness last night.*
> *As I rose and looked out of my window,*
> *I beheld a beautiful scene.*
> *What before was brown and unlovely*
> *is now a blanket so clean.*

Early the next day we left Ohio and drove across a snow-covered land. The roads were plowed until we reached the beltway that surrounded Washington, DC. Strips of packed snow lay in the roadway, narrowing lanes without warning. Cars were few and drivers were cautious.

In the morning, I crawled over a waist-high snow bank and entered the building that housed my studio. Snow began to fall soon after I settled in. Snow upon snow. White sky. White earth. From my fifth-floor window, I noticed a clump of snow on the rooftop across the alley beginning to flow over the edge like a thick white wave. I made myself a cup of chai and sat at the table in front of the window. There was nowhere to go and nothing to do. The city had stopped. Schools were closed. The government was closed. I sat as people have sat and watched snow fall since time began.

That studio on the top floor of a building in the heart of the city was my forest hut, my sanctuary, my room of my own. It fell into my hands when I most needed a haven, overwhelmed as I was with the enormity of the losses and tragedies of WWII and devastated by the rejection of family. Every morning I walked the ten blocks from our apartment, turned the key in the lock, and opened the door, amazed to find it still here, silent and waiting with shelves of books and space to breathe. There was no pressure in my room. I could watch the birds and the clouds, silent signs of life in the midst of a busy world. I could sit on my cushion and meditate for as long or as short as I liked.

That day I sat at my writing table and looked out over a white city of snow-covered rooftops, chimneys, and buildings that rose to meet an ever-changing sky. I thought about my mended family—I knew who they were, and alive or dead, they lived in me. The people I came from, those with whom I shared a common history, no matter how joyful or traumatic, were part of me, and I belonged to a family that included all of us. My thoughts turned to Dorothy and Mickey. Thankfully, Mickey's cancer was in remission, and Dorothy had told me the day before that she'd live to be 100.

Here, where silence restored me to myself and privacy allowed me freedom to think my own thoughts and feel my own feelings, I thought of Elinor. She had no room of her own, or even a speck of privacy, for seventy-two years, except what little she could create, as she did when she pulled her blue sweatshirt over her face for respite from the noisy crowd around her. From the time she was twenty-three until her death at ninety-five, Elinor had lived with people who were filled with unease and confusion. She'd had one narrow bed in a ward full of beds, sometimes sixty in one room, and little choice except in how she related to herself and to those around her. She chose to call the people who took care of her "Mother," and other women by her sisters' names, inspiring affection when it would be easy to give up, forget, or turn bitter. Seen as pleasantly confused, Elinor was able to get away with that, but her way of relating to the people around her as family was eminently sane.

I looked out the window. Clouds moved over the white city. It was almost dark when I opened my computer and found a message from Sandra.

Hi Susan,

I found the wedding book of my parents. They were married January 27, 1934 in the First Presbyterian Church in Pittsburgh, PA. I have actually been in that church when I was a student nurse. I remember it as being very large and beautiful. I wonder why they were married in Pittsburgh instead of East Liverpool? There were quite a few gifts. My mother recorded the guests and the gifts. Her handwriting was quite fancy. How very tender to see her handwriting.

I wrote back:

I guess Grandpa with his strict Presbyterian ways didn't want to have the wedding in East Liverpool if Elinor was pregnant, or maybe it was Mame's influence—Grandpa's second wife who hated Grandpa's daughters.

Sandra responded:

I was thinking the same thing about Grandpa Ben being ashamed of his daughter for being pregnant. But the Del Vecchio family seemed to come through for them. My grandmother's best friend, Mrs. McClain, made the wedding cake. I can relate to that because she was always serving us sweets when we visited them. This is making their wedding and their relationship seem so real to me. I know my father loved her so! What could have been, we will never know, but only imagine. I am able to do that now.

What great news to know when Elinor and Floyd were married, and most of all, to know that they had a wedding with parties and gifts and a wedding cake. Floyd's mother, Martha, probably stepped in when Grandpa Ben spurned the idea of a church wedding. I can imagine Martha and Elinor planning and making the arrangements together, a happy time in Elinor's mostly difficult life. Even now, many years later, Sandra and I shared her happiness. It was not quite a memory, because we hadn't been there, but it was an image that connected us with Elinor and with each other in a joyful way.

———

When we were in Ohio I stopped by the nursing center to pick up the music box and a few things, all that remained of Elinor's belongings. Betty had handed me a binder. "It was Elinor's notebook," she told me. "From time to time we'd give her a piece of paper and a pencil or a pen and tell her to write whatever she wanted to. Elinor liked to write."

I ran my hand over the faded blue cloth cover and thanked Betty for saving it. We left Canton with a little bit of Elinor still with us.

On that snowy day I sat at my writing table and opened the binder. Elinor had filled ten pages of lined notebook paper with her writing; the rest were blank. The first few were written with purple ink in an easy-to-read, round, cursive script. At the top of the first page she had written, "I need glasses. We read all the time. Do you understand Italiano, American? Do you understand English?"

"Whoa," I said out loud. Four sentences and I was hooked. Did she ever get her glasses? What did she read? With whom was she trying to communicate, to find a common language?

Skimming through the next eight pages, I saw the effects of dementia as her handwriting deteriorated toward the end. Turning back to the beginning, I read, "Now is the time for all good men to come to the aid of their children . . . our father which art in Heaven. Halloween thy name." Chuckling, I imagined the off-kilter quotes to be Elinor's droll way of addressing an absent and sometimes spooky father.

There were allusions to a life I'll never know, but Elinor took me a little closer through charged sentences that added up to a sort of scrambled autobiographical collage of her life beginning with her marriage to Floyd and the coming baby: "Our honeymoon isn't far away. We go again in our nice new car. I'm expecting a baby and if anything I need help taking care of it (the baby) . . . You were tied with a big Beau . . . Bless pretty boy Floyd too." Here again she inventively mixed positive and negative when referring to her husband as she had earlier, with her father. Although they were written in the nursing home when she was in her nineties, she dated one of the pages June 19, 1937, which was when Floyd was taken ill with a heart infection, a week before he died.

She wrote as if talking to a friend, in a style both warm and poignantly understated. "Would you like to take a walk with me? How long have you been here and when are you going home? Seven years. Look at the calendar in the kitchen." In her writing as in her caged life, Elinor created friendships: "a friend still here, Ruth. Remember that root beer we had at the drugstore? That was good wasn't it? Maybe we'll receive something similar to lemonade or orange juice. I haven't much news but remember I still like you. Do you still like me?"

She was honest and witty in life and her honesty and her wit lived on the page. "Everybody thinks it is too hot in here but I'm cold. It's supposed to rain but we only have an umbrella to keep the rain off. Of course we have feathers."

She pressed her family for help. "I'm Elinor, John, and I don't know anybody. Please pray for us. Blessed Virgin pray for us . . . speak to me William honey . . . How am I going to get home if you don't cooperate? You see, this hospital is a [she'd drawn a big zero] . . . Why not call us? Come on, pick up the phone . . . maybe you forgot to call. Please don't wait any longer. I don't know what else to write, right, left, right, left out . . . I really don't know just where I do belong."

Elinor, who was abandoned by every one of us, did not abandon herself. She was there in her writing about her father's betrayal, her need for help with the baby, her husband's death, friendship, affection, and godforsaken loneliness. Near the end her words formed a poem.

Oh the sun will shine today
and a few flowers grow. Mother
didn't know that we were coming,
but all of us are ready for love.

Acknowledgments

This book owes its life to the generosity of so many. To my husband, Jack—his intelligent sleuthing unearthed major clues and his loving companionship sustained me throughout every long search and the writing. To my children, Jacques and Sarah, for their joyful support and encouragement during their own years of exploration and new beginnings.

To my siblings, Amy Henkel, Dan Henkel, Ellen Kingston, Clare Henkel, and John Henkel, whose openness and wonder outshone their hesitation about disturbing the family ghosts; especially to Dan, who read every word twice with his keen editor's eye, and to John for the website he attentively and skillfully created. To Sandra Berkley and Amy Korsgard and Dorothy and Mickey Sasko, whose acceptance, enthusiasm, and humor filled the empty places with love and new life.

To Julie Bondanza for unfailing friendship. To Linda Miller for insightful questions and comments. To Richard Brady for listening deeply and suggesting new possibilities. To Elisabeth Dearborn and Mary Levin for their hearty responses and to Diane Shandor for her generous care throughout. To Lisa Fliege for laughter and useful criticism. To Valerie Stains, who loved Elinor and sent her music. To Brother Phap Doo who helped me understand my father and myself. To Jeffrey Paine, whose engaging thoughtfulness expanded my thinking and kept me going. To Marilyn Smith for sharing the writing journey and for her generous editorial help. To Lynn Stearns, whose editorial skill sharpened my writing. To Brooke Warner for offering a new mode of publishing and to Brooke, Cait Levin, and Krissa Lagos for guiding me through and making it happen.

To the American War Orphans Network, without whom the search for my father would not have begun, and especially to Ann Mix, whose nourishing companionship and know-how about searching for lost fathers changed my life. To the men of the 782nd Tank Battalion and to my father's friends in Oshkosh, WI for their stories, and for seeing him in me. To the Washington Mindfulness community, a source of refuge and joyful peace.

To Megan Smolenyak for finding Dorothy. To Kathy and Randy Heckert for peanut butter cookies and gracious hospitality, for chasing clues and providing contacts, and for Elinor's Christmas visit. To the Massillon Library Genealogy Department—especially Jean Adkins, whose skill and perseverance led me Elinor and to Sandra. To Sharon McConnell, Elinor's guardian, for staying with Elinor to the end. To the Colonial Nursing Center in Canton, Ohio and to every doctor, nurse, aide, volunteer, and resident who made Elinor's life more bearable.

Credits and Permissions

About the Author

S usan Johnson Hadler, PhD is the co-author, with Ann Bennett Mix, of *Lost in the Victory*, a book that broke the silence surrounding mention of fathers who died in WWII and how their deaths affected their children. She has published articles in the *Washingtonian*, *Reader's Digest*, and *The Mindfulness Bell*, and appeared in the *Ancestors* series on PBS. She formerly lived and taught in Tanzania, East Africa. Hadler worked for over twenty years as a psychotherapist in Washington, DC. Visit her online at www.susanhadler.com

SELECTED TITLES FROM SHE WRITES PRESS

She Writes Press is an independent publishing company
founded to serve women writers everywhere.
Visit us at www.shewritespress.com.

Splitting the Difference: A Heart-Shaped Memoir by Tré Miller-Rodríguez
$19.95, 978-1-938314-20-9
When 34-year-old Tré Miller-Rodríguez's husband dies suddenly from a heart attack, her grief sends her on an unexpected journey that culminates in a reunion with the biological daughter she gave up at 18.

A Different Kind of Same: A Memoir by Kelley Clink
$16.95, 978-1-63152-999-3
Several years before Kelley Clink's brother hanged himself, she attempted suicide by overdose. In the aftermath of his death, she traces the evolution of both their illnesses, and wonders: If he couldn't make it, what hope is there for her?

Don't Call Me Mother: A Daughter's Journey from Abandonment to Forgiveness
by Linda Joy Myers $16.95, 978-1-938314-02-5
Linda Joy Myers's story of how she transcended the prisons of her childhood by seeking—and offering—forgiveness for her family's sins.

Renewable: One Woman's Search for Simplicity, Faithfulness, and Hope
by Eileen Flanagan $16.95, 978-1-63152-968-9
At age forty-nine, Eileen Flanagan had an aching feeling that she wasn't living up to her youthful ideals or potential, so she started trying to change the world— and in doing so, she found the courage to change her life.

The Outskirts of Hope: A Memoir by Jo Ivester
$16.95, 978-1-63152-964-1
A moving, inspirational memoir about how living and working in an all-black town during the height of the civil rights movement profoundly affected the author's entire family—and how they in turn impacted the community.

Where Have I Been All My Life? A Journey Toward Love and Wholeness
by Cheryl Rice $16.95, 978-1-63152-917-7
Rice's universally relatable story of how her mother's sudden death launched her on a journey into the deepest parts of grief—and, ultimately, toward love and wholeness.